D1571414

Zones of Instability

PUBLISHING FOR THE WORLD
125 Years
THE JOHNS HOPKINS UNIVERSITY PRESS

Zones of Instability

Literature, Postcolonialism, and the Nation

Imre Szeman

The Johns Hopkins University Press
Baltimore and London

The Johns Hopkins University Press
2715 North Charles Street
Baltimore, Maryland 21218-4363
www.press.jhu.edu

Library of Congress Cataloging-in-Publication Data
Szeman, Imre, 1968–
   Zones of instability : literature, postcolonialism, and the nation /
Imre Szeman.
    p.   cm.
Includes bibliographical references (p.   ) and index.
   ISBN 0-8018-6803-3 (hardcover : alk. paper)
   1. Commonwealth literature (English) — History and criticism.
2. Nationalism and literature — Commonwealth countries — History —
20th century. 3. Postcolonialism — Commonwealth countries.
4. Commonwealth countries — In literature. 5. Caribbean Area — In
literature. 6. Postcolonialism in literature. 7. Decolonization in
literature. 8. Nationalism in literature. 9. Nigeria — In literature.
10. Canada — In literature. I. Title.
PR9080 .S97 2003
820.9'9171241 — dc21
2002154083

A catalog record for this book is available from the British Library.

For Maria, Joseph, and Maya

A Brechtian maxim: "Don't start from the good old things but the bad
new ones." — WALTER BENJAMIN, "Conversations with Brecht"

. . . of reanimating already existing themes, of arousing opposed strategies, or giving way to irreconcilable interests, of making it possible,
with a particular set of concepts, to play different games . . .
— MICHEL FOUCAULT, *The Archaeology of Knowledge*

I do not say that the world will be reduced to the expedients and
grotesque disorder of the South American republics; or that perhaps we
may even return to a state of savagery, and prowl, gun in hand, in search
of food, through the grass-covered ruins of our civilization. No, for
such adventures would imply the survival of a sort of vital energy, an
echo of earlier ages. Typical victims of the inexorable moral laws, we
shall perish by the thing by which we thought to live. Machinery will
have so much Americanized us, progress will have so much atrophied
our spiritual element, that nothing in the sanguinary, blasphemous or
unnatural dreams of the Utopists can be compared to what will actually
happen. — CHARLES BAUDELAIRE, *Intimate Journals*

It is not enough to try to get back to the people in that past out of
which they have already emerged; rather we must join them in that fluc-
tuating movement which they are giving a shape to, and which, as soon
as it has started, will be the signal for everything to be called in question. Let there be no mistake about it; it is to this zone of occult instability where the people dwell that we must come; and it is there that our
souls are crystallized and that our perceptions and our lives are trans-
fused with light. — FRANTZ FANON, *The Wretched of the Earth*

Contents

Acknowledgments

This book was written with the assistance of fellowships from the Social Sciences and Humanities Research Council of Canada, travel funding from the Ford Foundation, and, at the very end, a grant from the Arts Research Board at McMaster University.

Like all projects of this kind, this book could not have been produced without the support and assistance of a large number of people who collectively form (whether they know it or not) the extended community within which I live and work. I want to thank Chris Andre, Davina Bhandar, Ilidia and Tony Botelho, Will Coleman, Chris Coupland, Arif Dirlik, Peter Fitting, Mark Frankel, Don Goellnicht, Larry Grossberg, Michael Hardt, Peter Hitchcock, Eva-Lynn Jagoe, Zubeda Jalalzai, Michael Ma, Dan Moos, Valentin Mudimbe, the Ordnance Street gang, Andrew Pendakis, Chuck and Alissa Whiteman, and the late Ted Davidson — they all know why. Caren Irr provided immeasurable help at two key moments in the process of writing this book and offered me a model of how to think philosophically and politically (though I'm still not sure what that Soviet movie was about). Nicholas Brown and Susie O'Brien have been willing to be my partners-in-crime on numerous projects and have acted as the kind of intellectual interlocutors anyone would be fortunate to have in their lives. I was fortunate to have Eric Cazdyn drop into my life as I thought through the last stages of this project. Finally, Henry Giroux, Fredric Jameson, and Marty Kreiswirth have to be singled out for special thanks. Their influence and advice have helped to make me a far better thinker than I could ever have hoped to become on my own, even if I still have a long way to go. They deserve effusive and boundless praise for making the world a more interesting place to be.

Carolyn Veldstra did an incredible job of getting the manuscript into final shape in a very short amount of time.

Finally, to Maria and Joseph, for their support and everything else.

Parts of this book have been published elsewhere in substantially different form: portions of Chapter One as "Who's Afraid of National Allegory? Jameson, Literary Criticism, Globalization" in *South Atlantic Quarterly* 100, no. 3 (2001): 801–25; portions of Chapter Two as "Literature, Federation, and the Intellectual's Nation: Rereading Lamming's *The Emigrants*" in *Journal of Caribbean Literature* 3, no. 1 (2000): 28–50; and finally, parts of Chapter Four as "The Persistence of the Nation: Interdisciplinarity and Canadian Literary Criticism," in *Essays on Canadian Writing* 65 (1998): 16–37.

Zones of Instability

The Politics of Postcolonial Nationalist Literature

To an irresolute nation, irresolute literature! But as soon as the elements of a people approach some unity, the elements of its literature draw nearer together and condense into a great prophetic work. Let us now bemoan the fact that we lack this great work, not because we lack it but because it is a sign that we are not yet the great people of which it must be a reflection; for it must reflect, it must be the reflection. — JOSÉ MARTÍ

Everywhere throughout the world one finds the same bad movies, the same slot machines, the same plastic or aluminum atrocities, the same twisting of language by propaganda, etc. . . . [O]n the one hand, [the developing world] has to root itself in the soil of its past, forge a national spirit, and unfurl this spiritual and cultural revindication before the colonialist's personality. But in order to take part in modern civilization, it is necessary at the same time to take part in scientific, technical, and political rationality, something which very often requires the pure and simple abandonment of a whole cultural past. — PAUL RICOEUR

At the confluence of these quotations from the writer José Martí and the philosopher Paul Ricoeur it is possible to locate both the highest hopes for literature in the formerly colonized world, as well as the most serious challenge to the attainment of these hopes. For Martí, literature is an important sign of the existence of the nation; it is only when a great work of literature exists that the unity of the people that is the nation can itself be thought to exist. But if the function of literature for Martí is merely to "reflect" the progress made in the formation of the nation, writers such as Chinua Achebe, Wole Soyinka, George Lamming, and many other postcolonial writers have envisioned a more active role for literature in the production of the nations that would come into existence at the end of colonialism. For these writers, a (genuine) literature is less a sign of the nation than an important — perhaps even the most important — force for bringing about a substantive political transformation of the colonial situation; it is literature that is seen as laying the cultural groundwork that allows the nation to become a reality. In addition to reflecting prenational political and social formations, literature is thought by these writers to be uniquely able to form and foster the values, identities, and culture of the new nation. For both Martí and these other writers, there is thus an essential role imagined for literature in the creation of the postcolonial nation: literature and the nation are conceptualized as being mutually dependent on one another in a way that gives to the writing of national literature an urgency and importance that it has perhaps entirely lost in the West.

If in the decolonizing world the great work of literature is, in Martí's sense, a sign of the nation, the nation can itself be seen as a sign — a sign that true political independence, authentic sovereignty, and real self-determination have now either been brought into existence or are, finally, even possibilities at all; a sign indicating the end of colonialism and, concomitantly, the completion of the long, painful struggle to throw off the shackles of foreign rule. But if the achievement of the nation thus signifies a whole set of political possibilities, Ricoeur's words suggest that the very form in which this politics is made possible must also be seen as threatening or limiting the actualization of these possibilities. For the nation is also a sign of modernity. With modernity comes progress, science, technology, market capitalism, a rationalized bureaucratic state, and the end of a whole series of what were often seen as constraining traditional practices and beliefs — all of which may be taken as an "improvement" over the situation of colonialism by both the colonized and the former colonizers, a step "forward" (in the terms of Eurocentric history and modernization theories favored by international development organizations) into the main currents of the stream of Western history. But this is only one side of what modernity represents. Modernity also names a cultural system that places economic practices at the center of social existence. More than anything else, it is this system, often described in terms of a "cultural imperialism" that persists even after the formal end of political imperialism, that works to undermine the often radical experiments that it was hoped could be carried out in the decolonizing world under the sign of the nation. The promise of the nation in the decolonizing world was not only located in its brute assertion of political independence, but in the possibility of introducing ways of organizing social existence different from those assumed or imposed by the West. If this is a promise that has remained tragically unfulfilled, it is, at least in part, because the nation is a political form that, as Ricoeur's words imply, denies possibilities as much as it actualizes them; this in turn means that the relationship between literature and the nation celebrated by Martí must itself be seen as complex and problematic, fraught with dangers as much as it is filled with possibilities. For as much as literature would like to produce the unique collective cultural identity that forms the basis of the nation, it is not at all clear whether the nation is a suitable form "within" which such an identity can best be fostered and expressed.

In this book, I undertake a comparative examination of the ambiguous, difficult, and often contradictory attempt by writers in three regions of the former British Commonwealth — Nigeria, Canada, and the British Caribbean — to create unique national cultures and literatures in the context of a global modernity whose chief *modus operandi* seems to be the erosion of particularity and uniqueness. What makes the creation of a national culture an especially difficult and ambiguous task in these regions is in part the number of discourses with which these writers have to contend and work through: anti-imperialist and imperialist discourses; the discourses of nativism and Western philosophy; modernist discourses promising progress and development; the discourse of nationalism related to modernism *and* anti-imperialism; and discourses concerning the role and political efficacy of literature, which of necessity must deal with imperialism, modernism, and nationalism all at once. These multiple, heterogeneous, and, in many cases, contradictory discourses and practices together form the "zone of instability" within which writers in these regions had to operate; and if the title of this book speaks of "zones" rather than a singular "zone," it is because in each of the situations that I examine the space(s) carved out by these discourses and practices must be seen as unique, bearing the traces of particular historical, social, and cultural trajectories, even though they are also related by their common link to the British Empire. What makes these zones unstable — like Venn diagrams in perpetual motion, in which overlapping areas are suddenly rendered singular, while elsewhere, at the very same time, other lines of force cluster thick and black, forming new and unexpected limits and possibilities — is not only the number of discourses and forces that these writers had to contend with and work through, but the fact that in the postwar period, these discourses and forces are themselves in states of profound instability and indeterminacy as the shape of the world rapidly undergoes an enormous number of important changes, changes that have been described, for instance, as the shift from Fordism to post-Fordism, from production to consumption, and from internationalism to globalization.

My particular focus here is the relationship between literature and nationalism in the two decades following World War II, decades in which the future prospects for the colonies went from extreme political optimism to extreme political disappointment. In the case of Nigeria, this is roughly the period from the publication of Amos Tutuola's *The Palm-Wine Drinkard* in 1952 to the publication of Chinua Achebe's *The Anthills of the Savannah* in 1987; in the British Caribbean, the period from the publication of George Lamming's *In the Castle of My Skin* in 1953 to the collapse of the West Indies Federation in 1962; and in Canada, the two decades from the 1951 Massey Commission to the 1970 F.L.Q. (Front de Libération du Québec) crisis. The regions that I examine in this study differ enough politically, socially, and historically (not least in the way in which they were interpolated into the project of empire) that it will be immediately apparent that my aim is not to uncover some general logic that will be able to connect indiscriminately the literary production of all three regions, as proposed, for example, in some versions of postcolonial theory.[1] At the same time, my comparative emphasis suggests that it is important that these literatures and the zones of instability in which they were produced be examined against the common background not only of the Commonwealth, but also in terms of the unprecedented changes in the organization of the globe following World War II, which had particularly serious consequences for areas that were — and in many senses continue to be — peripheral to the West. Of course, "peripherality," as expressed in the dominant narratives of modernity (and of globalization), is an invented conceptual apparatus, an ideology that manipulates time and space in order to legitimate existing relations of political, economic, and cultural power — which is not to say that it doesn't have effects and consequences. While the confrontation between literature, modernity, and the nation takes different forms in each of the situations that I examine, it is only a comparative examination that reveals the extent to which this confrontation was (and is) an importantly *global* one, with widely different regions of the globe facing surprisingly similar problematics in the (belated) production of literature and the (equally belated) creation of nations and national cultures.

The need for the literatures of formerly colonized regions to grapple with the consequences and effects of modernity while attempting simultaneously to fashion nations has been noted from the very first studies of Commonwealth, world, or postcolonial literatures. In Bruce King's 1980 book, *The New National Literatures*, for example, the issue of modernity is identified as the central concern of the various new national literatures,[2] and the "double consciousness" experienced by a third-world intelligentsia trapped between cultures — the "local" culture of the colony and the cosmopolitan "world" culture introduced by Western civilization — has been a frequent theme of both colonial and postcolonial fiction, as well as of the criticism of this fiction. What has been left out of these accounts, however, is an attempt to problematize and interrogate the concept of "national literature" itself. While this has become a theme of much recent writing that attempts to make sense of what the global means for the continued salience and relevance of national (and nationalist) literatures,[3] certain assumptions about the function of literature with respect to the nation (ideologies of literature) and of the nation with respect to literature (nationalist ideologies) continue to remain largely unquestioned. Paik Nak-chung's recent defense of the contemporary necessity of a (South) Korean national literature rests, for example, on an idea of literature as perhaps the last cultural artifact that can embody the values and particularity of Korean national culture. Literature is seen as able to "contain the invasion of global consumerist culture" by preserving Korea's cultural heritage and offering Koreans the possibility of a "dignified life."[4] Paik is readily willing to concede that the notion of national literature is now a problematic one. At the same time, "literature" and the "nation" continue to function in his account in predictable ways: literature embodies/reflects/expresses a culture that happily resides in the defined and determined space of the nation. And while there is some truth to this equation of literature with the nation, it seems to me that what modernity (and later postmodernity) puts into question in those areas of the world whose cultures are threatened by the global is precisely this set of relations between literature, culture, and the nation that has been part of our conceptual vocabulary since Romanticism. One of the central imperatives of this book is to examine the post–World War II literatures of Canada, the Caribbean, and Nigeria by continually destabilizing the category of national literature and by interrogating both nationalist ideology and the ideologies of literature, in order to produce a more nuanced account of this period of literary history and of the relationship of literature to the nation more generally.

There are a number of other issues that arise in this study of national literature and culture, all of which may be broached through another theme that emerges out of a consideration of the belated national projects of these regions. It is here again that a consideration of these literatures through a contemplation of their zones of instability becomes important. In each region, the attempt to produce a national literature is most often expressed through an explicit concern with *space*. It is this interest in space, and the questions that it opens up, that will underlie my examination of the intersection of literature, the nation, and modernity in the period immediately following World War II—a largely "forgotten" period of literary and intellectual history whose politics have been repeatedly portrayed in an overly simplistic and reductive manner. What precisely I mean by space — a concept that has now become a fixture in a contemporary academy trying either to undo the tyranny of time (modernity) or to come to grips with the meaning and significance of globalization[5] — and how I propose to investigate it needs to be carefully laid out, since it is bound to be easily misinterpreted and misunderstood. By way of introduction to the overall project of this book, I want to discuss the multiple and related ways that space can be read in postcolonial literature. One of the reasons to think about space before the nation is in order to open up a different way of conceptualizing the nation: not as a preformed political structure that everyone already knows the shape of (say, the modern European nation-state), but as a problematic that draws together the hope of forming new collectivities, the role of culture and literature in the production of these collectivities, the political problems of organizing space, and, finally, the relationship of the writer or intellectual to the people — the specific zone of instability to which Fanon refers in the last of the epigraphs that begin this book.

From Space to Nation

There are many ways in which the concept of modernity and its effects can be described and explained, ranging from concepts and themes first introduced in the work of nineteenth-century sociologists such as Max Weber and Karl Marx to the work of contemporary theorists such as Marshall Berman, Cornelius Castoriadis, Jürgen Habermas, and Michel de Certeau.[6] In terms of the postcolonial world, the works of literature and the literary and intellectual formations that I examine suggest that it may be most useful to understand modernity as a specific way of organizing lived social space, which threatens the aspirations of these regions to form distinctive nations — nations that may try to be "modern" in terms of their political organization but nevertheless attempt to refuse the "pseudo-rationality" of modernity (Castoriadis), its rationalization of the lifeworld (Habermas), and/or its collapse of the consumer's space of "use" (de Certeau). The nation in the decolonizing world is thus envisioned as a potential buffer against modernity as much as it is seen as a sign of independence, that is, as an enclosed space (geographically, politically, culturally) that modernity cannot easily penetrate, a specific space (or place) as opposed to the abstract ones (or nonplaces)[7] increasingly produced by modernity. If space appears as a concern of postwar writing in Canada, the British Caribbean, and Nigeria, it is in part because of the unique relationship between literature and space that is assumed

by writers in all three of these regions. There is, first, the relationship of literature, and of print culture more generally, to nationalism that has been so well
described by Benedict Anderson in *Imagined Communities*. For Anderson, the
novel and the newspaper first introduce the possibility of social "simultaneity,"
that is, the ability to imagine the existence of an extended community in time,
even without direct knowledge of other members of this community who exist at
the distant edges of national space: "the idea of a sociological organism moving
calendrically through homogenous, empty time," Anderson writes, "is a precise
analogue of the idea of the nation, which also must be considered as a solid
community moving steadily down (and up) history."[8] But if these literatures
express a particular concern with space, it is also because literature — and especially the novel — is seen as the privileged intellectual tool by which it is possible
to delineate space, domesticate it, concretize it, manage it, and make it less
abstract. In other words, the relationship of literature to the nation is but one
dimension of the relationship of the novel to space more generally. The fact that
the overriding concern of writers in the period and regions that I am studying is
to produce the space of the nation (as opposed to other possible spaces) has
usually been attributed to the widespread sense that the nation was the only
legitimate discourse of political space available at the time. And while this is in
part true, it has tended to rule out an examination of the actual uses of the
concept of the nation in the decolonizing world, especially in the writing of
literature. It has also ruled out a more detailed and explicit examination of the
reasons for the conjunction of literature and the nation in the process of decolonization, which asks not only *why* the nation, but also why it is *literature* that was
assumed to be a particularly potent spatial technology, questions which again
probe at the ideologies of both nation and literature.

Writers in Canada, the Caribbean, and Nigeria in the period following World
War II are concerned with space first as an attempt to reorganize the geographic
space of empire, to produce against or within this space the sovereign space of a
nation. This is a movement beyond earlier literary attempts to produce or reproduce an authentic connection between language and geographic space that
the colonial experience was thought either to have severed or to have made
impossible (as in attempts to adapt the language of British Romantic poetry to
descriptions of the Canadian Rockies, the Africa savannah, or the Backpit country of Jamaica).[9] The necessity of the space of the nation is not argued for in terms
of an appeal to a mythic or primordial past that gives it an historical reality and
solidity — the usual means by which nationalisms are articulated — but in terms of

a communal political project whose aim is to create a promising future out of a terrible past. This is due to the specific circumstances facing colonial nationalisms, which make it impossible, as Fanon puts it, "to try to get back to the people in that past out of which they have already emerged." It is also due to the specific *form* that the project of the nation took in all three of these regions: *federalism*. Federations are specific kinds of national spaces: separated by geography, language, race, ethnicity, legal structures, and so on, the disparate spaces of federations have to be linked together in other ways. It seems to me that this is the specific project of the literature of these regions in the 1950s and 60s, which not only makes arguments for the existence of the postcolonial federation, but takes literature itself to be a "substitute" for this otherwise missing "historical logic" necessary for the production of the nation, the missing conceptual framework that might make a national federation work.

It is a project that is necessarily short-lived. For in the process of this first attempt to define space — an attempt that comes to be seen as somehow incomplete or that fails to account for some deeper, more widespread, organization of space in which the synecdochic relationship of the "nation" to a whole international system is revealed — the literatures of these regions already begin to turn their attention to the global space of modernity initiated by imperialism that makes national space transparent and permeable, turning it into an obvious fiction that is in the late-twentieth century no longer able to contain both the political and cultural differences that these literatures would hope to define *and* produce. The works that I will examine in this study are, therefore, among the first to confront what is now referred to as "globalization," a phenomenon that itself has been described in spatial terms as, for example, a "time-space compression of unprecedented intensity."[10] They are also among the first texts to see the central problem of intellectual practice in the global space of modernity to be a problem of *representation*. In the initial attempt to create the nation there is a sense that (especially) the novel could still represent "totality" in Lukács's sense; this is increasingly placed into question as space becomes abstract and globalized. If, following the collapse of projects of cultural nationalism in the 1960s, many writers were forced to abandon or seriously rethink their earlier ideas about the relationship of literature to space (Lamming writing *Water with Berries* eleven years after *Season of Adventure*, Achebe waiting twenty-one years between *Man of the People* and *Anthills of the Savannah*), this is due, it seems to me, not simply to the political failure of the various national projects, but to a sense of the inability of literature to adequately counteract the (increasingly) global space of modernity, a task that writers in these regions had perhaps come to identify too closely with that of writing itself.

The concern with space in the literature of the colonial and postcolonial world has already been noted by (among others) Fredric Jameson and Edward Said. While my approach to space — which is to read *through* (the problem of) space, rather than to read *for* its characteristic manifestations — differs from both of these authors, it is nevertheless useful to position my approach in the context of the intriguing proposals they set forth about third-world literature. In "Yeats and Decolonization,"[11] Said suggests that there are two moments of nationalist revival in the third world. The literature of the first moment, which Said calls "the period of nationalist anti-imperialism," is characterized above all by "the primacy of the geographical in it";[12] in Fanon's tripartite division of colonial literature, this moment corresponds roughly to the final stage of "national literature."[13] Said writes: "Imperialism after all is an act of geographical violence through which virtually every space in the world is explored, charted, and finally brought under control. For the native, the history of his or her colonial servitude is inaugurated by the loss to an outsider of a local place, whose concrete geographical identity must thereafter be searched for and somehow restored. From what? Not just from foreigners, but also from a whole other agenda whose purpose and processes are controlled elsewhere."[14]

If the language of loss, revival, and restoration does not apply equally to all of the spaces formed by imperialism, including those of the Caribbean and Canada, where there is in a very real sense no possibility of recovering a mythic past that is not associated with imperialism (since it is imperialism that first brought these spaces into existence), the general spatial logic of imperialism that Said describes nevertheless appears as an important literary concern in these regions. This is true not only in the period that Said associates with this first moment of nationalism in the third world, the period from World War I to the 1950s, but extends as well into the second moment, that of the "liberationist anti-imperial resistance"[15] that attempts to go beyond the limits of the discourse of nationalism to a more profound transformation of imperial relations. Indeed, it seems wholly inappropriate to speak of the period after the 1950s, as Said argues, as no longer "nationalist" but as newly "liberationist." For while such a periodizing schema may adequately describe the historical experiences of regions such as Algeria, Vietnam, Cuba, Palestine, and South Africa — the areas that Said addresses — in much of the rest of the decolonizing world, and especially in the former countries of the British Empire, nationalism and the transformation of space suggested by nationalism continues to be an important determinant of literary production well into the 1960s and 1970s. While it is true that following the disappointing results of the initial wave of nationalism in the Third World there is no longer the same confidence in nationalism as a liberatory discourse, in the periods and regions that I examine here, the movement toward liberationist discourses seems nevertheless of necessity to have to pass through the matrix of the nation. As writers work through a definition and development of a national space that would provide the grounds for identity, self-determination, and political sovereignty, there is, of course, a realization by many of them that the discourse of nationalism is in many respects complicit with imperialism — complicit in its reproduction of the old colonial structures of government operated by the new nationalist bourgeoisie that Fanon discusses in *The Wretched of the Earth;*[16] in the ways in which the nation masks global capitalism's "differentiation of national space according to the territorial division of labour"[17] under the banner of sovereignty and independence; and in terms of the modernizing agenda that the nation ultimately shares with imperialism itself. At this point, one might imagine that the discourse of nationalism would be abandoned in favor of a more radical attempt to redefine postcolonial relations. Yet the discourse of the nation, and thus of space as well, continues to persist much longer than Said suggests, a fact that cannot entirely be accounted for by the idea that the discourse of the nation was the only one available after the war that might be thought to adequately effect a reorientation of space; once again, an explanation must be sought elsewhere, by reading the function and utility of the space of the nation in a different manner from that of critics who prefer to see the nation as an historical idea that has now run its course.[18]

The "whole other agenda" that Said discusses in exploring "the primacy of the geographical" in third-world literature is, of course, what I have been describing as the colonization of space by a global capitalist modernity, whose ultimate aim is to eliminate anything outside of itself. If in addition to the natural world, imperialism generated a "second" nature through its "domination, classification, and universal commodification of all space, under the aegis of the metropolitan center,"[19] Said suggests that "it is therefore necessary to seek out, to map, to invent, or to discover, a *third* nature, which is not pristine and prehistorical ... but one that derives historically and abductively from the deprivations of the present."[20] How exactly *this* space is to be produced is perhaps the best way of characterizing the challenge undertaken by the writers of the decolonizing spaces of Canada, the British Caribbean, and Nigeria in the second half of the twentieth century. The fact that this "third nature" continues to be described within the general problematic of the nation is less an indication of a failure to move from a nationalist to a liberationist discourse than an indication of the diverse uses of the concept of the nation in the postwar period.

In "Modernism and Imperialism," Fredric Jameson argues that—with the exception of the "special case" of Irish literature, and specifically the work of James Joyce—imperialism leaves its traces "spatially, as formal symptoms, within the structure of first-world modernist texts themselves."[21] Colonialism means that a significant portion of the economic structure is located "outside" of the West, a fact that creates a crisis of representation: "daily life and existential experience in the metropolis—which is necessarily the very content of the national literature itself, can now no longer be grasped immanently; it no longer has its meaning, its deeper reason for being, within itself."[22] For Jameson, modernism and a distinctively modernist "style" offer a solution to this crisis through their attention to space: the self-subsisting interiority of modernist writing manages to contain things "within" in order to make up for what cannot be represented "without." As validation of this hypothesis concerning modernism, Jameson proposes an assessment of a border situation, "one of overlap and coexistence between these two incommensurable realities which are those of the lord and the bondsman altogether, those of the metropolis and of the colony simultaneously."[23] This border case is found in a national situation whose underlying structure is that of the third world, while the "surface" of its social reality, "perhaps through the coincidence of its language with the imperial language,"[24] is more akin to the first world. Literature produced in such a situation would transform the style of modernism by its very different, colonial relationship to space, while still retaining many characteristic features of first-world modernist writing. The national situation that Jameson has in mind here is Ireland, and it is not entirely surprising that it is James Joyce's *Ulysses* that is the exemplary text in the validation of his hypothesis, with its objective rather than symbolic treatment of space, and its ability to explore the (physical and psychological) space of Dublin instead of dealing with space only by transfiguring it into the formal and aesthetic space of modernism.

While Jameson suggests that texts that would validate his hypothesis are "not, in this period, to be found in what will come to be called the Third World,"[25] meaning presumably the period of European modernism at the beginning of this century, by the second half of the century the countries and regions that I examine occupy the same kind of border situation as Ireland—belonging (in a sense) to the first world through their desire for political modernity as well as through their linguistic similarity with the center of Empire and to the third world by virtue of their experience with colonialism. If earlier third-world texts were interested only in refusing and repudiating imperial culture (as Jameson suggests), the novels of the second half of the twentieth century are much more aware of the need to deal with the totality of the imperial relationship. It is precisely in terms of their exploration of space in the form of the nation that this awareness is exhibited. The novels that I will be examining in Canada, the Caribbean, and Nigeria do not (with few exceptions) exhibit the same degree of linguistic or formal experimentation as *Ulysses*.[26] But like Joyce's novel, these novels do not represent space as a symptom that can be identified only formally or structurally. It is rather *everywhere* apparent, available to be read in terms of theme and content as well as form. One of the reasons that it is difficult to find large numbers of texts in the regions that I will be examining that are clearly modernist is because the relations constitutive of imperialism, or rather, the undoing of these relations, are central concerns of the texts: imperialism is not elsewhere, as it is in E. M. Forster's *Howard's End*, the text that Jameson examines, and so space does not appear as a formal symptom of something that cannot otherwise be represented. What Jameson finds exemplary about *Ulysses* — the existence of history, the signs of community, the possibility of public space, and so on — is to be found in all of the texts that I will examine, since, like *Ulysses*, they constitute explorations of spaces that are modern but not yet *of* modernity.

This study, then, is an examination of these writers' attempts to create, in Said's sense, the "third" nature that is the continuation of a literary process begun by *Ulysses*. But here I would like to begin to move back from space to nation. What I will examine is not what *space* is a symptom of, but rather, what the *nation* is a symptom of in the writing of third-world literature. In other words, I am not interested in producing a catalog of the appearance of space or of spatial discourses in the *content* of the literature of the decolonizing world, nor in showing the historical conditions that make possible certain formal innovations that may be described (as Jameson does in the case of modernism) as "spatial." Instead, what I will explore in each of the situations under analysis is the "intellectual field," the zone of instability, within which all of the issues of space (as a form of defensive nationalism, the privileged role of literature to space, the literary reworking of imperial space, the mapping of a nascent globalization, etc.) that I have outlined above arise. The nature of these zones, and the set of questions that an investigation of them prompts us to ask about the conjunction of literature and the nation in the third world, are the subject of the first chapter of this book. Overall, what I will explore, with respect to the difficult and paradoxical task of trying to create national cultures in the midst of the belated modernity brought about by colonialism, is what problems the practice of writing literature was intended to solve and, further, the significance of the conjunction of literary practices with the discourses of nationalism and the nation.

Postcolonial Spaces

Examining the literature of these regions and this period with the idea of space in mind is also to explore and critique simultaneously three other related areas of contemporary critical concern from a new vantage point. The first of these involves the theories of nation-formation that have become widespread over the past decade or so — the amount of recent theoretical writing seeming to make up for decades of comparative silence about so important a topic as the nation. With respect to literary and cultural studies, some of the most influential of the many contemporary writers to deal with the subject of the nation have been Benedict Anderson, Ernest Gellner, Eric Hobsbawm, and Anthony D. Smith.[27] There is no agreement among these writers on the exact mechanisms that produce nations and nationalisms, on the relationship of contemporary nationalist movements to "classical" European models, or on the future of the nation as the primary organizing unit of the globe. If there is one strand of agreement among these competing models, it is an awareness of the artificiality of the nation, an artificiality that nationalisms manage to transform into "facts of nature." It is only by seeming to persist through time and by being linked to imagined, mythic pasts — pasts often defined in ethnic terms — that what are inventions of national elites for their own purposes can become objects of mass loyalty. The process by which the artifice of the nation is suppressed, and the nation reified into a fact not of history but of nature, would thus appear to be an important, even essential, characteristic of both the nation and nationalism.

In all three of the cases that I examine in this book — and this is indeed part of my rationale for proposing to study these specific regions together — the nation is formed (or tries to be formed) under very different conditions. In Canada, the Caribbean, and Nigeria, it is the very artificiality of the nation that is an essential component of the literary attempt to create the nation. This is perhaps inevitable not only because of the belatedness of the nation but also because nation building involved a federal project in each case. The artificiality of the nation is highlighted not as something to be overcome, but as the starting point for the new nation. Of the three cases that I examine here, Nigeria has had the most potential to develop a nation through the evocation of a mythic past that was suppressed by the colonial experience. Yet while various discourses of nativism and negritude very actively and forcefully suggested the need for just such a revival of a lost cultural past, its orientation was always *extranational*, claiming either a pan-African perspective or one that spoke to the entire situation of the global African Diaspora. The two Nigerian writers that I will be examining in detail, Chinua Achebe and Wole Soyinka, are both known as outspoken critics of negritude, seeing in its focus on the past and its decision to embrace uncritically one side of the West's Manichean division between black and white, an inadequate basis for a national culture that they believe is essential for Nigeria.

For both Achebe and Soyinka, the beginning point of the Nigerian nation is the spatial boundary of the Nigerian state. The boundary is, however, artificial even as far as nations are concerned, being merely a legacy of European colonial struggles to control as much of the continent as possible. Both authors are aware of the impossibility of creating a nation whose boundaries are congruent with its ethnic divisions, since over 250 ethnic groups exist in Nigeria, of which the Hausa-Fulani, Yoruba, and Ibo are merely the largest. These facts may suggest that there is no possibility of creating a Nigerian nation. Yet both Achebe and Soyinka see the nation as essential to Nigeria. If the nation cannot be created around the pole of ethnicity or through the evocation of a mythic past, it is then for both authors to be anchored in the possibilities of African modernity and, in particular, the possibility of a nation whose identity comes from the fact that it is *not* a nation in the usual senses of this term: rather than being tied to the past, Nigeria is to be a nation that is relentlessly modern. If most nationalisms are invented through a process in which its invention is subsequently forgotten or suppressed, for these writers the Nigerian nation is to be created through a nationalism in which its invented, artificial nature is foregrounded. For both Achebe and Soyinka, Nigeria is to be a nation whose defining cultural difference from other nations is the fact of cultural difference itself; and it is literature that they see as playing an important part in making a shared national space across the lines of ethnic difference possible. Both writers express an enormous amount of confidence in the power of literature to assist in the cause of the nation; one of the central issues that I look at in my chapter on Nigerian literature is how this faith in literature changes (or doesn't change) as a result of the collapse of the Nigerian nation-state in the ethnic strife of the Biafran war—a collapse from which it is perhaps only now beginning to recover.

If it is difficult to create the Nigerian nation through either the invention of a common mythic past or by claims of a continuous ethnic occupation of a certain portion of the space of West Africa that colonialism had interrupted, in the British Caribbean and Canada these modes of nation-formation are even more tenuous and problematic. National space in the British Caribbean would seem to be less arbitrary than in Nigeria or Canada, simply because of the physical fact that—with the exceptions of Belize and Guyana—the former colonies are all islands. It is important to note, however, that prior to the political independence of the three major island-states (Jamaica, Trinidad and Tobago, and Barbados) in the 1960s, there was a concerted attempt to produce a larger political unit in the Caribbean: the West Indies Federation (1958–62). The rationale for federation was driven in part by the demands of modernization. Many intellectuals saw the federation of the islands as the only viable form of Caribbean sovereignty, since it would produce a political unit with a larger population than any one individual island (and so one better able to compete with other nations), while also assuring that there would be no unnecessary and costly duplication of bureaucratic and political structures. The other rationale for federation had little to do with the evocation of a mythic past or with claims about a shared ethnicity that could link these disparate islands together, for although much of the population of the West Indies is of African ancestry, for the large East Indian populations in Trinidad and Guyana such claims about a common ethnicity could only appear as a threat to their place in the federation. Rather, as in Nigeria, the argument for federation was made on the basis of the essentially multiethnic character of the Caribbean. This unexpected outcome of British colonialism in the West Indies was to give the British Caribbean a distinctiveness among nations that correspondingly gave the new federation an advantage over older nations: the diasporic, worldwide movements of peoples that was already beginning to provoke crises in Europe, and the ethnic strife and struggle for the self-determination of ethnic minorities that would become such an enduring feature of the postwar world, were issues that the Caribbean was already uniquely equipped to deal with in a way that other nations were not. Of the authors whose work I examine in my chapter on the Caribbean, it is George Lamming who most forcefully makes these points about a common multiethnic West Indian space. While V. S. Naipaul, the other author whose work I examine in detail, expresses doubt over the possibilities of West

Indian modernity, parodying the attempts to create workable political structures, his negative vision of the political future of the Caribbean throws into relief the problems and dilemmas of meaningfully creating such a peculiar national space within global modernity.

What I have been describing in Nigeria and the Caribbean is an attempt to create the nation *negatively*, that is, through an appeal to what other nations were *not*, or at least, *not yet*.[28] This process reaches its apotheosis in Canada, which in 1971, after decades of intensive debate about Canadian nationalism and Canadian identity, became the first country in the world to declare itself to be "officially" a multicultural state, that is, to proclaim an *identity* of *nonidentity*, at least insofar as identity is normally configured within the nation. While Canada did not undergo a process of political decolonization in the same way as Nigeria or the Caribbean states did in the 1960s (indeed, it could be argued that Canada experienced intensified cultural and economic imperialism), and while the issue of space in Canadian politics and literature has a much longer tradition than in either of my other two cases (being a theme taken up by both Harold Innis and Marshall McLuhan), it is significant that anxiety over the tenuous existence of the Canadian nation also reached a peak in the decades following World War II. A major consequence of the war was to reorient global power away from Britain toward the United States. The dissolution of empire and the sudden (newly) hegemonic presence to the south of a linguistically and culturally similar state, though one much more assured of itself as a nation, brought about the urgent need for a specifically Canadian definition of the nation. With respect to issues of American cultural and economic imperialism, Canada — which Peter Worsley has called "the world's richest underdeveloped country"[29] — understood itself as being in much the same position as third-world countries whose cultural life and economic and political sovereignty was daily in danger of collapse. The physical proximity and cultural similarities of the United States and Canada made the threat appear even greater: the encroachment of Americanization cum modernity had to be resisted at all costs to preserve what was specifically Canadian, even if what *this* might be was only to be decided in the very process of resistance.

Given the extent to which this process of Americanization was felt to be a threat, and, perhaps more important, given Canada's far greater economic resources, it is perhaps no surprise that while in Nigeria and the Caribbean the task of producing a national culture fell to intellectuals and writers, in Canada the state itself was actively involved in the production of the Canadian nation during the period from 1945 to 1970. Following the 1951 Massey Commission Report on National Development in the Arts, Letters and Sciences, which made resistance to the American cultural threat official government policy, the state established the National Library (1953) and brought into being the Canada Council (1957), the major cultural funding body of the federal government. The latter had an enormous and direct impact on literary production, both by providing funding to individual authors and by making funds available to book and magazine publishers in order to provide outlets for Canadian literary production. The most important literary initiatives to grow out of these programs were the establishment of the New Canadian Library series (1957), which practically invented a Canadian canon where none had existed before and first made the widespread teaching of Canadian literature in universities and high schools a possibility,[30] and the production of *The Literary History of Canada* (1965), which was (incredibly) the first such history produced in Canada. Even given these overdetermined conditions for the production of Canadian literature in the 1950s and 60s, it is in literary criticism rather than in literary production itself that it is possible to see the explicit creation of a national literature. The Canadian situation is thus already different from the Caribbean and Nigeria. It is interesting to note that both the literary and nonliterary attempts (the establishment of Canadian Broadcasting Corporation TV in 1952, the opening of the Trans-Canada Highway and the launch of the Alouette I communications satellite in 1962, the adoption of the Maple Leaf flag in 1964, etc.) to forge a unitary Canadian nation — a space, in essence, infused with "Canadianness" — were unable to include Quebec in any significant manner. The obsession with the creation of a distinctively Canadian culture was an anglophone one, even if ironically the high point of this national quest for self-definition was reached at the 1967 World Exposition in Montreal. While in Nigeria and the Caribbean the project of nation-formation began with an acknowledgment of the multiethnic character of the nation, the adoption of multiculturalism in Canada in 1971 must be seen as the rear-guard action of a national project whose failure was announced with the murder of Pierre Laporte by the F.L.Q. in 1970.

Given the regions and the period that I examine, it is inevitable that this study must adopt a position with respect to the field of postcolonial theory. A rearticulation of the postcolonial problematic offers a second point of connection between the issues addressed in this study and those of contemporary theory. The critical work of many of the writers that I will be considering in this study have been important in defining and giving coherence to the field of postcolonial criticism[31] — or at least giving it whatever coherence it now enjoys: in recent years, it has seemed that the field of postcolonial criticism has become equivalent to the body of articles and books that hope either to define and clarify or to contest and deny the utility of the concept of the postcolonial itself.[32] It therefore seems necessary that I take on directly the major themes and theories of post-colonial criticism in this study. Yet, if I seem to shy away from "using" or "de-ploying" postcolonial theory in my consideration of what are, after all, a group of amongst the most canonical postcolonial writers and situations, it is because I feel that it is important to consider the work of these writers in the context of the problems that they attempted to address and sought to resolve. Reading these works retrospectively means that the "true" concerns of these writers are often distorted and issues are imposed on them that properly originate only within contemporary critical work. This is, of course, in one sense, an inevitable part of any kind of intellectual endeavor, the inescapable hermeneutical circle that one enters into in the process of all interpretation. Nevertheless, as much as possible, in this study I undertake what I understand to be an examination of the immedi-ate "prehistory" of postcolonial theory and criticism in part in order to excavate some of its hidden desires and buried logics, rather than starting with the work of Said, Bhabha, Spivak, and others and "applying" it to what has been already identified in advance as postcolonial literature. Without wishing to suggest that there is a narrative of development in postcolonial theory (e.g., Achebe [early] — Said [middle] — Bhabha [late]), it seems to me that what these "early" works suggest is the degree to which the postcolonial problematic continues to be haunted by the specter of the nation. It is a haunting that contemporary post-colonial theory has sought to exorcise or repress; Said's division of third-world literature into "nationalist" and "liberationist" phases is but one example of the mechanisms through which this repression has operated. Making the nation and space central issues in postcolonial theory is, it seems to me, one way of overcom-ing the frustrating and limiting "culturalism" of contemporary postcolonial the-ory that has been identified by critics such as Arif Dirlik and Aijaz Ahmad.[33] My argument here should be seen as one that stresses the importance of a dimension of postcolonial studies that seems to have been neglected or sidelined in the pursuit of other (equally important) questions. Postcolonial studies have taught us an enormous amount about the problems of identity and subjectivity as these are inflected through race, ethnicity, gender, and various forms and modalities of power. I see this book as supplement to such studies, one that looks at the ways in which the texts and contexts of the postcolonial also speak to the problem of the *collective;* at least in part, it is this problem that made postcolonial studies so urgent and important in the first place.[34]

A second point with respect to the postcolonial: as with any comparative project, my choice of regions and authors to examine is hardly accidental. Part of the reason that I have chosen to examine Canada, the Caribbean, and Nigeria is to examine the entire range of situations in which postcolonial literature is, or at least has been thought to be, produced — from a consideration of a situation of explicit colonial intervention (Nigeria), to a country whose status as a colonized country is both more complex and much less certain (Canada), to a region like the Caribbean that, having been both colonized like Nigeria and "settled" like Canada, acts as a bridge between these two extreme poles of postcolonial situations. While I explore these three regions in order to address a range of questions regarding the conjunction of the literature and the nation in the decolonizing world — the explicit question of "space" in the Caribbean, the involvement of the state in Canada, and the politics of literature after the nation in Nigeria — I also examine the literature of these particular regions in order to work simultaneously within and against the "postcolonial" in an effort to probe the limits of its utility as a general descriptive term of the contemporary global condition.

Finally, this study constitutes in many ways an elegy for a certain vision of the function of artistic activity, a specific understanding of the role of the artist that reached its fullest expression in the twentieth century. If the various laments over the absence of public intellectuals in modern life, the worries over the decline of a reading public for serious literature, and the concerns of the "public art" movement are any indication, it is a vision of the artist's or intellectual's role that is still with us — even if it is beginning to seem clear that such a role may no longer be a viable one. I am speaking of the relationship in the twentieth century of the artist to politics, whether this has taken the form of the avant-garde or the official doctrines of socialist realism. If the twentieth century has witnessed the greatest separation of art from life, as in the establishment of the bourgeois credo of "art for art's sake" that Pierre Bourdieu has examined,[35] there has also been a concentrated effort by various avant-gardes to overcome the false autonomy of art, to bring art back to the public, back to the life-world.[36] Postcolonial writers do not necessarily see their work as belonging to the tradition of the European avant-garde; indeed, writers such as Achebe and C. L. R. James are critical of the overly intellectual quality of European writing and of the Western vision of culture (limited mainly to "high" culture) in general. Nevertheless, their explicit desire for their literary work to bring about political effects, to break through impasses at the level of politics or economics by a modification of culture or consciousness, aligns them with the avant-garde against bourgeois conceptions of culture. And yet, there is something in this commitment to literature, regardless of how much it is transformed in order to make it more amenable to mass consumption, that, especially in an era dominated by electronic media, betrays certain bourgeois inclinations and limitations. The novel in the third world is supposed to be a transgressive form. But as Timothy Brennan writes,

> It is precisely here that the greatest paradox of the new novel can be seen. For under conditions of illiteracy and shortages, and given simply the leisure-time necessary for reading one, the novel has been an elitist and minority form in developing countries when compared to poem, song, television, and film. Almost inevitably it has been the form through which a thin, foreign-educated stratum (however sensitive or committed to domestic political interests) has communicated to metropolitan reading publics, often in translation. It has been, in short, a naturally cosmopolitan form that empire has allowed to play a national role, as it were, only in an international arena.[37]

It is in the postcolonial literature of the 1950s and 1960s that it is perhaps most clearly possible to assess what remains for literature with respect to politics today.

In the context of the unstable zone of questions and concerns that I have outlined, the overall plan for this book is comparatively straightforward and stable. The first chapter establishes the theoretical framework by which these various nationalist literatures will be examined. Through an examination of the wealth of contemporary writing on the nation, and on the relationship of literature to the nation, as well as through a detailed consideration of the work of Frantz Fanon, Benedict Anderson, and Fredric Jameson, I argue that the "nation" in postcolonial literature must be seen as a concept or a figure that ultimately relates back to the practice of "literature" itself in these regions — its possibility, its political efficacy, and its potential ability to transcend the divisions between intellectuals and the people in order to form new polities in the decolonizing world. In the post–World War II period, ideologies of literature and nation fold unstably in on one another as they try to articulate a new politics of the collective. Chapter Two explores the ideology of literature with respect to the nation in the Caribbean, as exhibited both by the theme of exile and by the literary attempt to forge a new kind of national space: the short-lived West Indies Federation. The third chapter examines the fate of nationalist literature after the hopes for the nation have been all but crushed. It does so through an investigation of the post-Biafra novels of Wole Soyinka and Chinua Achebe in the context of their earlier formulations of the intimate connection between literature and the nation in Nigeria. Chapter Four explores the persistence of the theme of the nation in Canadian literary criticism. In particular, it considers the function of nationalist (and antinationalist) criticism in light of the (relative) absence of an explicitly nationalist literature in Canada in the postwar period and in the context of the long-standing collective neurosis regarding Canadian national identity. The conclusion considers the limits of the nation with respect to global space and the challenge that this new space presents for any future understanding of the concept of culture.

CHAPTER ONE

The Nation as Problem and Possibility

The formation of national collectives . . . common in the detestable jargon of war that speaks of the Russian, the American, surely also of the German, obeys a reifying consciousness that is no longer really capable of experience. It confines itself within precisely those stereotypes that thinking should dissolve. It is uncertain whether something like the German as a person or German as a quality, or anything similar in other nations, exists at all. The True and the Better in every people is surely that which does not integrate itself into the collective subject and if possible resists it.

— THEODOR ADORNO (1965)

It is not the concept of the nation that is retrograde; it is the idea that the nation must necessarily be sovereign.

— PIERRE ELLIOT TRUDEAU (1968)

Literature and the Nation

The nation and literature have had a long history together. The intimate connection between land and community that is the foundation of the link between the geographical and cultural specificity of the nation is often traced back to Romanticism, and in particular, to the writings of Johann Gottfried Herder.[1] Herder claimed that "every nation is one people, having its own national form, as well as its own language."[2] This Romantic theory of nationalism, echoed in the work of William Morris, Percy Bysshe Shelley, and others, influenced the development of nations and literature in the nineteenth century.[3] In Europe, the nation quickly became the only legitimate form of political and social organization, as reflected in the consolidation and production of national languages out of diverse dialects, and by the development of numerous social and cultural techniques, processes, and institutions whose intent was to produce a homogeneous body of citizens loyal to the nation-state.[4] Just as the nation became a seemingly natural way of organizing groups of people, so too did the belief that literary and cultural products reflected the unique national soil from which they organically developed. The system of "national literatures" that was developed during this period and that continues to define contemporary literary studies provides ample evidence of this fact. Premised on the belief in the deep connection between "race, milieu and moment" (in Hippolyte Taine's terms),[5] the invention of national literatures was an outgrowth of the political concept of the nation, but also helped to determine and define the conceptual basis of the nation by highlighting the supposedly unique features of the national character. This can be seen, for example, in the British writer Henry Morley's description of the connection between English literature and the English nation in 1873: "The literature of this country has for its most distinctive mark the religious sense of duty. It represents a people striving through successive generations to find out the right and do it, to root out the wrong and labor ever onward for the love of God. If this be really the strong spirit of her people, to show that it is so is to tell how England won, and how alone she can expect to keep, her foremost place among nations."[6] The first professor of American literature, Fred Lewis Pattee, began his introductory text on the subject with a description of the relationship between literature and the nation that by the end of the century had become all but indisputable: "The literature of a nation is the entire body of literary productions that has emanated from the people of the nation during its history, preserved by the arts of writing and printing. It is the embodiment of the best thoughts and fancies of a people."[7]

The relationship of literature to the nation and of the nation to literature remains an important part of contemporary literary and cultural theory, if on somewhat different terms. Over the past few decades there has been an outpouring of articles and books that have addressed the nation from the standpoint of literature, and literature from the perspective of the nation.[8] This renewed — or perhaps simply new — focus on the nation and literature is due in part to the increased attention that has been paid to the nation itself.[9] Though these various studies draw different conclusions about what the nation is, as well as about the mechanisms that produce nations and nationalism, they share a common incredulity about how long it has taken for the nation to become an object of serious inquiry and a sense that the nation is, all things considered, a form of political, cultural, and social organization that is as theoretically suspect as it is empirically dangerous; Anthony D. Smith, for instance, writes that "at best the idea of the nation has appeared sketchy and elusive, at worst absurd and contradictory."[10] Changes in the academy that have allowed for and encouraged interdisciplinary work have also been important, permitting forms of textual analysis and inquiry that extend beyond a strict formalism to a consideration of such supposedly "extraliterary" factors as the nation or the national "context" of a literary work.

Perhaps the most important factor in prompting a renewed attention to the nation in literary studies, however, has been the emergence and institutional legitimization of the field of postcolonial studies. Though Edward Said's *Orientalism* has often been seen as the founding text of postcolonial theory, the theoretical and ethical roots of postcolonial studies can be found in the enormous burst of political and cultural energy that emerged from the widespread and rapid decolonization of the European imperial empires around the world. Many of the questions that consume the activities of critical intellectuals today — questions located at the intersection of concepts of migration and transmigration, nationalism and transnationalism, cultural hybridity and cultural imperialism, globalization and localization, and so on — have their origins in the events and texts of this period. The form in which decolonization took place was without exception through the establishment of new nations (if not always nation-states)[11] that both produced and were produced by the new national literatures that exploded into Western consciousness in the period following World War II. Postcolonial studies and the study of the phenomenon called "globalization," which mine the rich historical deposits of this period both implicitly and explicitly, thus of necessity have to deal with the nation over and over again, both in terms of the reemergence of the Romantic coupling of nation and culture in the decolonized world *and* in terms of the apparent dissolution of the nation and its implications for culture in the wake of the recent intensification of the processes of globalization.

In her overview of the development of postcolonial literature, Elleke Boehmer notes that there are two distinct phases of nationalism and nationalist literature in the (post-)colonial world.[12] The first phase occurred in the period between the world wars. The guiding principle of this phase was Woodrow Wilson's assertion in his fourteen points that each people should have the right to self-determination. This principle became a rallying point for nationalist movements around the world, however disingenuous its articulation may have seemed in light of the consequent reentrenchment of the political and economic positions of the colonial powers between the wars. The movement against colonialism thus began in earnest long before the first colonies were to gain independence after World War II, a fact reflected both in political events and literary and cultural production: the explosion of new literatures in the former colonies was made possible by literary precedents established by prewar writers (in the Caribbean, for example, the prewar novels of C. L. R. James and Alfred Mendes paving the way for George Lamming, V. S. Naipaul, Vic Reid, etc.), just as the postwar political struggle for decolonization built on the gains established by prewar independence movements. There are definite continuities between this first phase and the anticolonial efforts of the postwar period that the trauma of World War II has tended to obscure. Nevertheless, as Boehmer notes, after World War II there was "a marked intensification and radicalization in nationalist activity. The key difference was the extent of support for outright, and even violent opposition . . . in politics this meant nation-state independence and new institutions, while in the economic realm it entailed control over productive resources and, in some cases, national ownership."[13] The nationalist literature of this second phase saw itself as the necessary cultural counterpart to this revolutionary nationalism, forging through the written word the new individual and collective identities necessary for the creation of new nations.

It is the second phase of nationalist literature that has come to be most frequently associated with the category of postcolonial literature. Though it is very common in discussions of postcolonial literature to characterize everything, from the "new national literatures" of the 1950s and 1960s to writing by contemporary authors such as Ben Okri, Salman Rushdie, Bharti Mukherjee, Jamaica Kincaid, and Rohinton Mistry, as *generically* postcolonial (obscuring significant differences in both geography and history) and, for that matter, also to include writing from the late-nineteenth and early-twentieth century into the category of postcolonial,[14] it has been equally common to introduce a periodizing schema to account for differences *within* this second period. One of the most common ways of dividing up the postcolonial phase of nationalist literature is by limiting the degree to which the postcolonial is to be identified with nationalist literature as such, that is, by defining nationalism as an explicit characteristic only of the *early* part of this phase. In these schemas — and they can be found in works from Fanon's *Wretched of the Earth* to Said's *Culture and Imperialism*[15] — nationalist literature wanes alongside the waning of nationalist hopes in the third world. As the promise of independence is transformed into the reality of neoimperialism and democratic governments are replaced by military dictatorships, so too (or so the story goes) writing turns away from the nation as a site of political hope or as a form that can productively mediate culture and politics.[16] Bolstered by much of the recent scholarship on the nation that suggests that it is nothing more than "a thing of social artifice — a symbolic rather than a natural essence,"[17] there is therefore a developmental narrative built into these periodizing schemas. The early, explicitly nationalist literatures are seen as overly simplistic in intent and design, as overconfident in the political effectiveness of what are mostly imported cultural forms (preeminently, the novel), and so are doomed to political failure just as Third World nationalism itself is. The nation itself comes to be seen as a dangerous form. Paul Gilroy's view of the nation has become a common one: without exception, it is now assumed that "raciologies and nationalism promote and may even produce certain quite specific types of collectivity, characteristically those that are hierarchical, authoritarian, patriarchal and phobic about alterity."[18] Instead of engaging in the process of "imagining" the nation, more recent postcolonial literature and theory is therefore characterized as embarking on what is seen as a much more sophisticated examination of identity and hybridity. Unlike earlier, explicitly nationalist literatures, for example, recent postcolonial writing is seen as paying greater attention to those internal differences of ethnicity, race, gender, and class that nationalism attempted to suppress or mask. The nation has thus been transformed from the potential solution to imperialism to the chief cause of the inability of postcolonial societies to get beyond imperialism; it has come to represent "not freedom from tyranny, but the embodiment of tyranny."[19]

It might seem that contemporary postcolonial studies have thus dispensed with the nation, and with good reason. And yet the theme of the nation inevitably reappears over and over again, in both implicit and explicit ways. There is, first of all, the general theme of resistance that is inevitably connected to postcolonial literature. Although the very concept of the postcolonial tends to produce an idea of a world divided into two large opposing blocks (the colonizers and the colonized, the West and the Rest, etc.), resistance is very rarely conceived of in these large, abstract categories. Resistance is rather a way of preserving or defining the integrity and autonomy of one's own community against threatening outside forces; as often as not, this community continues to be conceived of in literature as a national community.[20] The vexed questions surrounding cultural autonomy and cultural imperialism are similarly conceived in terms of national cultures, even in recent discourses of globalization that propose to suspend the nation and focus instead on the relations between the "local" and the "global." It is striking, for instance, that, in Benjamin Barber's rather hysterical meditations on the production of the global "monoculture" he calls "McWorld," it is only cultural policy at the level of the nation that is seen as able to preserve any sense of global cultural difference; at the opposite end of the political spectrum, Fredric Jameson has said much the same thing (if for different reasons) in his reflections on the fate of national cultures in the era of globalization.[21] Finally, however much the production of the nation in literature has been put into question, there certainly seems to be no sign of a similar challenge to the idea that nations produce their own distinctive literatures that are expressions of a unique national character.

Even if these literatures may no longer be explicitly "nationalist," postcolonial literatures continue to be conceived institutionally as a conglomeration of numerous national literatures, each of which can only be appropriately studied against the framework of the national situation in and through which they have been produced.

Many writers have, of course, suggested that all of these lingering remnants of the nation should simply be purged from our thinking. Christopher Clausen, for instance, has argued that the concept of national literatures should be abandoned once and for all. He writes that "despite the fact that the notion of national character has long been discredited, the link that nineteenth-century cultural nationalism forged between the status of the nation to which it belongs and the status of the literature that expresses it has never been broken."[22] It is important to break this link, he believes, because "it elevates parochialism into an axiom of study for historical reasons that have rarely been challenged in recent criticism . . . Holding onto the model in which a national literature serves as a badge of independence [for postcolonial nations] now actually defeats the original purpose by excessively identifying each writer with his or her local 'tradition.'"[23] Similarly, the apparently obvious link between nation and culture that has predominated since Herder, and continues to form the basis for the national cultural policy of almost every nation on earth,[24] has been challenged, for example, by the communications theorist Richard Collins, who writes that "the notion of 'national culture' is both an organizing category in the shaping of economic and cultural production, and a mystifying category error."[25] He cites Canada as an example of a country that has almost no common national culture shared between significant segments of the population (Anglophones, Francophones, and recent immigrants), but that nevertheless "holds together remarkably well" as a nation.[26] What both these authors suggest is that even if the nation continues to play a part in our reflections on literature as well as on everything else, continually returning even when it has seemingly been banished for good, it is perhaps only because the effort to go beyond it has not yet been undertaken with enough force. The solution would be to take up ever more forcefully Arjun Appadurai's suggestion that "we need to think ourselves beyond the nation . . . the role of [contemporary] intellectual practices is to identify the current crisis of the nation and in identifying it to provide part of the apparatus of recognition for post-national social forms."[27]

The ease with which Appadurai is willing to abandon the nation in virtually all of the essays collected in his recent book, *Modernity at Large*, comes from his unproblematized acceptance of the ways in which the world has fundamentally changed in recent years. Accepted definitions of national citizenship and national culture have been placed into question as a result of global mass migration, which has produced what he refers to as "diasporic public spheres"; a global mass-mediated imaginary has evolved that transcends all national boundaries; and the long-developing internationalization of consumption and production has reached levels that Lenin could barely have dreamed of when he characterized the imperialism of his day as "the highest stage of capitalism."[28] But as Masao Miyoshi, among others, has pointed out, it seems dangerous to take the new conditions of "globalization" as an inevitable, empirical fact about the present state of the world — as the beginning point, in other words, for critical reflection; to do so can blur the line between the imperatives of critical discourse and that of the celebratory discourse of globalization expressed by transnational corporations and nation-states alike.[29] After all, capital seems perfectly happy to exist in a "postnational" world of hybrid subjectivities, just so long as everyone continues to consume its products as well as its ideology. Furthermore, what Appadurai and others have taken as an actualized state of the globe — a world in which, it seems, everyone watches James Cameron movies, speaks on cell phones, and moves to take up a new life in some distant part of the globe (when they are not traveling to visit United Nations–designated world-heritage sites) — must itself be seen as an invention of a class of cosmopolitan intellectuals from whose vantage point the world may indeed look fully globalized. As other commentators have pointed out, the discourse of globalization is in many ways a political fiction whose intent is to transform the remaining spaces of the public in terms of the neoliberal logic of the private (capitalist) enterprise; it does so by claiming that the processes associated with globalization are inevitable — impossible to stop or alter in the slightest way.[30] By contrast, the discourse of the nation might still today fulfill a critical function, and not just because it represents "the least bad version of governmental practice,"[31] because it remains "the most universally legitimate value in the political life of our time,"[32] or because "all modern history demonstrates that proletarian dictatorships have only taken root where they fused with a national liberation."[33] The growing sense that the nation is an inherently negative, limiting political form that should be replaced by discourses that deal with "nomadism" or "deterritorialization" should be tempered not only by the continued empirical existence of nations, but by the real political possibilities that it might have once and may still represent, especially in those national situations in which the "global" alternative to the nation represents in many cases no alternative at all. In other words, as Henry Giroux argues, "what must be resisted is the assumption that the politics of national identity is necessarily complicitous with a reactionary discourse of nationalism and has been superseded by theories which locate identity politics squarely within the discourses of postnational, diasporic globalism."[34]

But whether or not the nation is still an important political force today — an issue that has generated endless, if necessary, debate — it remains essential to an understanding of the literature of the decolonizing world. In part, this is, of course, a historical necessity, that is, it is only through an understanding of the nation and its relationship to literature that we can make sense of the national and nationalist literatures that emerged in various parts of the British Commonwealth after World War II.[35] It is thus important to continue to pay attention to the relationship between literature and the nation in order to avoid the creation of a historically undifferentiated, homogeneous body of postcolonial texts. But the nation remains important in yet another way. By failing to deal with the nation in postcolonial literature, we are in danger of misunderstanding the significance of the aesthetic and political problems confronted by the writers of the fifties and sixties, for the larger political imperatives underlying contemporary postcolonial literature and theory as a whole. One of the most troubling problems for recent postcolonial criticism has been, for example, the question of the "cosmopolitanism" of many postcolonial writers and of much of postcolonial literature.[36] Writers such as Salman Rushdie, Ben Okri, V. S. Naipaul, and George Lamming produce works of literature that in content may be about the third world, but that are intended to be read and consumed mainly by first-world audiences; indeed, most contemporary postcolonial writers reside in the first world, and may even be citizens of first-world countries. The worries that this raises about the political or cultural authenticity of these contemporary texts begs the question of the conditions assumed for authenticity, that is, the organic connection between the writer, his or her people, and the national soil that is thought to be a guarantee of authentic cultural expression. These questions of authenticity, of their possibility or impossibility, are already central to the problem of writing nationalist literature in the 1950s and 1960s. The answers to the questions concerning the authenticity of contemporary texts, and so many of the other questions concerning the politics of the postcolonial, can be found in the way in which these earlier writers handled the aesthetic and political dilemmas they faced — or if not the answers themselves, perhaps a more sophisticated way of posing the question that doesn't turn the issue of authenticity (as just one example) into an antinomy for which there is no solution.

It has been relatively easy to move beyond the question of the nation in literary studies largely because the relationship of the literature of the "nationalist" period of postcolonial literature — for the purposes of this study, the literary fields that developed in Canada, the British Caribbean, and Nigeria in the 1950s and 1960s — to the concept of the nation has rarely been analyzed in the depth that it deserves. There are at least two reasons for this. First, with perhaps the exception of Marxist studies of African literature,[37] the "literary" status of the literature of these three "postcolonial" nations has never been properly placed into question. While Marxist literary critics such as Terry Eagleton and Raymond Williams have drawn attention to the fluid and shifting definitions of "literature" over time, the reified bourgeois notion of literature that undergirds most contemporary Western literary criticism has tended to be applied unquestioningly to non-Western or postcolonial literatures. What this obscures is an understanding of postcolonial national literary production as a specific mode and form of intellectual practice with its own specific conditions of possibility; the focus instead has been on the analysis of literary meaning rather than on an examination of what historical, intellectual, and material conditions made it possible for these texts to "mean" in the particular ways that they do. If there has been relatively little attention paid to the question of *why* postcolonial intellectuals produced literary objects as a mode of political activity in the postwar period, it is largely as a result of the second reason why the relationship between literature and nation has been undertheorized. For the most part, the Romantic coupling of literature to nation (or more generally of culture to nation) continues to be assumed as the only relationship between these terms in the period of nationalist literature. It seems obvious to most critics that during a period of revolutionary energies, revolutionary literature would be written, and that during a time in which the nation was seen to be the only possible mode of politics, that it is the nation that would be invoked by a political literature. The dyad nation-literature has thereby managed to retain its identity as a kind of literary natural kind, the name for a species of creature no longer extant but about which textual fossil records allow us to theorize. Yet a closer analysis suggests that the "nation" in nationalist literatures must be seen as functioning in a more complicated way, and one that cannot be easily dispelled when the Romantic connection of literature and nation is brought into question.

In what follows, I develop more fully the general theoretical orientation that I will take in my examination of the intersection of literature and the nation in each of the historical and geographical sites I have chosen to examine. I do so by looking closely and critically at some of the prominent models that have been offered regarding the relationship of literature (and culture) to the nation (and politics), adopting from each certain important themes that need to be addressed in any account of the function and meaning of nationalist literature. I begin by looking at Frantz Fanon's essay "On National Culture," which offers one of the most sophisticated interpretations of the relationship of culture to the politics of nationalism written during the period of decolonization itself. Second, I examine what has become a canonical text on the relationship of literature to nation: Benedict Anderson's *Imagined Communities*. Finally, through a careful rereading of Fredric Jameson's much (and unfairly) maligned essay, "Third-World Literature in the Era of Multinational Capitalism," I propose a way of thinking about the nation that lets us see it as a fluid conceptual zone in which the difficult problems of what Jameson calls "cultural revolution" are posed and explored in a manner from which we still have much to learn.

"This Zone of Occult Instability": Fanon on National Culture

Frantz Fanon's "On National Culture," constitutes one of the first attempts to theorize the relationship between culture and political struggle in the process of decolonization.[38] Originally delivered to the Second Congress of Black Artists in Rome in 1959, which was attended by such internationally prominent intellectuals as Langston Hughes, Pablo Neruda, and Nicolás Guillen, and later published as a chapter of *The Wretched of the Earth* (1963), it has been an influential and formative text in establishing the framework for the study of postimperial and postcolonial culture and cultural production. As is perhaps most clearly visible in *Black Skin, White Masks*,[39] Fanon emphasizes throughout his work the ways in which colonialism and imperialism operate through a form of cultural exploitation and degradation just as much as through the political and economic control of the colonies by their colonial masters. At the same time, in "On National Culture" he expresses a great deal of skepticism about any form of resistance to colonialism that addresses cultural imperialism without also engaging in the revolutionary work of bringing about an end to political and economic forms of colonialism. It is this aspect of the essay that has often been elided by critics who have chosen to emphasize Fanon's discussion of "the reciprocal bases of national culture and the fight for freedom" (ONC 236–48), which appears to place culture and politics in a more dialectical relationship than is really the case in Fanon's work; and though it has certainly been a foundational essay in thinking through the significance of culture for revolutionary politics, what it thus tells us about the politics of culture has sometimes been simplified in a manner that betrays both the complexity of the issues Fanon addresses and the complexity with which he attempts to address them.

The primary questions that Fanon addresses are announced only at the end of "On National Culture": "What are the relations between the struggle — whether political or military — and culture? Is there a suspension of culture during the conflict? Is the national struggle an expression of culture? Finally, ought one to say that the battle for freedom, however fertile a posteriori with regard to culture, is in itself a negation of culture? In short is the struggle for liberation a cultural phenomenon or not?" (ONC 245) These are useful and important questions. The task of making sense of Fanon's answers to these questions is, however, made difficult because of the multiple and ambiguous ways in which he uses the term "culture" throughout the essay. At times, culture is used in its anthropological sense as a term to describe a "collective mode of life, or a repertoire of beliefs, styles, values and symbols."[40] In this sense, Fanon clearly believes that the struggle for liberation *is* a cultural phenomenon: the independence struggle necessarily produces a new culture that is no longer in the thrall of colonialism nor simply resumes a cultural inheritance that colonialism interrupted. But when he speaks dismissively of "men of culture" (intellectuals), and of the presumed politics of various cultural artifacts (literature, jazz, etc.), the opposite seems to be the case. While liberation is, for Fanon, a cultural phenomenon, it is not a product of "culture" understood in this latter sense — "culture" as the collection of predominantly "high" cultural objects, like paintings, novels, elite forms of music, and so on, that in a complex, mediated manner produce liberation by effecting (among other things) a change in the consciousness of the colonized.

The critical energy of Fanon's essay comes from its attack on the politics of negritude. His critique is one that has since become familiar, echoed, for example, by Chinua Achebe and Wole Soyinka.[41] For Fanon, the problem with negritude is both temporal and spatial. The program advocated by intellectuals associated with negritude (Léopold Sedar Senghor's "Negritude: A Humanism of the Twentieth Century" constituting the most cogent defense of negritude)[42] has two aims: the recovery of a rich, vibrant African cultural past that imperialism sought to negate and destroy, and the affirmation of a common African culture shared by various African nations as well as by the communities of the African diaspora around the world. Fanon takes exception to both of these aims. While he believes that the recovery of a devalued cultural heritage is an important first step in opposing colonialism, it is also a limited one, because it consigns African culture to the past, to a world of tribal villages rather than reflecting the present-day reality of an Africa of skyscrapers and freeways. Intellectuals concerned with revolutionary change must, for Fanon, concern themselves with the dynamic culture of the present, and of the future, that is being generated through the very process of the struggle against imperialism. There is for Fanon a second problem with extolling the riches of an African cultural past: the evocation of Africa's cultural glories does not produce the political effect that proponents of negritude would want to claim for it. As he writes, "you will never make colonialism blush for shame by spreading out little-known cultural treasures under its eyes" (ONC 223).

To his criticism of negritude's inverted temporality—a concern for the past that should be an interest in the future—Fanon adds a second criticism. This has to do with negritude's excessive spatial generality, expressed in the form of a cosmopolitanism that seems to negate the determining and determinate importance of social, historical, and geographical context. By claiming a cultural inheritance that extends geographically to virtually every part of the world, negritude negates the fact that profound differences exist, for example, between the experiences of Africans in Chicago, Nigeria, and Tanganyika (ONC 215–16). Fanon sees the spatial generality of negritude emerging as a genuine reaction to the logic of colonialism. He writes that since "colonialism did not dream of wasting its time in denying the existence of one national culture after another," it makes sense that "the reply of the colonized peoples will be straight away continental in its breadth" (ONC 212). An emphasis on the continental or intercontinental dimensions of black culture tends, however, to impede a more materialist exploration of the relationship of culture to the particularities of history, economics, and politics in different parts of the globe. What negritude fails to account for as a result is, Fanon claims, that "every culture is first and foremost *national*, and that the problems which kept Richard Wright or Langston Hughes on the alert were fundamentally different from those which might confront Léopold Senghor or Jomo Kenyatta" (ONC 216; my emphasis).

As expressed in the series of questions posed at the end of "On National Culture," it is the question of the relationship of culture to politics that is Fanon's primary concern. Yet if "every culture is first and foremost national," then this question must itself of necessity proceed through a consideration of the shape and meaning of the nation. What the nation means for culture and for politics, how it is connected to each of them, and how it produces or is produced by them, therefore, become important questions. Why the nation is the appropriate "unit" or "container" of culture, that is, why culture is *national* as opposed to international, or (in all of the numerous modalities of these terms) local or regional is a question that Fanon never addresses directly. Indirectly, as a response to negritude's cultural idealism, the assertion of the national basis of culture can be understood as an attempt to assert a more materialist analysis of culture by counteracting a spatial generality with that of a more specific space. Nevertheless, in the context of Africa, it would seem to be difficult to see the nation as anything other than a colonial imposition on the continent, a division of peoples and geography that fails to comply with even the most basic logics of the typical (i.e., European) nation, formed as a geographic division of space on the basis of ethnic or linguistic grounds, however violently invented these might be. The nation in Africa reflects the struggle of imperial powers over the resources of the continent — nothing less, nothing more. By presuming a necessary identification between culture and nation, Fanon appears to be in danger of repeating the error he and others have identified in negritude, implicitly supporting the Manichean logic of colonialism through an affirmation of its invented divisions: white/black, rational/emotional, modern/premodern, *national/African.*

It needs to be remembered, however, that for Fanon, if culture is somehow necessarily "national," it is not because of its link to some primordial ethnic or national past. The "national culture" that interests Fanon is the one being produced in the present struggles for independence for the future. The struggle for independence and cultural autonomy is framed by the nation, it seems, because of the importance of a specifically national independence for *international* political legitimacy. Indeed, the importance that Fanon attributes to the nation arises out of his suspicions regarding a false cosmopolitanism or internationalism — what the Second Comintern identified as a first-world, "petty bourgeois internationalism"[43] — that argued for the irrelevance of the nation on the eve of national independence in the third world. In this respect, Fanon echoes views expressed by other third-world political leaders, such as Sun Yat-sen, who cautioned that first-world nations, "hoping to make themselves forever secure in their exclusive position and to prevent the smaller and weaker peoples from again reviving . . . sing praises to cosmopolitanism, saying that nationalism is too narrow; really their espousal of internationalism is but imperialism and aggression in another disguise."[44]

Fanon addresses this issue explicitly in the conclusion of the essay. In the final paragraphs, he attacks the notion that "national claims . . . are a phase that humanity has left behind" (ONC 246–47). Rather, national consciousness — which he states "is not nationalism" (ONC 247) — is the starting point for any genuine internationalism. As he writes, "it is at the heart of national consciousness that international consciousness lives and grows" (ONC 247–48). It is not, then, a regressive or parochial nationalism that Fanon is advocating, but simply a sense of the nation as the space where a people's culture takes place, a space that correspondingly defines who "the people" are, or rather, who they will come to be as a result of revolutionary struggle. National culture is therefore in a sense the culture of the dictatorship of the proletariat (given Fanon's Marxist inclinations), though with its own regional or national inflections. This sense of the nation is not without its problems, as can be seen by looking at a related formulation in Amilcar Cabral's "National Liberation and Culture."[45] Cabral describes "national culture" as the "master line" that connects across the diversity of a nation's "cultural panorama"; to create a national culture means to bring diversity into a "confluence," to "resolve contradictions and define common objectives . . . within a national framework."[46] There is something potentially sinister about this forward-looking, revolutionary nationalism. But the possibility that a national culture might limit a diversity of cultural expression *within* the nation — which is presumably the kind of thing that Fanon associates with "nationalism" rather than the nation — is not one that Fanon is either concerned with or seems prepared to address.

In contrast to various forms of nativism, Fanon emphasizes the continual transformation of culture: the shifting modalities of present reality that form "the seething pot out of which the learning of the future will be formed" (ONC 225). For Fanon, intellectuals who focus on reviving the nation's cultural past forget that "the forms of thought and what it feeds on, together with the modern techniques of information, language, and dress, have dialectically reorganized the people's intelligences and that the constant principles which acted as safeguards during the colonial period are now undergoing extremely radical changes" (ONC 225). One of the essay's central issues — perhaps *the* central one — has to do then with how intellectuals can contribute to the development of the anticolonial revolution, how one form of national culture (the "culture" of books, treatises, plays, etc.) can contribute to the production of national culture understood as a whole way of life. In this sense, Fanon's essay often reads like an African version of Mao's instructions and warnings to the intellectuals and writers assembled at Yan'an.[47] At the core of this discussion is a familiar antinomy: "The first duty of the native poet is to see clearly the people he has chosen as the subject of his work of art. He cannot go forward resolutely unless he first realizes the extent of his estrangement from them" (ONC 226). The separation of the intellectual from the masses has to be overcome if she is to be able to participate in the fight for freedom in a meaningful way. Yet it seems as if this estrangement, insofar as it appears built into the very definition of what constitutes an intellectual, is a logical and epistemological impediment as much as a political or ethical one. Fanon commonly ascribes only two positions to intellectuals: either they are nativists, "hypnotized" by the "mummified fragments" of the "dead-husk of culture" (ONC 227); or they have been seduced into mimicking the colonizer's national culture. Both of these positions distance the intellectual from the national culture (and it is safe to assume therefore that what is meant by "national," is a national *popular* culture) that is being forged through the process of national liberation. So, too, does the association of intellectuals with various forms of cultural production that Fanon characterizes as separate from the actualities and realities of "lived" or "revolutionary" culture. Writing literature, for example, is treated at times by Fanon as little more than a second-order activity whose importance to and utility for the struggle for national independence is precisely one of the things that needs to be established in "On National Culture," since, on the surface at least, writing literature seems to be little more than a waste of revolutionary energies that could be better expended on the direct struggle for independence.

In "On National Culture," the role of the intellectual or cultural producer in establishing national culture is therefore always suspect. In one sense, for Fanon, intellectuals *can* play a role in forming national culture, as long at they commit themselves to being one with the people. Their role is that of a "cheering section," urging on the political struggle without truly participating in it or explicitly affecting it. At one point, Fanon describes "national culture" as *just* this sort of activity: "the whole body of efforts made by a people in the sphere of thought to describe, justify, and praise the action through which that people has created itself and keeps itself in existence" (ONC 233). This stands in sharp contrast not only to his earlier claim that national culture emerges out of "the fight which the people wage against the forces of occupation" (ONC 223), but also with his subsequent discussion of the "reciprocal bases of national culture and the fight for freedom" (ONC 236–48), the section of the essay to which most critical attention has been paid.

This final section of "On National Culture" appears to express a more dialectical relationship between culture and politics and culture and the nation. This is exemplified in Fanon's description of the "literature of combat," the only true or authentic national literature, that is characterized by the native writer's decision to address his or her own people (ONC 239–40). A literature of combat "calls on the whole people to fight for their existence as a nation . . . it moulds the national consciousness, giving it form and contours and flinging open before it new and boundless horizons; it is a literature of combat because it assumes responsibility, and because it is the will to liberty expressed in terms of time and space" (ONC 240). As Fanon describes it, true national literature functions as a kind of technology of freedom that does not simply praise revolutionary efforts, but generates and shapes the national consciousness that makes national revolution possible. Fanon's description of the storyteller opens up a similar political role for culture: "The storyteller replies to the expectant people by successive approximations, and makes his way, apparently alone but in fact helped by his public, towards the seeking out of new patterns, that is to say national patterns" (ONC 241). It is the nation that is born out of this dialectic between the intellectual and the people through "successive approximations" as the storyteller produces his stories with the people (who are themselves in a constant state of transformation) in mind. Even here, however, Fanon is careful to assign to the nation a *priority* over national culture. The nation, he claims, gives life to national culture "in the strictly biological sense of the phrase" (ONC 245),[48] and not the other way around.

Where are we then left with respect to Fanon's questions that I set out at the beginning of this discussion? If nothing else, what we can see is that "national culture," an apparently obvious and straightforward concept, employed constantly in all sorts of political discussions and debates, is in reality an enormously difficult and ambiguous concept that can be utilized rhetorically in all kinds of ways. Fanon is never clear about what the concepts "nation," "culture," and "national culture" finally signify, and even less so about how these concepts intersect. Does culture create the nation? Or is the nation necessary for culture? What role does the writer play in producing national revolution and what role do the people play? And why a *national* revolution? Though there is a temptation to try to wrest a single meaning for all of these concepts, to assign to Fanon a particular position on the efficacy and utility of culture in the pursuit of revolutionary activities, it is perhaps by highlighting the multiple valences of each of these terms and their multiple links both to each other and to a complex set of political questions, that this essay is most useful. It is, in other words, precisely by *not* settling any of these issues that we can grasp that for Fanon the nation and national culture name a political problematic rather than a concrete solution, a problematic to which there are no easy answers.

What seems to me to most complicate Fanon's attempt to address the questions he poses at the end of "On National Culture" — as if it is only after working through all of the various combinations I have outlined here that the questions themselves finally emerge clearly — is the introduction of the "nation" into what is really a meditation on the politics of culture. The concept of the nation seems to bring with it all sorts of ambiguities that multiply the already difficult questions that he tries to address. In one respect, the anticolonial "nation," understood in Benedict Anderson's sense of the nation as an "imagined community," is only brought into existence through the struggle against colonialism; in another sense, both in terms of the people conducting the struggle and the space in which the struggle takes place, it must already be presumed to exist: the independence struggles in Algeria and Guinea-Bissau, for example, are separate ones, each responding to their own historical circumstances and their different colonial legacies, however much they might also be animated by theories and philosophies that circulate internationally. In one sense, "national culture" can simply denote the whole way of life of the people within the space, either the preexisting culture or the one to come; in another, it refers to a much more determinate and determining set of discursive and institutional practices (those of the "literature of combat," for example) that presumes to define the very essence of the people of the nation. In "On National Culture," the concept of national culture also swings ambiguously from high to popular culture, with one often pitted against the other in an attempt to define the soul of the nation. Finally, to all of this must be added Fanon's sense of the nation as a kind of generative principle that exists prior to and is the condition of national culture: "the nation gathers together the various indispensable elements necessary for the creation of a culture, those elements which alone can give it credibility, validity, life, and creative power" (ONC 245). It is not entirely surprising that to the multiple questions that Fanon poses regarding the political efficacy of culture in the independence struggle, his essay suggests multiple answers: yes, no, maybe.

What is it that introduces all of these various formulations, all of these possible meanings of national culture? Or to put it another way, what is specifically *national* about culture? The answer to this question is to be found not in Fanon's opposition of the nation to a bourgeois internationalism, but in one of the key themes that emerges out of Fanon's consideration of national culture, and one that will prove to be an essential component of any examination of literature and the nation in the third world: the question of the role of intellectuals in the revolutionary anticolonial struggle. Fanon rejects any easy connection between, for example, the writing of nationalist literature by an intellectual elite and the creation of the nation or of national culture. As in so many of his writings,[49] in "On National Culture" Fanon expresses what I have already described as a deep suspicion about the third-world intellectual. The intellectual seems to be an inevitably compromised figure, positioned between worlds in such a way that his or her contribution to the revolutionary struggle must always be treated as suspect; she is necessarily estranged from the people by virtue of being an intellectual and must resolve this estrangement before engaging in politics. And yet, the intellectual appears to have something important to contribute to political struggle *as* an intellectual—in the case of Fanon's analysis, the production of a "national consciousness" through the writing of a literature of combat. In part, this literature can only be written once the writer overcomes his or her estrangement and decides to address the people genuinely; and yet, it must also be recognized that it is only the intellectual's estrangement that makes possible the introduction of this largely foreign concept—"literature"—into the midst of the revolutionary struggle in the first place.

There are thus two points to take from "On National Culture" regarding the relationship between culture (and literature) and the nation (and politics). First, Fanon's analysis reveals a much more theoretically sophisticated attempt to deal with national culture than that presumed in the Romantic coupling of culture to nation: we are here already well beyond the simple equation of race to national culture or revolutionary writing to revolutionary results. Second, what begins to emerge is that the "nation" is the name for a specific problem of cultural production in the postwar world as much as it is the name for a geopolitical formation. In other words, what is "national" about culture is in part an expression of the difficulties faced by third-world intellectuals with respect to politics, a fact that is performatively enacted in Fanon's own ambiguity with respect to national culture. One aspect of this difficulty is located in the politics of culture with respect to the people—the problem of how to speak to and for the people, how to direct them while being directed by them. The nation forms the conceptual and rhetorical space within which this difficulty is worked out. It is in this sense that the nation is the "zone of occult instability where the people dwell" that the intellectual must travel to in order to be suffused with light. The nation is also a concept that balances out the third-world intellectual's inevitable cosmopolitanism (or modernity), which threatens his or her claim to authenticity. Fanon's famous claim that "it is at the heart of national consciousness that international consciousness lives and grows" (ONC 247–48) is by itself an incomplete thought. To this should be added the final words of "On National Culture," which directly follow Fanon's more famous statement: "And this two-fold emerging is ultimately the only source of all culture" (ONC 248). If culture is born at the intersection of the national and the international, the local and the global, then the claim that "every culture is first and foremost national" means something different from what is normally assumed. It is another dimension of the meaning of this phrase and its significance for nationalist postcolonial literature that will become clear through an examination of Benedict Anderson's *Imagined Communities.*

The Imaginary Nation: Anderson's *Imagined Communities*

Benedict Anderson's *Imagined Communities*[50] articulates what has become the most common and perhaps least contested understanding of the connection of literature to the nation in the academy today. The influence of the book on the discipline of literary criticism and on virtually every field that touches upon the question of the nation has been staggering: the description of the nation as an "imagined community" has become ubiquitous, though what is meant by either of these terms ("imagined" or "community"), let alone what they mean when taken together, has rarely been examined in detail. In projects as different as Gregory Jusdanis's and Stathis Gougouris's work on the development of Greek national culture to Robert Lecker's assessment of the work of the nation in Canadian literary criticism to Arjun Appadurai's description of the new work of the imagination that follows the end of the nation, the idea of the nation as an "imagined community" acts as a fertile and suggestive term, with "imagined" being used both in a technical sense as essentially equivalent to the psychoanalytic "imaginary" (in Gougouris's *Dream Nation*) and in a simpler, everyday sense to suggest that it is possible through a collective force of will simply to "imagine" the nation in an entirely different way (in Lecker's *Making It Real*).[51]

It is easy to understand why Anderson's theory of the nation as an imagined community has enjoyed particular success in the field of literary criticism. For instead of having to make sense of the more abstract or mediated ways in which literature contributes to the formation of the nation — as one element, for example, of the institution of state-sponsored education discussed by Gellner in *Nations and Nationalism* or as a device or *techne* that reinforces ethnic or linguistic particularities within a nation — in Anderson's account the central disciplinary object of literary criticism, the novel, is placed at the epicenter of the nation's raison d'être. Instead of having to devise complicated models by which the writing and reading of literature can be understood as having an effect on the formation and perpetuation of the nation and national culture (to have to spell out, with great difficulty, the operation of "levels," "mediation," and so on), Anderson makes the novel and the nation roughly congruent. This means that the theoretical and pragmatic questions with which Fanon and Cabral struggled regarding the relationship of culture to politics are resolved immediately, and all sorts of otherwise very difficult epistemological and critical questions are rendered easy and unproblematic.

One effect of Anderson's model has been then to close off the analysis of the relationship of literature to the nation, or if not to close it off entirely, to limit it to a contemplation of literary content, that is, to the ways in which various novels "imagine" the nation or how through novels the nation is imagined by readers.[52] This has obvious problems, not the least of which has been to render the nation into nothing more than a set of ideas shared by a community and, even more restrictedly, to ideas that are expressed or manifested uniquely in cultural objects like the novel. Even though Anderson himself deals with different national circumstances and situations, the concept of the nation as an imagined community has circulated in such a way as to have made it into a universal expression of the form of modern nation, limiting work on the specific function of the novel in various national formations. Finally, foregrounding the impact of "print-capitalism" in the formation of the modern nation has tended to sideline its role in producing transnational connections as much as national ones, as well as the development of other communication technologies in the late eighteenth and nineteenth centuries (such as semaphore, telegraphy, national road systems, etc.) that were also understood explicitly as technologies of nation-building.[53]

This is not to suggest that Anderson's understanding of the relationship of the novel to the nation is not useful or that it is (to put it too bluntly) incorrect. *Imagined Communities* remains an important and essential text on the nation, and on literature with respect to the nation, for at least two reasons. First, Anderson's claim that the idea of the nation developed outside of Europe in the form of the "creole nationalisms" of South America has challenged the largely Eurocentric terms in which third-world nationalisms have been examined. No longer the space to which the nation is exported as an alien category, the colonies become instead a site to which the nation "returns" after a prolonged, transformative detour through Europe in the eighteenth and nineteenth centuries. Second, as misleading and open-ended as the idea of the nation as something "imagined" has become, it nevertheless introduces a way of thinking about the nation that emphasizes its discursive character — an important corrective to social scientific studies of the nation that have tended to look primarily at the historical and institutional elements of the nation in exploring its growth and development.

It is in this second sense that the novel is seen by Anderson as playing a key role in the production of the nation. Anderson's chief insight about the relationship of the novel to the nation, besides that of the shared period of their historical genesis, is to see that the novel did not merely represent the nation, but was a form that "provided the technical means for 're-presenting' the *kind* of imagined community that is the nation" (IC 25). It does so in a number of ways: by helping to encourage a standardized national language; by encouraging literacy; and, in Timothy Brennan's words, "by objectifying the 'one, yet many' of national life . . . mimicking the structure of the nation, a clearly bordered jumble of languages and styles."[54] Indeed, the particular form of the realist novel seems to be an almost exact homology of the kind of imagining that is required to produce the defined space of mutual identification and group solidarity that is the nation. Anderson exemplifies this in terms of José Joaquín Fernandez de Lizardi's 1816 novel, *El Periquillo Sarniento* (The itching parrot): "Here again we see the 'national imagination' at work in the movement of a solitary hero through a sociological landscape of a fixity that fuses the world inside the novel with the world outside. This picaresque *tour d'horison* — hospitals, prisons, remote villages, monasteries, Indians, Negroes — is nonetheless not a *tour de monde*. The horizon is clearly bounded: it is that of colonial Mexico. Nothing assures us of this sociological solidity more than a succession of plurals. For they conjure up a social space full of *comparable* prisons, none in itself of any unique importance, but all representative (in their simultaneous, separate existence) of the oppressiveness of *this* colony" (IC 30).

In the spirit of Régis Debray's "Marxism and the National Question" and Tom Nairn's *The Break-Up of Britain*, Anderson's book originates as an attempt to deal with what Nairn refers to as "Marxism's great historical failure" — its lack of attention to the nation.[55] Anderson's reflections on the nation emerge out of his specific attempt to make sense of the emergence of nationalism throughout the 1970s in South Asian communist countries where one might have expected a commitment to internationalism rather than to nationalism. His theory of the emergence and development of the nation is nevertheless intended to be universal — a global theory of nationalism as opposed to simply a discussion of nationalism in South Asia. It is the universalizing character of Anderson's theoretical reflections in *Imagined Communities* that has drawn a good deal of the criticism directed toward the book. Gopal Balakrishan and Partha Chatterjee, for instance, have suggested that Anderson's discussion of the development of the nation has limited applicability to the postcolonial nation.[56] Chatterjee in particular is critical of Anderson's description of third-world nationalism as essentially "modular" in character, a nationalism sutured together Frankenstein-like from preexisting models of nationalism developed elsewhere: the "creole nationalisms" of the Americas, the linguistic nationalisms of Europe, and the "official nationalism" typified by Russia. Chatterjee asks: "If nationalisms in the rest of the world have to choose their imagined community from certain 'modular' forms already made available to them by Europe and the Americas, what do they have left to imagine? History, it would seem, has decreed that we in the postcolonial world shall only be perpetual consumers of modernity. Europe and the Americas, the only true subjects of history, have thought out on our behalf not only the script of colonial enlightenment and exploitation, but also that of our anti-colonial resistance and postcolonial misery. Even our imaginations must remain forever colonized."[57]

Chatterjee suggests that anticolonial nationalism can in fact only be understood as premised "not on an identity but rather on a *difference* with the 'modular' forms of the national society propagated by the modern West."[58] This is a point that is often misunderstood when looking at anticolonial nationalisms, Chatterjee claims, because nationalism in the decolonizing world has been taken "much too literally and much too seriously" as a political movement, even though "anticolonialism nationalism creates its own domain of sovereignty within colonial society well before it begins its political battle with the imperial power."[59] Using India as his primary example, Chatterjee shows how anticolonial nationalism works through a division of "the world of social institutions and practices into two domains — the material and the spiritual."[60] He writes: "The material is the domain of the 'outside,' of the economy and of statecraft, of science and technology, a domain where the West had proved its superiority and the East has succumbed. In this domain, then, Western superiority had to be acknowledged and its accomplishments carefully studied and replicated. The spiritual, on the other hand, is an 'inner' domain bearing the 'essential' marks of cultural identity. The greater one's success in imitating Western skills in the material domain, therefore, the greater the need to preserve the distinctiveness of one's spiritual culture. This formula is, I think, a fundamental feature of anti-colonial nationalisms in Asia and Africa."[61]

In his criticism of Anderson's universalistic tendencies, Chatterjee unfortunately produces a universalism of his own. For while the substance of his criticism of Anderson might be generally correct, it is nonetheless not at all clear whether the "formula" that he outlines can itself be easily transposed to all other anti-colonial situations. One of the things that makes the division of the "spiritual" and the "material" possible in India is, as Chatterjee points out, the evolution of Bengali in India as the language of national culture, with English reserved for the business of the country — both its political and economic business. The dynamics of colonialism are such, however, that in many former colonies, such a division is rendered difficult and problematic by the fact that there is no linguistic cultural "reservoir" available other than the colonial language, which thus has to act as the language of business *and* of national culture. The trauma experienced by many postcolonial writers is precisely to be found in their sense of a lack of an authentically indigenous language or literary form that could act as the "spiritual," "inner" domain of cultural identity, although forms of creole and regional English complicate this to some degree.[62] In nations such as Canada, those of the West Indies, and Nigeria, the "inner" therefore *also* seems to be a realm in which the West has proved its superiority. In these three regions, it is possible to see a continuum along which the colonization of the inner, spiritual domain can be measured — the "settler colony" of Canada experiencing the collapse of the "inner" and "outer" to the greatest degree (though here one needs to be careful to distinguish between French and English Canada), while Nigeria, with its rich cultural and social traditions that existed prior to colonialism, experiencing it to a more limited degree. Nevertheless, even in Nigeria, the language of the spiritual domain seems *of necessity* to be English, the only possible language shared by an elite (made up of an unhappy and unstable combination of Igbo, Hausa-Fulani, and Yoruba) for the purposes of running the country, but also, as Achebe and Soyinka both argue, for the writing of a truly national literature.[63]

The greatest problem with extending Anderson's equation *novel=nation* to these postcolonial sites, however, has to do with historical, cultural, and technological circumstances that have made the novel (or print-culture more generally) an increasingly difficult site at which to imagine the imagining of the nation. Since the end of World War II, it could be argued that representational technologies such as radio and television have largely supplanted the novel and have come to be almost coextensive with what is left of the contemporary public sphere.[64] In Nigeria and the Caribbean, illiteracy, lack of the leisure time and disposable income required for "serious" reading, and an underdeveloped tradition of reading for noninstrumental purposes (i.e., for "pleasure" as opposed to school examinations), has made the novel a minor cultural form with very little public or popular presence; in Canada, necessities of geography have meant that the discourse of nationalism has been mediated in the twentieth century by more highly developed technologies than by literature, for example, radio, television, and telecommunications. Whatever the importance of the novel in the creation of nineteenth-century European nations, it is simply too great a leap to imagine that the novel has played or can play a similar role in these postcolonial regions. This is true, I think, even if the idea of national culture or the nation is defined primarily as a concern of the elites,[65] since it is not at all clear whether the novel has played much role even in the deliberations of the postcolonial nationalist elite.

If the separation between the "spiritual" and the "material" that Chatterjee claims is definitive of anticolonial nationalism in India has a counterpart in Canada, the Caribbean, and Nigeria, it is to be found precisely in the relationship of the novel to these other representational technologies. In these regions, it is the aesthetic and moral "seriousness" of the novel that has been seen as (potentially) the spiritual reservoir of national culture; in the postcolony, radio and television are by contrast too obviously extensions of the state's political and economic apparatuses, both in terms of their relationship to nation-state propaganda and as one of the primary means by which the "foreign" intrudes into national culture. As I hope will become apparent in my examination of each of the sites under consideration in this study, the formative character of the novel with respect to the nation is a theme that is raised by writers and critics in each of these regions. Yet it is difficult to reconcile this with the limited societal impact of the novel, and with the fact that the novel, along with other literary genres "borrowed" for use in these regions, must *also* be seen as forms of foreign "technology" that might impede the development of national culture as much as they could help to produce it. So while it may not be possible to see the relationship of the novel to the nation in the way that Anderson imagines, it is perhaps as a means of resolving this absence of a language that could operate definitively as the "spiritual dimension" of national culture that the writing of literature assumes an important place in the intellectual production of the nation. The problem faced by Fanon returns here again with renewed force. For if this relatively minor cultural form contains the "spirit" of the national culture (and thus of the nation itself) it becomes imperative to reconnect it to "the people" by whatever means possible; this imperative arises as a common theme of third-world literature and criticism, particularly in that literature that sees itself as nationalist.

It should be noted that the suitability of "print-capitalism" as an explanation of third-world nationalism is something that Anderson himself has begun to question. In "Imagining East Timor," he tries to account for the "the very rapid spread and development of Timorese nationalism," which poses a problem for his general thesis. He writes: "My theoretical writings on nationalism have focused on the importance of the spread of print and its relation to capitalism, yet in East Timor there has been very little capitalism and illiteracy was widespread . . . What was it then that made it possible to 'think East Timor'"? Anderson's conclusion is that the nation imagined as "East Timor" — "an expression which comes from the Mercatorian map, on which a penciled administrative line divides Timor in half" — has in fact been produced by the gaze of the colonial state of Indonesia. Just as in the colonial Dutch East Indies, where all of the natives understood that they were all seen simply as (generic) colonized subjects in the eyes of the colonizers regardless of difference in island of origin, religion, or ethnicity, so too the Indonesian state has consistently referred to the people of East Timor as the "East Timorese," even though there are at least thirty different ethnic groups living there. Another factor that Anderson points to is the state-sponsored spread of religion in Indonesia, originally devised as a response to the official atheism of the former Communist regime. Prior to the state requirement that each Indonesian have an official religion, the East Timorese were primarily animists; afterwards, due to historical and geographic circumstances, East Timor became almost entirely Catholic. Anderson writes that "this Catholic community in some sense substitutes for the kind of nationalism that I have talked about elsewhere, which comes from print capitalism."[66]

Anderson sees the situation of East Timor as an exception to his general thesis regarding the relationship between print capitalism and the nation. But, at least with respect to the development of postcolonial nations, the case of East Timor seems to represent the rule rather than the exception. This *negative* form of nation-formation, one in which the affinities of national identification are the result of external definitions that blur race, ethnicity, and class into one category —

the "colonized" — seems to provide the founding moment of national identity in almost every postcolonial situation (a fact that Chatterjee captures in his phrase "anti-colonial nationalism"). Even so, the situation of the former British colonies is once again further complicated in terms of language. In East Timor, Tetun has become the language of religion and of national identity, functioning in the same manner as Bengali in nineteenth-century India, while Indonesian in East Timor has played the same role as English in India, providing access to the larger, outside world. Again, in the British Commonwealth there is no such internal *elite* language distinct from the language of the colonizer that might provide the basis for the creation of a national culture, nor is there the high degree of religious differentiation that characterizes the relationship of East Timor to Indonesia.

As provocative as Anderson's thesis regarding the place of the novel in the formation of the nation might be, it thus hardly seems to be an adequate way of assessing postwar, postcolonial nationalist literature. A straightforward reading of numerous literary manifestos from Canada, the Caribbean, and Nigeria regarding the revolutionary power of the novel with respect to the nation might of course suggest otherwise. From Wole Soyinka, Chinua Achebe, and Ngugi wa' Thiong'o in Africa, to George Lamming, Wilson Harris, and C. L. R. James in the Caribbean to Dennis Lee and Robert Kroetsch in Canada, writers have proclaimed the imaginative power of literature to create nations along very similar lines to Anderson's thesis. The connection that these writers make between literature and the nation is, however, nevertheless different from that made by Anderson, for whom it is the *form* of the novel and the newspaper rather than its content that makes national imaginings possible. For these writers, the connection largely remains that of the Romantic coupling of culture and nation, even if literature seems to have very limited material force in these regions.

Instead of addressing questions either of literary content or form when mapping out the function of literature with respect to the nation, what is needed is a different way of looking at this relationship that emphasizes the production of nationalist literature in the postcolony as a form of intellectual practice with its own specific limitations and possibilities and that takes into account the way in which the "nation" functions as a conceptual space for the articulation of the political dilemmas faced by third-world writers with respect to the people. This new model of national literature must also be able to assess the way in which "literature" acts as the "spiritual" dimension of the nation in the absence of an unique national language. It seems to me that, built on the insights into the category of national literature offered by a reading of Fanon and Anderson, such a model is offered by Fredric Jameson's idea of "national allegory," which not only takes into account both of these elements of nationalist literature in the decolonizing world but extends and develops them further. This is, however, by no means a clear, straightforward reading of Jameson's essay on third-world literature. What I will do is draw out the ways in which Jameson's discussion of national allegory points to both a mode of interpretation of postcolonial texts that focuses on its collective, political dimension and to a way of thinking about the nation that makes it more than just the name for a primitive political stage that we're lucky to have left behind. This may be true of the nation-state; the nation, perhaps not just yet.

"By Way of a Sweeping Hypothesis": Jameson's National Allegories

Fredric Jameson's proposal that all third-world texts be read as "national allegories" has been one of the more influential and important attempts to theorize the relationship of literary production to the nation and to politics. Unfortunately, its influence and importance has thus far been primarily *negative*. For many critics, Jameson's essay stands as an example of what *not* to do when studying "third-world" literature from the vantage point of the first-world academy. His attempt in the now infamous essay, "Third-World Literature in the Era of Multinational Capitalism," to delineate "some general theory of what is often called third-world literature"[67] has been attacked for its very desire for generality. The presumption that it is possible to produce a theory that would explain African, Asian, *and* Latin American literary production, the literature of China *and* Senegal, has been (inevitably) read as nothing more than a patronizing, theoretical orientalism or as yet another example of a troubling appropriation of Otherness with the aim of exploring the West rather than the Other. The best-known criticism of Jameson's essay along these lines remains Aijaz Ahmad's "Jameson's Rhetoric of Otherness and the 'National Allegory.' "[68] More informally and anecdotally, however, within the field of postcolonial literary and cultural studies, Jameson's essay has come to be treated as little more than a cautionary tale about the extent and depth of Eurocentrism in the Western academy, or, even more commonly, as a convenient bibliographic marker of those kinds of theories of third-world literature that everyone now agrees are limiting and reductive.[69]

Looking back on Jameson's essay through the haze of fifteen years of postcolonial studies, as well as through the equally disorienting smoke thrown up by the explosion of theories and positions on globalization, one wonders what all the fuss was about. In hindsight, it appears that almost without exception critics of Jameson's essay have willfully misread it. Of course, such misreadings are to be expected. The reception given to this or that theory has as much to do with timing as with its putative content. As one of the first responses to postcolonial literary studies from a major critic outside the field, Jameson's essay in the mid-1980s provided postcolonial critics with a flash point around which to articulate general criticisms of dominant views of North-South relations expressed within even supposedly critical political theories, like Marxism. It also provided a self-definitional opportunity for postcolonial studies: a shift away from even the lingering traces of Marxist interpretations of imperialism toward more deconstructive ones exemplified by the work of figures such as Gayatri Chakravorty Spivak and Homi Bhabha.[70] While criticisms of Jameson's views may have thus been useful or productive in their own way, they have nevertheless tended to obscure and misconstrue a sophisticated attempt to make sense of the relationship of literature to politics in the decolonizing world. I want to argue here that Jameson's "general" theory of third-world literary production offers a way of conceptualizing the relationship of literature to politics (and politics to literature) that goes beyond the most common (and commonsense) understanding of the relations between these terms.[71] Indeed, what the concept of "national allegory" introduces is a model for a properly materialist approach to postcolonial texts and contexts, one that resonates with Kalpana Seshadri-Crooks's recent characterization of postcolonial studies as "interested above all in materialist critiques of power and how that power or ideology seems to interpellate subjects within a discourse as subordinate and without agency."[72] The question I will pursue here is the relationship of allegory (as a mode of interpretation) to the nation (as a specific kind of sociopolitical problematic) and what this relationship entails for an examination of the nation in postcolonial literature, specifically in the decades immediately following World War II.

One of the first things that has to be made clear about Jameson's account of third-world literature is that the concept of "national allegory" is exhausted by neither of its component terms. Jameson is aware of the fact that the "nation" and "allegory" are concepts that have both fallen into disrepute: the nation, because of the historical experiences of first- and third-world countries with the virulent nationalisms of the twentieth century, as well as the vigorous criticism that has been directed toward the nation over the past several decades; allegory, because of the naive mode of one-to-one mapping that it seems to imply, a presumed passage from text to context that is epistemologically and politically suspect. Attaching these terms to a theory of third-world texts has a tendency to conjure up once again the whole specter of development theory and practice, in which technologies that have become antiquated in the West are passed along to countries where such outmoded technologies (including conceptual technologies such as the "nation" and "allegory") might, in Hegelian fashion, still be of some use. There is no doubt that some of the initial discomfort felt by many critics with the concept of "national allegory" arises out of a resistance to the political implications of each of its component terms — resistance to the sense, that is, that either of these terms still has a relevance for the "underdeveloped" third world that the terms have (as Jameson admits) lost in the "developed" first (in this way becoming the literary-critical equivalent of pesticides long banned in the West that continue to be produced in the U.S. for sale in the third world).

Jameson writes (infamously) that "all third-world texts are necessarily . . . allegorical, and in a very specific way they are to be read as what I will call *national allegories*" (TWL 69). Here again, the claim that Jameson makes about third-world texts ("by way of a sweeping hypothesis" [TWL 69]) cannot help but distract from his broader aim, which is not to pass aesthetic judgment on third-world texts, but to develop a system by which it might be possible to consider these texts *within* the global economic and political system that produces the third world *as* the third world. For Jameson, third-world texts are to be understood as national allegories specifically *in contrast* to the situation of first-world cultural and literary texts. He argues that there is a political dimension to third-world texts that is now (and has perhaps long been) absent in their first-world counterparts. This corresponds to a difference between the social and political culture of the first and third worlds — a difference that must, of course, be understood as broad and conceptual and that should not be seen as unreflexively rendering homogeneous two extraordinarily heterogeneous categories.[73] Jameson believes that in the West, the consequence of the radical separation between the public and the private, "between the poetic and the political," is "the deep cultural conviction that the lived experience of our private existences is somehow incommensurable with the abstractions of economic science and political dynamics" (TWL 69). In terms of literary production, this "cultural conviction" has the effect of limiting or even negating entirely the political work of literature: in the first world, literature is a matter of the private rather than the public sphere, a matter of individual tastes and solitary meditations rather than public debate and deliberation. The relations between the public and the private in the third world are entirely different: they have not undergone this separation and division. Literary texts are thus never *simply* about private matters (although, as Michael Sprinker points out in his review of Jameson's essay, they are never *simply* private in the first world either, however difficult it might be to see this now).[74] In the third world, Jameson claims, *"the story of the private individual destiny is always an allegory of the embattled situation of the public third-world culture and society"* (TWL 69).

This is a strong and sweeping claim, whose precise meaning in "Third-World Literature in the Age of Multinational Capitalism" can be grasped only by careful attention to Jameson's description of allegory, his claims about the relationship of psychology to politics in the first and the third worlds, and his description of the significance of the term "culture" and the relationship between culture and politics more generally. Of the concept of "allegory," Jameson writes that "our traditional concept of allegory — based, for instance, on stereotypes of Bunyan — is that of an elaborate set of figures and personifications to be read against some one-to-one table of equivalence: this is, so to speak, a one-dimensional view of this signifying process, which might only be set in motion and complexified were we willing to entertain the more alarming notion that such equivalencies are themselves in constant change and transformation at each perpetual present of the text" (TWL 73) Read in this more expansive way, the allegorical mode is not limited to the production of morality tales about public, political events — tales that could just as well be described in journalistic terms as in the narrative structure of novels or short stories. On the contrary, "the allegorical spirit is profoundly discontinuous, a matter of breaks and heterogeneities, of the multiple polysemia of the dream rather than the homogenous representation of the symbol" (TWL 73). If in the third world, private stories are *always* allegories of public situations, this does not thereby imply that of necessity third-world writing is narratively simplistic or overtly moralistic, or that all such texts are nothing more than exotic versions of Bunyan, as might be supposed in the terms of a more traditional sense of allegory. The claim is rather that the text speaks to its context in a way that is more than simply an example of Western texts' familiar "auto-referentiality": it necessarily and directly speaks to and of the overdetermined situation of the struggles for national independence and cultural autonomy in the context of imperialism and its aftermath (TWL 85).

Why third-world texts speak more directly of and to the national situation has to do with what Jameson sees as the very different "relationship between the libidinal and the political components of individual and social experience" (TWL

71) in the first and third worlds. One of the results of the deep division between the public and private spheres in the first world is that "political commitment is recontained and psychologized or subjectivized" (TWL 70). Again, for Jameson, the very opposite is the case in the third world. The division between public and private that is characteristic of the West is *not* characteristic of most third-world societies, or perhaps this should be read (in 1986 if not in the present) as *not yet* or *not yet completely.*[75] This assertion could be taken (again, in Hegelian fashion) as a claim that socially and aesthetically, the third world lags behind the first in its development.[76] But—and I think that this is how Jameson intends it—it also highlights a genuine, material difference between the first and third worlds that is expressed socially and culturally. The attempt to maintain a different form of social life while accepting the material and technological advantages offered by the West has constituted one of the major challenges faced by non-Western societies for whom modernity *has* been belated; it does not seem to me inconceivable to imagine a different organization of private and public in societies that were the subjects of colonialism as opposed to its agents.[77] In any case, the lack of a corresponding division between public and private in the third world means for Jameson that "psychology, or more specifically, libidinal investment, is to be read in primarily political and social terms" (TWL 72). If political energies in the first world are psychologically interiorized in a way that divests them of their power, it could be said that in the third world the "sphere" of the psychological does not function as a containment device in which what is dangerous in the public is sublimated and defused. In the first world, these sublimated energies may, of course, return to the public sphere in the mediated form of various cultural products; even so, unlike the situation of the third world, in the first world such cultural products would nevertheless be taken to be imbued with only *private* significance or with only the most banal form of larger public meaning, that is, as indicators of "styles" or "trends," the Hegelian *Geist* reborn as successive waves of (essentially similar) commodities. Another way of characterizing this division between first and third worlds within Jameson's own vocabulary is to say that the history that is everywhere actively repressed in the first world is still a possible subject of discourse in the third world (consider, for instance, his discussion of the repressed spaces of Empire in British modernism).[78] Of course, this characterization of the large-scale societal differences between the first and third worlds, Jameson adds, must be read as "speculative" and general and open to "correction by specialists" (TWL 72).

Jameson's characterization of the different relationships in the first and third worlds between private and public, and so of the psychological or the libidinal, must be read further in terms of his subsequent discussion of the concept of "cultural revolution"; otherwise, it is possible at this point to see his characterization of the vast social, political, and cultural gulf separating the first from the third world as a form of Eurocentrism or exoticism in which—as in the early moments of Modernist art—what is lacking in the civilized West is found at the heart of its "uncivilized" exterior. Jameson links the idea of "cultural revolution," which has most commonly been used to refer to the massive set of social and cultural changes undertaken by communist regimes (in China in particular), to the work of figures with "seemingly very different preoccupations": Antonio Gramsci, Wilhelm Reich, Frantz Fanon, Herbert Marcuse, Rodolph Bahro, and Paolo Freire. It is in the connection that Jameson makes between cultural revolution and "subalternity" that the significance of "national allegory" as an interpretive strategy for third-world texts begins to come into focus:

> Overhastily, I will suggest that "cultural revolution" as it is projected in such works [Gramsci, Reich, et al.] turns on the phenomenon of what Gramsci called "subalternity," namely the feelings of mental inferiority and habits of subservience and obedience which necessarily and structurally develop in situations of domination—most dramatically in the experience of colonized peoples. But here, as so often, the subjectivizing and psychologizing habits of first-world peoples such as ourselves can play us false and lead us into misunderstandings. Subalternity is not in that sense a psychological matter, although it governs psychologies; and I suppose that the strategic choice of the term "cultural" aims precisely at restructuring that view of the problem and projecting it outwards into the realm of objective or collective spirit in some non-psychological, but also non-reductionist or non-economistic, materialist fashion. When a psychic structure is objectively determined by economic and political relationships, it cannot be dealt with by means of purely psychological therapies; yet it equally cannot be dealt with by means of purely objective transformations of the economic and political situation itself, since the habits remain and exercise a baleful and crippling residual effect. This is a more dramatic form of that old mystery, the unity of theory and practice; and it is specifically in the context of this problem of cultural revolution (now so strange and alien to us) that the achievements and failures of third-world intellectuals, writers and artists must be placed if their concrete meaning is to be grasped. (TWL 76)

It is *this*, then, that the concept of "national allegory" points to—the ways in which the psychological points to the political and the trauma of subalternity finds itself "projected outwards" (allegorically) into the "cultural." Very crudely, the cultural is what lies "between" the psychological and the political, unifying "theory and practice" in such a way that it is *only* there that the "baleful and crippling" habits that are the residue of colonialism can be addressed and potentially overcome. A "cultural revolution" aims to do just this — to produce an authentic and sovereign subjectivity and collectivity by undoing the set of habits called subalternity. While these are not habits that can be modified by the transformation of political and economic institutions alone, this does not mean the exclusive attention to the subjective (the psychological) *or* to the cultural is sufficient in and of itself either. The idea of "habit" is for this reason a particularly apt way of understanding the legacy of subalternity, since it draws attention to the ways in which subalternity cannot be reduced simply to "mental" or "psychological" states, but must be seen as residing in the unconscious and inscribed somatically in a whole range of bodily dispositions. The problem of cultural revolution accounts for the presence of the political in the psychological by means of a level of mediation comprised of cultural objects like literary texts and provides a framework in which it is possible to assess "the achievements and failures of third-world intellectuals" (TWL 76) with respect to the task of reclaiming something positive from the colonial experience.

The relationship between the cultural and subalternity may be seen, of course, as almost generically definitive of the intellectual work that has been produced under the sign of "postcolonial" theory and criticism. For example, to point to one of the earliest works (retrospectively) in postcolonial criticism, what other than the "habit" of subalternity does Frantz Fanon address in *Black Skin, White Masks?* One of the most important things that postcolonial critics have added to our understanding is the degree to which cultural and discursive domination was (and is) a necessary and essential aspect of colonialism and imperialism. Where Jameson differs from most postcolonial critics, however, is in his insistence that "culture":

> is by no means the final term at which one stops. One must imagine such cultural structures and attitudes as having been themselves, in the beginning, vital responses to infrastructural realities (economic and geographic, for example), as attempts to resolve more fundamental contradictions — attempts which then outlive the situations for which they were devised, and survive, in reified forms, as "cultural patterns." Those patterns themselves then become part of the objective situation confronted by later generations.

He continues:

> Nor can I feel that the concept of cultural "identity" or even national "identity" is adequate. One cannot acknowledge the justice of the general poststructuralist assault on the so-called "centered subject," the old unified ego of bourgeois individualism, and then resuscitate this same ideological mirage of psychic unification on the collective level in the form of a doctrine of collective identity. Appeals to collective identity need to be evaluated from a historical perspective, rather than from the standpoint of some dogmatic and placeless "ideological analysis." When a third-world writer invokes this (to us) ideological value, we need to examine the concrete historical situation closely in order to determine the political consequences of the strategic use of this concept. (TWL 78)

There are then (at least) two levels of mediation that must be considered in the movement from the psychological to the political (and back again) through the cultural. Culture mediates; to understand precisely how it does so, it must be understood that the cultural forms and patterns that produce this mediation are themselves the product of an earlier process of mediation — now reified into the forms and patterns of culture that are to be used as the raw materials of cultural production. While few critics now would object to the need for the analysis of any form of cultural production to take into account the circuits of economics and politics that make the text possible in the first place, the significance of this second mode by which culture mediates remains all too often unexplored. In other words, what is often missing is the realization that all mediation in the present takes place through the reified cultural forms (and culture in general) of the past; all attempts to resolve the "fundamental contradictions" of the present through cultural production must pass through the concretized history of previous attempts to solve the contradictions of earlier infrastructural realities that have since changed in form and character. This is not to say that culture must be understood as somehow necessarily belated, or that it therefore always "misses" the present, which is to misunderstand in any case what it might mean for cultural forms to attempt to resolve historical contradictions. It is, rather, to point out the need for a more complicated understanding of the process of mediation that considers not simply the site of mediation (say, the text), but also the way in which this site is itself the product of mediation. It is this sense of mediation to which Adorno was trying to draw our attention, too, when he said that "mediation is . . . not between the object and the world, but in the object itself."

Far from reducing the complexity of third-world literary production, the concept of national allegory enables us to consider these texts as the extremely complex objects that they are and *not* just as allegories of one kind or another of the manichean binaries produced out of the encounter of colonizer and colonized (however ambivalently one might want to understand it). It also foregrounds (metacritically) the cultural-social situation of the reader of the texts, and, indeed, the very fact that every interpretation or reading is a kind of translation mechanism that it is best to acknowledge rather than to hide the workings of; the critic, too, works out of a cultural situation that forms the raw material for her readings that is the product of earlier mediations.[79] Understood through the lens of the idea of "cultural revolution" that Jameson outlines here, the concept of national allegory suggests a number of things about how we should think about postcolonial or third-world texts in the context of the period of decolonization and globalization. First, postcolonial literary production needs to be understood as forming "vital responses to infrastructural realities . . . as attempts to resolve more fundamental contradictions" (TWL 78). In other words, it is fruitful to look at this form of cultural production as a particular kind of cultural strategy (which may or may not be successful), rather than to "read" simply and immediately as "literature," in the sense in which this concept is well understood in the first-world academy.[80] Second, careful attention needs to be paid to the deployment of "ideological values" by third-world writers themselves, values that sometimes have a resonance in the Western academy because of the ways in which they politically re-empower the project of Western literary criticism. One of the most important of these values may be that of the "nation" and its strategic use in the literature produced during decolonization; another is to be found in the unquestioned assumption on the part of many critics of the almost necessary social significance of postcolonial literature (or at least, it significance in a straightforward way). Another way of putting this last point is that, in the examination of postcolonial literature, what needs to be considered is the condition of possibility for the practice of writing *literature* in these regions, for it is only in this way that we can understand the precise and complicated ways in which this older, imported "technology" participates in the task of cultural revolution that is so important to third-world societies.

Whatever one might think of this formulation of mediation and of its utility for postcolonial literary studies, it might nevertheless seem as if I have come far afield from the initial concept of "national allegory" in producing it. This elaboration of national allegory appears to be more or less akin to the general interpretive schema that Jameson has developed with remarkable consistency over the course of his career, specifically in works such as *The Political Unconscious*. And if *this* is what national allegory is finally about, one has to wonder why Jameson would have generated a neologism that cannot help but invite confusion. Why, after all, *national* allegory and not something else? In elaborating how this mode of interpretation has specific relevance to the theorization of the role and function of culture and literature in the context of decolonization and postcolonial nation-building, I want to review briefly the history of national allegory in Jameson's own work. For if there is anything that is troubling about the use of national allegory as a mode of analysis of third-world literary texts, it is to be found in the changes that this concept undergoes throughout Jameson's work, coming to be, finally, nothing less than a substitute term for the kind of dialectical criticism that he would like to apply to *all* cultural texts — whether third world or not.[81] National allegory names a possibility and a limit for texts that Jameson first sees in the fiction of Wyndham Lewis, then in third-world texts, and finally, as a condition of contemporary cultural production as such. What is missing in Jameson's discussion of national allegory is a discussion of the *nation* to match that of allegory. Though it might seem as if the nation has an important role to play in understanding third-world texts, on the question of the nation itself, Jameson has surprisingly little to say in "Third-World Literature": the nation is more or less simply conflated with the "political" and, when it is not, it becomes a term that seems to make reference to a kind of collectivity or community that is idealized when it should itself be placed into question. It is in this lack of attention to the issue of the nation in the concept of "national allegory" that the strain of the transposition of this concept from an earlier formulation becomes apparent.

The term "national allegory" first appears in *Fables of Aggression* as a description of Wyndham Lewis's novel, *Tarr*. As it is presented in this early work, national allegory originates as a much more straightforward concept than it comes to be in the discussion of third-world texts: it refers to the way in which individual characters with different national origins stand-in for "more abstract national characteristics which are read as their inner essence."[82] When dealing with any one such correspondence between character and national essence, this allegorical mode becomes a form of "cultural critique." For Jameson, the unique characteristic of Lewis's texts is to have assembled numerous national types into one setting, thereby producing "a dialectically new and more complicated allegorical system . . . that specific and uniquely allegorical space between signifier and signified" (FA 90–91). In *Fables of Aggression*, "national allegory" is thus the name for a specific, formal characteristic of Lewis's novel rather than a concept that suggests an entire system or mode of reading and interpretation. Indeed, the more general logic that Jameson suggests as the only way to account properly for the possibility in Lewis's novel of this "now outmoded narrative system" (FA 93) seems to have become transformed with reference to third-world texts into the principle of what is now "national allegory" itself. In characteristic form, Jameson draws attention to the fact that an explanation for national allegory as a formal principle of *Tarr* can only be found in history — though not in the sense that historical conditions "caused" the formal organization of *Tarr* or that the novel is "a 'reflexion' of the European diplomatic system" (FA 94). Instead, he suggests, our attention should be directed toward "the more sensible procedure of exploring those semantic and structural givens which are logically prior to this text and without which its emergence is inconceivable. This is of course the sense in which national allegory in general, and *Tarr* in particular, presuppose not merely the nation-state itself as the basic functional unit of world politics, but also the objective existence of a system of nation-states, the international diplomatic machinery of pre–World-War-I Europe which, originating in the 16th century, was dislocated in significant ways by the War and the Soviet Revolution" (FA 94).

According to Jameson, all literary and cultural forms provide an "unstable and provisory solution to an aesthetic dilemma which is itself the manifestation of a social and historical contradiction" (FA 94). National allegory can therefore be seen as a once but no longer viable formal attempt "to bridge the increasing gap between the existential data of everyday life within a given nation-state and the structural tendency of monopoly capital to develop on a world-wide, essentially transnational scale" (FA 94). In other words, the formal qualities of *Tarr* point to the fact that life in England can no longer be rendered intelligible with the "raw materials" of English life alone; narrative resources must be sought elsewhere, and what lies "outside" England is for Lewis (objectively and structurally) a system of nation-states (and their attendant national cultures): "the lived experience of the British situation is domestic, while its structural intelligibility is international" (FA 95).

It is striking that the words that Jameson uses to describe the "problem" to which Lewis's national allegory is a solution are almost exactly those that he uses later to describe modernism's characteristic spatiality.[83] Jameson suggests that "space" is a formal symptom of modernist texts *in general*, because they, too, encounter the representational crisis exemplified in Lewis's *Tarr:* the need to make sense of life in a "metropolis" whose immanent logic — that of imperialism—lies beyond its national borders. Just as in his discussion of *Tarr,* the emphasis is on form, even though the term "national allegory" is not used. It is significant that in the reemergence in the third world of what was described as an "outmoded" category by the time of the Soviet Revolution, Jameson's discussion of national allegory is no longer posed in terms of the work of form on specific "aesthetic dilemmas," nor in the form of a "representational crisis" that involves and invokes the bounded space of the nation. Instead, national allegory names the condition of possibility of narration itself in the third world. It names it, further, as a *positive* condition, one in which there remains a link, however threatened, tenuous, and political, between the production of narrative and the political. It is this connection that in the first world has been shattered so completely that third-world texts appear "alien to us at first approach" (TWL 69).

What I think this suggests is that the nation *has* disappeared from third-world national allegories. What Jameson describes as "national allegory" could just as easily have been called "political allegory": the nation seems to serve little purpose here and can only inhibit analyses of third-world literary texts insofar as it seems to point to the nation as the (natural) space of the political in the third world. So again, why *national* allegory? It does not have to do with the historical reemergence of the international system of nation-states—or of the emergence of a new form of this system, which we might too hastily identify as globalization—which formed the "structural and semantic givens" for Lewis at the beginning of this century. Nor does it seem to me that third-world literary texts face the representational problems of modernism: in the third-world, lived reality is *never* seen as intelligible only in terms of the "national" situation, and so there is correspondingly no aesthetic or formal necessity to grapple with what amounts to the "absent cause" of lived experience. The "nation" means something else entirely, something different from the empirical community or collectivity for which the cultural revolution is undertaken. Jameson's evocation of the nation in his discussion of third-world literature should be taken instead as a reference to a reified "cultural pattern" that "having once been part of the solution to a dilemma, then become[s] part of the new problem" (TWL 78).

Instead of seeing nationalist literature as a "vital response to infrastructural realities"—which I would not deny that it also clearly is—the evocation of the *nation* in the production of third-world literature must also, or perhaps even primarily, be read in terms of what Jameson describes in one of the long quotations cited above as a reified "cultural pattern" that "having once been part of the solution to a dilemma, then become[s] part of the new problem" (TWL 78). The "nation" is the name for a discursive, epistemological problematic as much as it the name for some collectivity; it names the problem of attempting to speak to and on behalf of this collectivity. This is especially the case for literature that is *explicitly* nationalist, literature, in other words, in which one aspect of the allegorical has been rendered literal, not just "conscious and overt" in comparison with the "unconscious" allegories of first-world cultural texts (TWL 79–80), but *conscious of this consciousness*. This means that a new proposition should be placed alongside Jameson's understanding of national allegory: *nationalist literature is always an allegory of the embattled situation of the third-world intellectual with respect to his or her culture and society.*

Just as Jameson suggests that it would be incorrect to "resuscitate" the mirage of the centered subject, it is important to see the crisis of intellectual authority with which we have become familiar in the first world — from Gramsci's reflections on the organic versus the traditional intellectual to Foucault's discussion of the specific versus the universal intellectual[84] — as a central part of intellectual practice in the third world as well. Jameson is, of course, well aware of this fact. Although he suggests that "in the third-world situation the intellectual is always in one way or another a political intellectual" (TWL 74), the enthusiasm for a third-world subject position that in the first-world has "withered away" (TWL 74) has to be tempered by his comments concerning the "poisoned gift of independence" (TWL 81) given to third-world writers. Radical writers in the third world face the dilemma of "bearing a passion for change and social regeneration which has not yet found its agents" (TWL 81). This is, Jameson points out, an "aesthetic dilemma, a crisis of representation: it was not difficult to identify an adversary who spoke another language and wore the visible trappings of colonial occupation. When those are replaced by your own people, the connections to external controlling forces are much more difficult to represent" (TWL 81). The postcolonial nationalist literature that I will be examining in the remaining chapters of this book constitutes both an attempt to resolve this dilemma, as well as a self-reflection on this dilemma and the problem of the lack of the agents necessary for political change.

Decolonizing the (Concept of the) Nation

Before embarking on an examination of some of the specific uses of the concept of the nation in the post–World War II literature of the British Caribbean, Canada, and Nigeria, I want to summarize the points I have been making in this chapter about how the concept of the nation should be understood in these contexts. Two general, theoretical points emerge out of the alternative genealogy of the nation that I have sketched out here—alternative, at least, to what I have claimed is the dominant position on the nation within postcolonial studies (and, indeed, with critical and cultural theory more generally), which sees the early fascination with the nation in postcolonial literature and theory as an empirical and theoretical error that we are fortunate now to have moved beyond. I have pointed out several problems with this view, not least of which is that it repeats and entrenches a progressivist (modernizing) view of the contemporary theoretical enterprise that it seems difficult to break out of: newer is better, and instead of seeing the nation as the name for a whole cluster of problems at a specific moment in time, we have tended to take the failure (has it been a failure?) or tentativeness of the nation-building project during decolonization as an indictment of the nation per se. What I am suggesting here should not be mistaken for an expression of nostalgia for the nation-*state*, which has been a political form premised on identity rather than difference in ways that are politically dangerous. Rather, what I have drawn attention to throughout this chapter is that the nation and national culture, especially as expressed in the literature of various decolonizing regions in (roughly) the 1950s and 1960s, is other than what it has been assumed to be. The aim of this project is to take the concept of the nation seriously in order to better understand what problems it names and what possibilities it represents; it does so because while we may believe that we are ready to think and feel beyond the nation, the issues and problems that circle around this concept in this first (or second) moment of postcolonial national literatures are *not* ones that we have gone beyond. Newer may be better, but we still have more to learn from even the immediate past.

This is really already the first of my general points: for writers and intellectuals in the third world, the nation names a *problematic*—not only the problem of how to create new collectivities (whose final shape may end up being very different than that of the European nation-state), but also the problem of creating the space of a new collectivity *as* an intellectual, *as* a writer, and *through* literature (most often, and certainly in the cases that I will be discussing here, through the novel). These problems are connected in ways that are almost impossible to separate out without altering the nature of the problematic. This I take to be the lesson of Fanon's brilliant formulation of the myriad questions that are involved in thinking about the nation, national culture, revolution, literature, and the intellectual. Fanon ends with questions instead of beginning with them; these same questions animate the textual readings in the chapters that follow. In this context, my examination of Benedict Anderson's *Imagined Communities* is meant to question the too easy link between the novel and nation within literary criticism, while Partha Chatterjee's perceptive criticisms of the utility of Anderson's formulations, especially with respect to postcolonial spaces, opens up another theme that runs throughout the rest of the book. If the model that Anderson develops is inappropriate for some of the former spaces of the British Empire, it is for reasons other than those that Chatterjee has suggested in his analysis of the nation in India.[85] In the regions I will be looking at, literature represents a "spiritual" dimension of the postcolonial collectivity that gives life to the possibility of the uniqueness of the nation even in the midst of a leveling modernity. This is true, of course, only for an intellectual elite who already believe that literature possesses such spiritual powers; a faith in these powers of literature constitutes one of the important elements of the larger problematic of the nation in the period of decolonization.

The second theoretical point emerges out of my reading of Fredric Jameson's attempt to produce what he describes as a "general theory of what is often called third-world literature." There are a number of lessons that can be learned from a more rigorous reading of Jameson's most maligned essay. What is especially pertinent for this study is Jameson's materialist recharacterization of the situation of the third-world intellectual. Instead of accepting at face value the claims and stated aims of postcolonial intellectuals and writers concerning the nation or seeing in literature a straightforward allegorization of the postcolonial nation, Jameson's discussion of national allegory prompts us to consider the entire cultural situation — and not just *empirically* (as historical "background"), but *theoretically* as the logic informing a particular historical formation. In particular, it forces us to consider the concept of the nation in the ways in which I have been arguing for it here: not as a pregiven, preunderstood political formation, but as a theoretical problematic that exists at the center of the struggle over subalternity and for a substantive cultural revolution.

Further, Jameson's formulation of national allegory reinforces Fanon's placement of the intellectual (and the activity of the intellectual) at the center of the problem of cultural revolution. In literary terms, what is produced under the "sign" of nationalist and national literature is a meditation on the problems and possibilities of cultural revolution and, correspondingly, on the politics of literature and of the intellectual. In each of the subsequent chapters I will keep an eye not only on the multiple ways in which literature corresponds to various "infrastructural realities," but also on the manner in which the idea of literature itself exists as one of the enduring colonial "cultural patterns" that has become "part of the objective situation confronted by later generations" (TWL 78). I do this as a way of grounding my analyses materially. I also think that such a procedure addresses a more general problem that exists today in contemporary postcolonial studies. Kalpana Seshadri-Crooks has recently described a malaise or melancholia that has beset postcolonial studies as it enters the new millennium.[86] It seems to me that revisiting Jameson's theory of third-world literature — both its problems and its productive potentialities — provides a (perhaps unexpected) way out of this malaise. One of the things for which Jameson has been criticized throughout his career is his insistence on totality as a central concept in social and political criticism. In the context of postcolonial studies, it is easy enough to see how this appeal to totality could be mistaken as a Eurocentric, universalist claim par excellence.[87] But this is to conceive of the concept of totality far too rigidly and unimaginatively, and in the process of doing so, to "fall back into a view of present history as sheer heterogeneity, random difference, a coexistence of a host of distinct forces whose effectivity is undecidable."[88] It seems to me that what is missing in many theories of postcolonial literary production (and what thus produces the malaise that Crooks points to) is just such a map of the relative effectivity of different forces in the globalscape.[89] In any case, my argument here should also be taken as an implicit argument on behalf of totality — not the "bad" totality that legitimates theories of modernization of development, but the totality constructed by an antitranscendental and antiteleological "insurgent science" that "is open, as open as the world of possibility, the world of potential."[90] In this study, at least, totality appears in part as the possibility of metacommentary — not as a secondary step in interpretation but as a condition of interpretation per se. What national allegory names is thus the conditions of possibility of a metacommentary that considers the problematic of the nation that I have outlined here.[91]

Two final points of clarification. First, even given the claims made on behalf of totality above, this study is not meant to call postcolonial studies into question, a set of critical practices that I have described elsewhere as the most important ones to have emerged over the past half-century.[92] It is not meant as a substitute or replacement for theories of identity and subjectivity that the postcolonial cannot do without. At the same time, this project does not simply constitute an addendum to theories that view totality with suspicion. One of the reasons that my readings concentrate on relatively canonical texts is to highlight points of difference *and* similarity with interpretations of these texts that have been offered from other viewpoints. It is perhaps in considering these similarities and differences that a much needed rapprochement can begin to be developed between theories of totality and those that focus on the (post)colonial subject.

Finally, as I hope is clear in the comparative character of this study, the utility of the theoretical frame that I have developed here is to be found, finally, in the examination of specific, concrete sites — in the relationship, in other words, of specific literatures to specific national problematics. As should be equally clear, it is the specific character of these sites that have framed the development of my theoretical orientation, though the linear structure of a book in which theory is presented before practice has a way of confusing this fact. What should be absolutely clear is that for all my discussion of *the* nation, even a cursory examination of the relationship between literature and nation reveals that there is not one relationship, but *many* — as many as the literatures that bear the names of nations (American literature, British literature, Nigerian literature, etc.), and even more, since these already accepted national designations leave out untold literatures that work across the boundaries of established nations in an effort to produce larger units of identification (Caribbean literature, African literature, etc.), as well as literatures that contest the formation of national literatures through the production of regional literatures that are often conceived of as the seeds of new national projects (Southern literature in America, Québécois literature in Canada, Basque literature in Spain, etc.). My aim is not to suggest that the spaces that I take up in this study are, finally, all the same. Whatever work the term "postcolonial" undertakes, whatever knowledges it produces, its function is not to level very different spaces into a single narrative about colonialism, imperialism and its aftermath. At the same time, there is a reason why comparing these three regions isn't simply arbitrary or beholden to that logic of Empire that these spaces have, in their own ways, tried to escape. The problematic of the nation in Canada, the Caribbean, and Nigeria shares what Wittgenstein would describe as a "family resemblance" to one another due to the circumstances and mode of their interpolation into the global world-system. Yet they also differ enough that my own desire for a certain order and logic to this book was exploded. In my examination of the problematic named by the nation in Canada in the 1950s and 1960s, it made no sense to offer the kind of literary readings that I present in the case of the West Indies and Nigeria. I hope that why this is the case will become apparent in the arguments that I present in the remainder of the book.

The ambiguous feelings James always expressed about the suitability of the novel as the best mode of cultural expression in the region are heightened in this book as he excavates and describes a practice that is both more "indigenous" and more deeply connected to the daily lives and practices of Caribbean peoples: in the shared love of cricket across the islands, he locates a different site on or through which a certain form of national space might yet be produced. And while James flirts with renewing the nation-space along this axis of identification, he ultimately opts for a politics of place that reveals some of the limits of the literary attempt to produce the space of the nation in the Caribbean.

The literary production of space for political purposes is an urgent issue for many decolonizing countries. The literary desire to produce the nation is expressed, for example, in both the criticism of Chinua Achebe and Wole Soyinka and in the writings of the proponents of negritude (though here the space is pan-African or international) whom both criticize. It is also a central component of much critical reflection about the literary situation of "settler colonies" such as Canada, South Africa, and Australia, where there exist numerous examples of literary attempts to map, name, and domesticate non-European spaces through European languages and concepts. In the Caribbean, however, space inevitably was and is an even more important concept because of the particular circumstances of its geography—its "empirical" space, in other words. The "West Indies" is a space that can only be produced through several apparently contradictory operations: they are a group of islands that do not extend a pseudo-pod toward other, geographically similar islands divided among the colonial powers (for example, a vast gulf of space separates Dominica and Guadeloupe even though the actual distance between them can be measured in tens of miles); at the same time, they include Guyana, a country on the South American mainland, though again, not Belize or Honduras, even though these were also British colonies. The operations of these novels during the period of the establishment of the federation shows a further heightening of these contradictions, as questions of race are introduced into the abstract difficulty of establishing some geographical relation between the countries of the West Indies (since this relation cannot be that of contiguity, which is perhaps the most basic requirement for the establishment of national space). Since even racially the islands are enormously diverse—a fact that Lamming seems at times to forget and that Naipaul sees as precisely the source of the West Indian "problem"—it seems that it is only the common experience with the British Empire that can hold the states of the West Indies together as a common nation. This is an inglorious and troubling basis for a federation of states intent on declaring their freedom from Empire, and introduces yet another problem that must somehow be accounted for and resolved in the creation of national space.

There is a further contradiction that needs to be addressed: exile. If exile is not the entire story of Caribbean literature, it is nevertheless difficult to analyze the literature of the 1950s and 1960s without considering the meaning and consequences of exile — what Simon Gikandi has called "the ground zero of West Indian literature."[6] The scale on which the generation of British Caribbean writers after World War II immigrated to London, the "literary capital" of Empire, is perhaps unprecedented in literary history. Between 1948 and 1953, Edgar Mittelholzer, William Richardson, Samuel Selvon, Andrew Salkey, Mais, and Lamming — a who's who of a whole generation of writers from the British Caribbean — all made the destabilizing move across the Atlantic; Naipaul, Harris, Jamaica Kincaid, Neil Bissondath, and others would leave the Caribbean in the years to come, now moving to Toronto or New York as well as to London as the latter's influence as a literary center declined and as immigration between the Caribbean and Britain became more difficult after the passage of the Commonwealth Immigrants Bill in 1962.

One reason the Caribbean has become a site to which an increasing amount of critical attention has been paid is because it has been seen as a paradigmatic space for the study of colonialism and postcolonialism, a space in which all of the contradictions and ambiguities of the colonial project have been revealed with particular acuteness. This is true of the Caribbean experience of exile as well: the social and cultural logic governing the exile of Caribbean writers reveals the underlying operations of the institution of literature in the colonies more generally (though specific historical differences always have to be taken into account). Unlike the positions of exile that Achebe, Soyinka and other Nigerian writers have had to occupy on and off since Nigerian independence in 1960 (especially following the Biafran conflict), the exile of Caribbean writers was not political (in the restricted sense of this term), but was motivated primarily by social and economic concerns: it was largely the desire of these writers to be *writers*, to write for an audience, and to make a career as writers that led them into self-imposed exile abroad. The economic and social conditions necessary to produce a viable local literature — a book publishing and distribution system, a relatively large and leisured middle-class, a high level of literacy — were not present in the Caribbean in the 1950s and 1960s. If Caribbean writing was to be a possibility, then the only option was to go abroad where the conditions for writing were more favorable. The decision to undertake exile has too often been seen as nothing more than the result of numerous individual career decisions. An assessment of the conditions of possibility of exile will show instead that it is one of the products of an attempt to connect literature and space — to write a *national* literature and a *literature* that is national.

Exile is important for an analysis of the interest in the nation-space in the Caribbean during the period of federation not simply because of the biographical circumstances of most Caribbean writers. I agree with Simon Gikandi, who suggests in his excellent book *Writing in Limbo* that "exile is not a subjective quest by the Caribbean avant-garde to escape the fixed and fetishized places in the colonial."[7] What is at issue in the exile of all these writers is, rather, a certain conception of writing as a particular kind of intellectual activity with a unique social and political function. To put this in a different register, what is assumed at the outset by these exiled writers is the whole of bourgeois aesthetics: the historical division of labor that makes writing into a specific career, the idea of literature as a special kind of writing whose privileged domain is that of subjectivity — in other words, a notion of the relationship of the writer and writing to the rest of the culture that from the outset positions its political effectivity within strictly demarcated limits. The distance and autonomy of modernist aesthetics that Pierre Bourdieu, for instance, shows to be yet another element of class distinction in the West reappears here in the emptiness and abstractness of a national space imagined from afar.[8] For what is imagined in these works is not the specificities of place, a home that would act as a resolution to exile and would also permit a reading of all the contradictory forces that go into the production of place and space, but the creation of a space that would make writing (and politics) possible: the abstract space of modernity so ably embodied in the form of the nation.

Writing Exile: "The Occasion for Speaking"

The interplay between nationalism and exile is like Hegel's dialectic of servant and master, oppositions informing and constituting each other. All nationalisms in their early stages develop from a condition of estrangement.

— EDWARD SAID[9]

Our workers in literature and art must carry out their own work in literature and art, but the task of understanding people and getting to know them properly has the highest priority. How have our workers in literature and art performed in this respect until now? I would say that until now they have been heroes without a bat-

tlefield, remote and uncomprehending. What do I mean by remote? Remote from
the people. Workers in literature and art are unfamiliar with the people they write
about and with the people who read their work, or else have actually become estranged from them. Our workers in literature and art are not familiar with workers, peasants, soldiers, or even their cadres. What do I mean by uncomprehending?
Not comprehending their language. Yours is the language of intellectuals, theirs is
the language of the popular masses.   — MAO ZEDONG [10]

Exile is one of many tropes in postcolonial criticism that has taken on important
epistemic and historical significance. It has been used to describe not only the
state of those who have been forced to make the traumatic transition from one
land to another but also to refer more generally to any kind of break with an
"authentic" relationship, whether to the land, to history, to language, or to place.
In this sense, it is possible to suggest, at least metaphorically, that one outcome of
the twentieth century has been to make exile a universal condition, whether this
takes the form of rootless suburban existence in the West, the collapse of traditional ways of life under the relentless pressures of modernization, or the global
diasporic movement of peoples.[11] It has also been asserted that this universal
condition is one that the figure of the literary or intellectual exile, in particular
the postcolonial intellectual, is in a unique position to understand and comment
on. As Edward Said writes, "liberation as an intellectual mission, born in the
resistance and opposition to the confinements and ravages of imperialism, has
now shifted from the settled, established and domesticated dynamics of culture
to its unhoused, decentred, and exilic energies, whose incarnation today is the
migrant, and whose consciousness is that of the intellectual and artist in exile, the
political figure between domains, between forms, between homes, and between
languages."[12]

    Whether or not Said's vision of the intellectual and the migrant are accurate,
in the Caribbean in the 1950s and 1960s exile must be seen as the result of a
process different from the one he suggests here. The energies of Caribbean exile
are not born out of the rejection of the "domesticated dynamics of culture," a
phrase that invokes the nation and national culture. On the contrary, exile is born
out of these very dynamics. Critics such as Said and Gikandi have suggested that
exile is a necessary first step in the project of decolonization.[13] Gikandi, for
instance, suggests that in the Caribbean the loss represented by exile provides the
only conditions from which national consciousness could develop.[14] This relationship between exile and nationalism is reflected in the works that I look at

here. What I will consider is how a missing third term in this relationship —
literature — mediates and transforms the connection between exile and nationalism in complicated ways that need to be clearly laid out.

The link between exile, the nation, and literature is perhaps most thoroughly
articulated in George Lamming's influential essay "The Occasion for Speaking."[15] Written in the midst of the region's experimentation with federation,
Lamming's essay is both the definitive attempt by a West Indian writer to provide
a rationale for his self-chosen exile and also a text that has been important in
establishing exile as a theme of postcolonial literary studies. The explanation of
the causes of exile is couched by Lamming in the Fanonian vocabulary of the
psychic pressures of colonialism on the Caribbean subject and, in particular, the
Caribbean writer.[16] For example, Lamming points out that the Caribbean writer
has no literary history, that writing appears to him as something that exists only
abroad, that his language is not "authentic" but borrowed, and so on. These are,
for him, the cultural conditions that form the psychic limits and possibilities of
writing in the Caribbean; they also form a set of problems that have been described as those commonly faced by the postcolonial writer. These conditions
produce two nearly contradictory impulses in Lamming's essay. On the one hand,
Lamming suggests that the writer must assume the role of exile because of the
enormous number of barriers that stand in the way of the colonial writer that
prevent him from being a writer at all. He writes that "these men had to leave if
they were going to function as writers since books, in that particular colonial
conception of literature, were not — meaning, too, are not supposed to be —
written by natives" (OS 27). On the other hand, Lamming articulates the unique
role and importance of the novel in producing a regional or national culture in
which these very same barriers would hopefully no longer be present. Just as the
reasons for exile are described in terms of an oppressive subjective structure that
disables writing, the specificity of the novel's task is explained in terms of its
ability to identify and counteract these subjective structures. A set of imbedded
contradictions develop, a knot of paradoxes that only exile can cut: the impossibility of writing at home until a writing has already taken place that would
produce the conditions of "home," i.e., a genuine nation; the writing of texts that
articulate a national culture only for an audience that will remain forever foreign
to this culture, since it is difficult for these texts to reenter the colonial space they
left behind.

In *Black Skin, White Masks*, Fanon hoped to bring about the end of the "massive psychoexistential complex" created by the "juxtaposition of white and black

races," in part through his analysis of it.[17] At the same time, he is aware that "there will be an authentic disalienation only to the degree to which things in their most materialistic meaning of the world will have been restored to their proper places."[18] Like Fanon, Lamming also identifies two levels on which the legacy of colonialism must be fought. There are, of course, political or economic reasons why, at the time Lamming was writing, the Caribbean was not yet politically independent. In the case of the Caribbean, however, Lamming identifies the real problem as due not to a failure to take definitive political action, but to "colonialism [as] the very base and structure of the West Indian's cultural awareness" (OS 35). Lamming suggests that for this reason the effects of colonialism on the Caribbean are unique in the entire colonized world: "What the West Indian shares with the African is a common political predicament: a predicament which we call colonial; but the word colonial has a deeper meaning for the West Indian than it has for the African. The African, in spite of his modernity, has never been wholly severed from the cradle of a continuous culture and tradition. His colonialism mainly takes the form of lack of privilege in organizing the day to day affairs of his country. This state of affairs is almost at an end; and its end is the result of the African's persistent and effective demand for political freedom" (OS 34).

What Fanon describes in *Black Skin* as an ontological condition arising throughout the colonized world based on the structural relationship of race and power between black and white, colonized and colonizer, Lamming claims here uniquely for the West Indies. The movements and actions against colonialism launched around the world following World War II have, in Lamming's view, not been mirrored in the West Indies because of this "absolute dependence" (OS 35) on the values of the colonizer. With apparent disregard for the prewar efforts of trade organizations and labor unions to bring about representative democracy in the region, and the political gains achieved by figures such as Norman Manley, Grantley Adams, Eric Williams, and Cheddi Jagan in the decade leading up to the achievement of formal political independence throughout the English Caribbean, Lamming writes that in the Caribbean "the desire to be free, the ambition to make their own laws and regulate life according to their own impulses, is dormant" (OS 35).[19] To rectify this requires above all a modification of this "structure of awareness" in the West Indies; and it is the novel that for Lamming has a privileged role in effecting this phase-change of awareness.

For Lamming, the Caribbean is a special case because unlike other colonial countries, "cultural awareness" has effectively become the base to the economic and political superstructure (an inversion of the typical relation between these terms), and so like any base-superstructure relationship the former must be changed before significant effects can be seen in the latter. It seems that for Lamming, this is what the novel alone is able to do, a fact that grants the novelist an important and historic role, and, indeed, Lamming says that the advent of the novel in the Caribbean is one of the three most significant historical events in the region (OS 37–38). This claim about the subjective energies of the novel is fraught with problems that reflect the complexities of bringing about (in Jameson's terms) a cultural revolution in the West Indies. For instance, the fact that the subject of the West Indian novel is, as Lamming claims, "peasant" as opposed to the middle-class orientation of the British novel (OS 38), does not alter the fact that the form of the novel, the very idea of its potential effects, as well as its place within the culture—the assumption of its deep link to subjectivity and inner experience, for example—remain middle class and Western. Of course, as Ngugi wa Thiong'o has shown in his own work, "the social or even national basis of the origins of an important discovery or any invention is not necessarily a determinant of the uses to which it can be put by its inheritors."[20] Nevertheless, rather than modifying or altering the "cultural awareness" of the West Indian subject, the novel may act in a contrary fashion, reinforcing the damage to the West Indian's awareness, not least through an emphasis on the cultural or political necessity of the novel itself. This possibility can be seen, for example, in Lamming's assumption that it is writing above all else, in a region with neither a large leisured middle class or a high literacy level, that will bring about political change. This causes him to misrepresent the political situation in the Caribbean—to render impulses toward independence "dormant" and to place the West Indian within a desperately disabling psychoexistential complex. But as Gordon Rohlehr writes, "long before the advent of the West Indian novelist, the peasant was visibly working against tremendous odds towards an essential independence . . . writers reflected an awareness which had been there for some time; they could neither create nor restore what was already present in the creative struggle, rebellion and movement of the West Indian people."[21]

What is it for Lamming that the writing of literature is supposed to accomplish that, one would presume, other avenues of experience and activity cannot? And why or how does the novel in particular help to dissipate the West Indian's colonial structure of thinking? The novel, more than any other cultural form, has long been seen by writers, critics, and theorists of varying orientations as being uniquely able to represent and reveal the workings of ideology (Fredric Jameson has described it as "the privileged instrument of the analysis of reality")[22] and also to disrupt this ideology. This is potentially true of even the most retrograde forms of literature, provided they are read in the right way: all literature expresses the political unconscious of its formative moment. This is essentially how Lamming views the operations of the Caribbean novel. In part, Lamming's way of understanding how the novel ruptures the West Indian's colonial awareness is through its ability to represent what György Lukács has called "totality." Gikandi suggests that Lamming is attracted to the novel because "narrative offered a form and strategy for restoring West Indian character to history."[23] But even more strongly expressed in "The Occasion for Speaking" is the idea that the political work of the novel is conducted through the specific operation of representation: the introduction to the novel of peoples and thematics that have never before been represented in this form. Lamming writes that "the novelist was the first to relate the West Indian experience from the inside . . . for the first time, the West Indian peasant became other than a cheap source of labour. He became, through the novelist's eye, a living existence, living in silence and joy and fear, involved in riot and carnival. It is the West Indian novel that has restored the West Indian peasant to his true and original status of personality" (OS 39).

By being admitted into the space of the novel, the peasant undergoes a momentous political change. If the novel has the power to give life to the peasant in the way Lamming describes, the importance of the novel for the Caribbean cannot be underestimated. But then again, the claims that Lamming makes for the novel seem excessive and politically suspect. While making the peasant the subject of the novel does have effects above and beyond simply prompting a reconsideration of the appropriate themes and concerns of literature (a strictly disciplinary politics), this shift in representation does not by itself constitute a corresponding shift in the position of the peasant in social and economic terms or, for that matter, in terms of a more general shift of their cultural awareness. Representation does not all at once break up the accreted habits of subalternity to bring about a cultural revolution.

The real appeal of the novel for Lamming is that it also represents a pedagogic technology: it is a means of transmission or education. The novel has the potential to be a didactic form unlike any other: it is a mode of transmission that accomplishes the miraculous feat of passing an incendiary note scribbled by one person to a multitude, enflaming an entire nation as it passes through it. It is because this form has the potential to be so widely dispersed, so universally consumed, that the act of writing a novel or of reading one can become a legitimate way of pursuing politics outside of the determinations of a dominant ideology that always limits the scope of what counts as the space of politics; the expansion of the space of politics in the twentieth century into that of cultural production and reproduction, which has been suggested by thinkers as diverse as Antonio Gramsci and Amilcar Cabral, has helped to reinforce the political viability of these acts. At one point in "The Occasion for Speaking," Lamming laments the fact that while in Nigeria writers such as Chinua Achebe and Cyprian Ekwensi also have the opportunity to be radio broadcasters, this same opportunity is not available to Caribbean writers, or at least not on native soil (OS 48). It is this, then, that seems to be Lamming's ultimate desire: the novelist as radio host. But while radio has the ability to reach a mass audience even in relatively poor areas of the world, the novel has much greater material and social constraints. This fact is, for Lamming, not something that should concern the writer; it does not mark a failure of the writer or indicate, potentially, the irrelevance of the novel to postcolonial politics. Rather, the lack of an audience for the Caribbean novel is seen as the responsibility of politicians, and it is they who must work to make the conditions for writing possible. On this point Lamming is clear: "These [Caribbean] writers will never be required in the West Indies until their meaning and their contribution have been established in national and political terms. And it is not their job to establish themselves in this way. Their business is to get on with writing their books. The rest must be done by men like Eric Williams, the Chief Minister of Trinidad, and C. L. R. James" (OS 48).

If there is no audience for the Caribbean novel, no native "peasant" audience on whom the novel can work its political effects, the question, "For whom, then, do we write?" must be raised. And while Lamming does pose this question, he does not seem to take it as a major epistemological or political problem. In "The Occasion for Speaking," he acknowledges that the primary readership for the Caribbean novel is a foreign audience, and not the Caribbean middle class, but he passes very quickly from this to ponder the question of whether or not Caribbean writers should market their works in Communist countries (OS 43). Other novelists, much more troubled by the gap existing between the postcolonial writer and his or her readership, have attempted to reconceive the character of the novel, to modify it in some way in order to bring about potentially wider effects, or have attempted to construct a hermeneutic operation or an epistemology of some sort, an interpretive machine that would help to bridge this gap. Perhaps the best-known example of this is Ngugi wa Thiong'o's decision to write novels in Gikuyu, altered not only in terms of their language, but in their form, and accompanied by a significant effort to overcome the usual problems of distribu-tion to a nonurban, non–middle class.[24] Lamming makes no such concessions to his audience: he asserts a connection, claiming that although "the education of these [Caribbean] writers is more or less middle-class Western culture, and par-ticularly English culture . . . the substance of their books, the general motives and directions, are peasant" (OS 38). The identity he affirms between West Indian writers and Western culture is not something that seems to require any sort of theoretical struggle before the peasant can, through the writer, speak in his or her "own" voice. The relationship to the peasant is simply asserted, and the fact that the peasant appears as the dominant subject of the novel — a fact about the Carib-bean novel that Rohlehr disputes[25] — is, for Lamming, guarantee enough of the necessity of the novel and of its positive political effects.

Realizing the need for more than an assertion of identity between writer and peasant, Lamming has proposed more recently an operation that might bring the novelist and his audience closer together:

> I would propose that the essential and supreme function of the critic/intellectual, in our circumstances, is to be a mediator of the text; and the area of mediation must travel beyond the enclave of the specialist and student, or specialist in contention with specialist. It must attempt to travel beyond this domain of mediation to link the human substance of the text to the collective consciousness, the continuing social reality which has, in fact, nurtured the imagination of the writers. So the critic/ intellectual, in our circumstance (which requires the compiling, preserving, and disseminating of the native inventory), needs also to cultivate the skills of the jour-nalist, the temperament of urgency so common in the evangelist, intervening in public debate over issues that he or she can easily identify in the literary texts that are mediated.[26]

But here, too, the text (and it is clear that Lamming is referring to the literary text above all else) remains essential. The literary text remains the starting point for politics, and Lamming's critic-intellectual must learn to speak to a wider audience in order, ultimately, to lead this audience back to the novel by means of his or her work of "mediation." If the earlier relationship between writer and peasant was undertheorized, it is now too one-sided: the mass must be trans-formed so that it may come to occupy the position of knowledge that the literary intellectual already occupies. After several decades of writing by feminist and antifoundationalist scholars that has attacked this notion of the intellectual as the figure who speaks for those who are unable to speak for themselves, Lamming's view of the intellectual is troubling, to say the least.

My main intent here is not to expose the failings of "The Occasion for Speaking," to question its claims, or to challenge its politics, but to show how a certain understanding of the function of literature or literary writing produces a specific framing of the nation and of the problem of cultural revolution. Lamming's essay begins with a division of intellectual labor into the spheres of culture and political economy. From this beginning, a series of conclusions are drawn that together produce the links between literature-nation-exile. There is, first, the idea that the central task with respect to colonialism involves the reparation of a damaged consciousness and subjectivity. Second, until this first task is accomplished, there is no possibility of conducting "normal" politics, as evidenced by the fact that nothing seems to be happening politically (or at least this is his claim). In other words, the politics of consciousness must precede any other politics. Third, the politics of repairing a damaged cultural awareness is seen to take place within literature, particularly in the novel, since it is the space in which individual and social consciousness is somehow represented and, by virtue of the transmissibility of its "message," the space that is able to turn a subjective politics into a social one. Or at least, it has the *potential* to do so: in the Caribbean, this potential is always delayed because there is no audience that could produce within itself this miraculous transformation. And so, because the entire space of politics is thus closed off, rendered impenetrable, the writer must go into exile. This exile only further confirms the very first and second conclusions, transforming them in the process into a truth about the character of the present that then becomes a guiding principle of intellectual practice.

It is the choice of exile that Lamming sets out to explain; in the process of explaining it, he misrecognizes it and produces it as an epistemological category. What produces the condition of exile—"exile" as opposed to a term such as "emigrancy"—is not, finally, some general structural condition of the (post)colonial subject, but perhaps only one aspect of it that has a resonance within an elite: a belief that literature is *more than* another form of writing, that it possesses almost magical powers that make possible a resolution of political problems at the level of the aesthetic. And this understanding of literature needs to be seen as intimately related to the concept of the nation. When Lamming discusses the life of the peasant as the central concern of Caribbean literature, he does so as a way of connecting the interests of the intellectual (literature) with the authenticity of people (the nation). Lamming makes clear that the responsibility of the novel is to make the Caribbean aware of itself as a national space, perhaps to even create this space for the first time. It is a very particular sense of the nation that is invoked by Lamming, with political consequences for both the peasant and the intellectual. It seems that the peasant enters the novel only as the citizen of a nation-space in which the writer also has a function. In other words, politics can return to the islands only when the particularities of peasant life, the specific practices and activities connected to life in particular places, have been subordinated or elevated to the more general space of the nation—when the peasants understand themselves no longer as inhabitants of a village, St. Mary's Parish, or even of Jamaica, but as citizens of the West Indies. This is the project of both federation and of Lamming's novel, *The Emigrants*.

The Intellectual's Nation: George Lamming's *The Emigrants*

"This West Indies talk is w'at a class o' doctor call symptomatic."
— GEORGE LAMMING [27]

The connection between space, nation, and literature in the figure of exile appears with particular force in Lamming's *The Emigrants*. It may be said that all of his novels attempt to deal with the West Indies as whole. Of all the Caribbean novelists writing in the 1950s, only Lamming does not attempt to write the history of a specific place, a particular segment of Caribbean experience. While Lamming's first novel, *In the Castle of My Skin*, bears a resemblance to a novel such as Roger Mais's *The Hills Were Joyful Together* in its intimate and detailed depiction of the life of a particular, isolated community, it is important to remember that the novel is set in San Cristobal, a fictional island that appears again in *Of Innocence and Experience*, *Natives of My Person*, *Season of Adventure*, and *Water with Berries*. It is not enough for Lamming to write about a specific place. His aim seems to be to write the history of the West Indies in general through the production of a typical Caribbean island that does not synthesize the differences between each island but, rather, attempts to distill their ontological and epistemological essence.

This process is made apparent in Lamming's use of the Caliban-Prospero relationship as a general philosophical model of the relationship between colonized and colonizer. This abstract model of intersubjective relations is used as the basis for character development in all of Lamming's novels, and as such they often read as the articulation of theoretical or philosophical positions that are exemplified rather than developed through novelistic situations. Since Lamming himself has highlighted the primacy of the Caliban-Prospero relationship in his work in *The Pleasures of Exile*, this is a model that has also somewhat unreflectively been employed as the primary critical means of reading Lamming's work as an attempt at an extended and consistent analysis of Caribbean experience.[28] Lamming's use of abstract models as a means of describing Caribbean experience can be seen as well in his use of the child characters Singh, Lee, and Bob, who appear in *The Pleasures of Exile* and *Of Age and Innocence*[29] and relate the story of the resistance of the "Tribe Boys" to European colonization. These children are intended by Lamming to represent allegorically the mixed racial composition of the islands (Singh and Lee, the children of Indian and Chinese indentured workers, Bob, the child of African slaves). These three boys also represent the political future of the islands, a future that is possible only if the internal racial problems of the islands are overcome through the production of such innocent clusters of friends. What is collapsed in the allegorical friendship of these three boys in the imagined setting of San Cristobal is the enormously different racial composition of each West Indian country. The continued Amerindian presence is also forgotten, as is the process of creolization that has made it difficult to assemble such racial "natural kinds" into mixed groups.

Lamming's second novel, *The Emigrants*, constitutes his most explicit attempt to define the essence of what makes up the space of the West Indies as a whole. From what has been said thus far, it is not surprising that this quest for essence should intersect with the project of defining a West Indian nation-state. In part because of the disappearance of the imagined island of San Cristobal and the reemergence of the real islands subsumed within it, *The Emigrants* is uncharacteristic of Lamming's other novels. Like his other novels, it explores one dimension of what will be an attempt (through the "system" of his entire literary output) to provide a complete account of Caribbean experience; unlike them, however, it is composed of an odd assortment of gestures and positions that never manage to cohere into a whole. While this can be seen as a modernist strategy whose intent is to exemplify the state of the colonial mind,[30] my reading will suggest that the explanation lies elsewhere. If San Cristobal does not appear in this novel, it is because the task of the novel is to produce this composite island — now called "the West Indies" — not from a more or less abstract determination of what the West Indies might be, but out of the fragments of real islands and the real inhabitants of those islands.

As the title suggests, *The Emigrants* explores the experience of a group of West Indians who emigrate to London in the early 1950s. In one respect, it is possible to view the novel as the natural continuation of the narrative begun in *In the Castle of My Skin*, both in terms of its autobiographical relationship to Lamming's own life and to the position that *The Emigrants* occupies in the total system of Lamming's novels. In terms of its exploration of the immigrant experience, specifically that of the colonized individual traveling "back" to the center of Empire, the novel is among the first texts to explore the psychological trauma of the racialized encounter with the reality of imagined imperial "home";[31] indeed, it explores in great detail the way in which the concept of "home" is in fact doubly displaced by emigration. One of the gravest consequences of emigration is that it brings about a total destruction of any notion of "home" or belonging: it is discovered that the new country can never substitute for the home that has been left behind; the home left behind is, correspondingly, nostalgically recreated from afar in such a way that any subsequent return to this place will find it wanting: no longer home, but a place from which the immigrant is also displaced. In its attention to the psychological and philosophical dimensions of the colonial and postcolonial experience, Lamming's novel reads like the English-language literary equivalent of Fanon's *Black Skin, White Masks,* a text that appears to have had an influence on *The Emigrants.*

If we see the novel in this context, it appears that its main function is the performance of the kind of sociodiagnostic that Fanon undertakes in *Black Skin.* Since the theme is emigration, this sociodiagnostic concerns the trauma of digging up one's roots in the hopes of transplanting them in more fertile soil elsewhere. With respect to colonialism, a *literary* examination of emigration might be thought to have the advantage of bringing to light all of its ontological effects, the deep homelessness that is felt in both the colonies and in the imperial center from which it was supposed that the meaning and logic of the colonies emanate. And the bulk of the novel largely fulfills these expectations. It is primarily a narrative of the difficulties and disappointments that the group of West Indian emigrants it follows experience after arriving in England with such high hopes. The first sight of England, viewed from the ship after its long journey from the Caribbean, marks perhaps the single greatest moment of crushed expectations in the novel. The imagined glories of England that had no doubt been ceaselessly trumpeted to all of the emigrants during their lives in the colonies crumble in the face of the remorseless reality of the ugly, squat-gray island lying before them:

> Beyond the first mild rising of the land a straight and narrow spate of red brick buildings covered the hills, and further on an anonymous greyness that held within it neither hills nor houses. On the other side in the distance there was a moderately high stone construction topped with a metal fan that spun in the wind. It looked like

the old plantation windmills of the tropics and Collis turned to ask his neighbour whether he could say what purpose it served . . .

"It's a working-class district," the man said, and Collis, feeling vaguely that he was being drawn into something he didn't understand, asked the man how he knew.

"You'll learn," the man said, pulling the beret tight over his head. The man kept his glance towards the houses, seeing, it would seem, some vision of the past or the future. Collis watched him suspiciously as though he were a dealer on the black market, a detective, or an illicit voyager. (E 99)

England is revealed as a place like any other. Instead of a land that can offer the emigrants the better life that they had hoped for, it bears a resemblance to the plantation economies left behind. Once the real England is substituted for the imagined one — a process that has slowly been taking place as the emigrants learn about housing and labor shortages in England and that is prefigured forcefully when Higgins learns that the cooking school he had planned to attend has been closed — the emigrants also immediately sense that too much has been given up for comparatively little in return. As the emigrants pass through customs, Lamming shifts perspective away from the emigrants to the customs officials, who question the desire of these colonial masses to come to England. Imagined from the side of England, it is impossible to comprehend why the emigrants would leave the paradisial lassitude of the sun-baked islands for the unpromising chill of England (E 108).

The emigrants have substituted a harsh set of living conditions for harsher ones, a world of perhaps numbing familiarity and limited possibilities for one in which they are marked forever as outsiders by their skin color and foreign accents. Yet while everything about *The Emigrants*, beginning with its title, suggests that the main project of the text is to explore the situation of those colonials that dared to make the trip "home," the novel's form and structure necessitate a different reading of its content, one that leads to different conclusions as to what this novel is finally "about." There is a potential in Lamming's text for a profound meditation on the effects of modernity on colonized subjects, the effects of its decomposition and recomposition of the subject at the moment when the boundaries between the center and the margin become forever blurred. If this potential is incompletely actualized, it is because *The Emigrants* is only incidentally about emigration. It is, in fact, less a text about the intrusion of modernity on Caribbean peoples, than about the possibilities of space, understood here as the possibility of a West Indian nation of the sort that federation attempted to bring into existence.

The Emigrants is divided into three sections: "1. A Voyage," "2. Rooms and Residents," and "3. Another Time." The last two sections of the novel are set in England: "Rooms and Residents" in the period immediately following the emigrants' arrival, when most of the characters are living together in a hostel (and then also, in an abrupt shift of time near the end of the section, the period immediately following the closing of the hostel); "Another Time" describes a period somewhat further along, two days in the future that are described (in the title of two subsections) as "Today" and "The Day Before." In terms of both page length and the novel's own temporality, the majority of the novel is concerned with describing the emigrants' experience in England. From even a brief description, it is possible to imagine the contents of these final two sections: the communal life the emigrants experience while at the hostel is broken up once the hostel is closed and the group that traveled together from the Caribbean becomes fragmented as each of them drifts in their own way into the "other time" of a tenuous existence in a racist postwar England.

This is indeed the narrative that guides these latter sections of the novel. But the specific moments or episodes of this narrative betray a different set of concerns. While Lamming shows the progressive alienation experienced by each of the emigrants over the course of the novel, the causes of this alienation are rarely located where one might expect: in the specifics of the racial and class discrimination that the emigrants experience as a result of their loss of community and place. At times it appears as if the episodes in the final two sections of the book are only incidentally set in England: England is more an abstract "backdrop" against which the emigrants' feelings of alienation are manifested than an active element, a reason for this alienation.[32] Each of the two sections builds toward the revelation of the "logic" that links together what appear to be disparate episodes in which various emigrants appear and disappear. It is this logic which is primary, whereas the setting (and causality) of England is secondary.

The major event of the second section appears initially to be Higgins's arrest for what is thought to be drug possession, which confirms his tragic fall from the position of the most self-assured of the emigrants to the one least able to deal with life in England. At the end of the section, however, it is revealed that the "powder" Higgins was carrying for Azi was burnt bull's testicles: an aphrodisiac. This "Love Vine" is a concoction made up for Frederick, the main British character in the novel, who is introduced into the narrative once the emigrants arrive in England; it is only through a combination of the Love Vine and the voyeuristic pleasure of watching his wife make love to a black man or woman that he is able to achieve orgasm. In a novel about Caribbean emigrants, it is Frederick's story and that of Azi, his African friend, that become disconcertingly the organizing principles of the narrative, however minimal this might be; it is this to which the stories in all of the other episodes ultimately relate. The third section is less organized, but its most important story, and the most startling example of plot-resolution in the novel, also concern Frederick. Miss Bis, who emigrated from Trinidad because she had become the subject of a well-known calypso for being "ruined" by a white man, becomes Frederick's lover; Frederick, who is remorseful about having ruined a woman when he served in the colonial office in Trinidad years earlier, decides to marry Miss Bis as a means of restituting his earlier error. Lamming expects us to believe that each does not recognize the other because they have changed so much in appearance in the intervening years — one of the "coincidences" that appear with regularity in Lamming's novels that Simon Gikandi characterizes as a "strategic narrative possibility that allows the writer to deconstruct the colonial vision and to introduce the narrative of Caribbean history into the text."[33] The point, however, is that once again Frederick's story comes to assume more weight than the emigrants': it is brought to the fore, whereas narratives of the other characters' experiences — Queenie, Higgins, and even Dickson — begin to appear with less frequency, growing slowly invisible over the course of the novel.

If the sexual peccadilloes and unusual personal history of an Englishman seem to be the organizing principles of the events in "Rooms and Residents," a fact that detracts from a consideration of what happens to each of the emigrants themselves, it is hard to resist a metaphorical or allegorical reading of Frederick's practices and the nature of his involvement with the emigrants. This is especially suggested by the fact that although Frederick is presented as a friend of the emigrants and is disdainful of the colonial project in which he himself was earlier involved (suggesting at one point, for example, a need for anthropologists to study the strange customs of the English instead of those of the Africans [E 157]), virtually all of the emigrants we meet on the voyage to England are drawn into the web of his perverse sexual practices. In the absence of specific episodes in which the emigrant experience is diagnosed and dissected, that is, specific moments in which the emigrants interact directly with the social environment that they now find themselves in, the presence of Frederick transforms the novel into one that is perhaps no longer literally about emigration, but one that pursues the theme of emigration through a narrative concerning the exoticization, objectification, and debasement of the body of the Other; this is, again, reminiscent of

Fanon's speculations about the sexual politics of race in *Black Skin, White Masks*, and, indeed, the sexualization of the Other figures in one way or another in all of Lamming's novels (most strikingly in *Water with Berries*). Higgins, Azi, Collis, Queenie, and Miss Bis are all used by Frederick in one way or another to satisfy his sexual desire, and with striking consequences; Higgins is psychologically devastated by his run-in with the police over the "powder," Queenie loses her life, Collis drifts into a deep anomie. The fact that the rest of the emigrants also grow more ghostly and ever more psychologically unstable over the course of the novel can be read as evidence of the effects of emigration and colonialism on the ontology of the Other.

Before such a reading becomes feasible (and readings of the novel as a text about psychology and alienation abound), it is necessary to consider the first section of the book and its relation to the sections that follow. That this novel is about alienation appears so obvious that critics have seldom bothered to describe the novel in detail, concentrating almost exclusively on the function of its fragmentary form. There is certainly an abundant vocabulary of alienation and objectification in *The Emigrants*. But it is significant that this vocabulary *does not* begin when the emigrants arrive in England. Rather, throughout the novel, specific characters undergo what can only be described as "existential" crises — crises of the will that manifest themselves in the evacuation of reason or meaning from the world and by the collapse of the ontological into the ontic. There are passages that without warning break away from the narrative: suddenly, living things become objects, characters find themselves transformed into mere things, and the contingency of history becomes an unbearable burden that mocks any human attempt at the production of meaning. Even in the second two sections, these moments of crisis are not only infrequently connected to Frederick's sexual objectification of the emigrants, but Frederick himself is beset by them: which suggests that whatever this crisis is it is a general one, a feature neither of a particular history or society, but of Being as such. In other words, whatever might be the cause of these crises is *already* a condition of the colonial subject, a condition that is not produced by emigration but only intensified by it.

It is then the significance of the first section of the novel that needs to be established. It would be a mistake to see "A Voyage," as simply providing a form of narrative continuity that shows how the main character of *In the Castle of My Skin*, G., makes it to England. This first section is not, in other words, simply a necessary literary passageway between the islands that makes possible a discussion of the circumstances faced by emigrants (circumstances that were faced by

Lamming himself). Rather, it seems to me that it is this section that is the real focus of the novel. For reasons that will become apparent, this focus cannot be sustained once the journey ends in England. The initial "logic" of the novel breaks down once the emigrants arrive, which is why the narrative fragments in the final two sections of the book and a governing logic needs to be located outside of the emigrants to pull the disparate episodes together. Once the emigrants become emigrants by arriving in England, the novel has lost its original direction and momentum, mainly because the project that it undertakes has *already* been accomplished, however paradoxically, however incompletely.

The voyage from the Caribbean permits Lamming to introduce the numerous characters in the novel whose fates will be intertwined when they reach England. The reason for the large number of characters that he introduces appears initially to be an attempt to exhaust all of the various possible dimensions of emigration through the presentation of a set of typical characters: Collis, the writer; Dickson, the teacher; Phillip, the student; the ex-RAF men, Tornado and the Governor; and Higgins, the working man. The emigrant women — Miss Bis, Queenie, and Lillian — are not presented as typical in this fashion. On the contrary, they are either mysteriously unknown (Queenie) or are attempting to render themselves anonymous (Miss Bis). In the end, however, the characters in *The Emigrants* are not meant to represent specific instances of emigrant experience. They are assembled on the ship from their separate islands in order to explore another possibility — the feasibility of a greater Caribbean nation and the means by which such a nation might be brought into existence.

"A Voyage" constitutes a literary experiment in nation-building; the remainder of the novel unintentionally reveals the consequences of this project. The journey to England by ship begins with a series of delays that are significant. When the ship winds its way through the Caribbean, picking up passengers from different islands, there is only waiting. The repeated lines concerning waiting — "We were all waiting for something to happen" (E 5), "We waited to see what would happen" (E 7), "We waited, sure that something would happen" (E 10), and so on — that so enervate the critic Mervyn Morris,[34] establish everything that will follow in the novel as the site of agency and action by comparison. Furthermore, the action that follows is carried out by a group, by a "we," rather than separately, by a number of "I"s. While Lamming shifts between first- and third-person narrative throughout the novel, these lines of waiting are the only moment in which one character, Collis, speaks for a collective "we." That it is Collis, one of the characters who "stands in" for Lamming's own experience as an emigrant, who speaks these lines is itself significant. The period of waiting lasts only until the ship has finally left the Caribbean altogether. It arises one last time after the ship sets out from the last Caribbean port in Guadeloupe: "The passengers, grouped or scattered here and there, were like men standing aimlessly at cross-roads waiting for something to happen, hoping however that nothing would happen except the usual things: a pleasant voyage, a safe arrival. At the crossroads they would have thrown dice or dealt cards or simply talked, expecting something to happen: gains or losses to be registered; and hoping however that nothing would happen: the police might not arrive and they would return to find their houses where they had left them waiting to be inhabited, playing their part in the pleasant, uneventful passage that began every day with waking and ended always with sleep" (E 25) The prosaic, everyday world has been left behind. Though there is a hope that the voyage will be as uneventful as a night at the crossroads, what is to come is unknown, unpredictable, and hardly uneventful.

In the midst of all this waiting, an unnamed narrator (who is eventually identi-fied as Dickson) recalls his reasons for leaving Trinidad. The central consider-ation is "freedom." Dickson has already experienced one sort of freedom, which he describes as "a child's freedom, the freedom too of some lately emancipated colonials" (E 8). This is the freedom he experiences as the result of leaving behind "the climate that caught [him] at birth" (E 8), by having left an unnamed island in the Caribbean to teach in Trinidad. Dickson has already experienced one kind of emigration, only to find that the freedom it offers is inadequate. Taking a day off from teaching in order to celebrate his birthday, the narrator stays at home reading a book called *The Living Novel:* "I read it as though by habit, page after page for several hours. The Novel was alive, though dead. This freedom was simply dead" (E 8–9). Later that night while drinking rum with a friend, the means by which he might gain a greater freedom that would presumably no longer be the "child's freedom" of "lately emancipated colonials" presents itself: the chance to leave the islands behind entirely and to begin all over again. Lam-ming suggests that the freedom for which Dickson searches and, for that matter, the "we" of the immigrants that Collis presumes to speak for, requires a clearing of the ground, a destruction of habit, a reconstitution of the self. This process will in some way also bring the novel back to life, so that *The Living Novel* in the West Indies is transformed into a tautology rather than an oxymoron.

The period of waiting that begins the novel is linked to the phenomenological weight of the Caribbean: even if Guadeloupe is a French-speaking island, its churches Catholic, its architecture a reflection of a different colonial history, the sheer physicality of its existence as one mode of the Caribbean does not yet permit an expression of the agency possible within the relative freedom of the ship. Once the ship is in open waters, between the reality of the Caribbean and England, the ship becomes "like home; and they regarded its limitations as the limitations of a home for which they were responsible" (E 33). Even as they leave the space of the West Indies behind, they carry with them a sense of it, now displaced to the geography of the ship. It is a space that needs to be constituted anew, given the spatial conditions suggested by the ship. The emigrants begin to speak to one another almost immediately after Guadeloupe has been left behind, and it is through these conversations that this substitute home is built. Emblematically, with the exception of the main characters that have already been introduced, the minor characters are identified only by their country of origin: "Barbadian," "Jamaican," and "Grenadian." The initial conversations revolve around the differences between the small and big islanders, the bigger islanders claiming that they are obviously more cosmopolitan and modern. Each emigrant proclaims the virtues of his own home island. There are debates over where the best beach is located, which island has the best educational system, and so on. In the midst of these friendly debates, the all-too-aptly-named character, the Governor, intercedes: " 'All you down here is my brothers,' the Governor said. He surveyed the men, cutting his glance where Dickson covered his face with a magazine. Dickson took no part in their discussions on the deck or in the dormitory. 'All you,' he said doubtfully, looking quickly towards the Grenadian, 'an' that's why I tell you as I tell you to stop this monkey-talk 'bout big islan' an' small islan' " (E 39).

From the moment the Governor's asserts that all of the emigrants are brothers, the discussions they have with each other change. Switching from their contentious assertions about the differences between the islands, the emigrants attempt to establish instead the common features of one West Indian people — a startling, and not entirely convincing, shift, brought about merely by Governor's suggestion of a shared brotherhood. At one point, the Jamaican summarizes what has been said in a form that would have been put to good use as a slogan for the West Indian Federation: "Different man, different land, but de same outlook. Dat's de meanin' o' West Indies. De wahter between dem islands doan' separate dem. Many o' man in Jamaica would expound de same view, an' dere's a worl' o' sea between me an' you" (E 61).

It is not merely in the content of this section that a concentrated effort can be seen to fashion a West Indian nation. Structurally, the novel enters an unexpected didactic mode when the group begins its discussions. The relatively long speeches made by each character as they put forth arguments and propositions about the nature of the West Indian character necessitates, it would seem, that long sections of "A Voyage" are transformed into the form of a play. Each character is clearly identified ("Jamaican," "Strange Man," etc.) and a lengthy soliloquy follows. The theme that repeatedly arises is that core characteristics connect the Jamaican, the Grenadian, and the Bahamian (the "Strange Man" is the one dissenting voice, and it becomes important for the emigrants to try to include him, to bring him back into the fold) and provide the basis for a larger national body that transcends the differences between the islands. This is made most explicit in the Jamaican's description of West Indians as "a sort of vomit you vomit up" (E 65). While "vomit" has a decidedly negative connotation, the way in which the Jamaican unpacks this metaphor transforms it into an apt and powerful one, shifting the valence of "vomit" from negative to positive. The metaphor of "vomit" contains the idea of the colonial disregard for the people that Britain forcibly "settled" in the West Indies; it turns this disregard into a source of strength. Numerous peoples, the Jamaican explains, have been vomited onto the Caribbean islands, never to return to the stomachs from which they came. This vomit keeps mixing together over history, stirred by the intervention of the imperial powers, until it begins "gradjally to stir itself" (E 66) and to desire a stomach into which it might be able to once again settle "'cause it realize that it is expose'" (E 66). The name for this "stomach" is the West Indies rather than any one individual island, since the people who are this vomit are "West Indians. Not Jamaicans or Trinidadians. Cause the bigger the better" (E 66).

As he develops his metaphor of the West Indian as "vomit," the Jamaican suggests that the realization that the West Indians are a common people can arise only when individuals are separated from their home-islands: "When them stay back home in they little island them forget a little an' them remain vomit; just as them wus vomit up, but when they go 'broad, them remember, or them get tol' w'at is w'at" (E 66). The "new home" of the ship provides Lamming with a setting in which discussions about a common West Indian identity can be articulated. It is only under such circumstances that individuals from different islands can be brought together, placed into face-to-face contact, displaced enough from their prosaic environments to overcome the allegiances that they have to their own islands. This displacement into the neutral space of the ship allows them to imagine a larger West Indies — one, for instance, in which the islands are no longer separated by the specific complexities engendered by their very different racial compositions (a substantial Indian population in Trinidad by comparison to Jamaica, Amerindians in Guyana, etc.).

It is paradoxical that the space required for federation, whose possibility is what this section introduces, can only be imagined as it is being physically left behind. Emigration seems to be a precondition for the construction of a nation-federation: the West Indies can be seen as a potential national space only from abroad. In one respect, this highlights the politically productive aspects of exile that Simon Gikandi has discussed with specific reference to the Caribbean and that Edward Said has explored as a more general feature of postcolonial nationalism. At the same time, *emigration is not the same as exile*, which means that the insights these characters have about the true nature of the West Indies are, in a sense, negated: their heightened awareness of the possibilities of the West Indies is wasted in England. It is not an insight that will go into fashioning a new nation, though the sense of commonality that they discover will find a place in the construction of a new black British identity. Reading this section of *The Emigrants*, one is reminded of C. L. R. James's suggestion that the reason for the breakup of the federation was the inability of its political leaders to break up the "Old Colonial System."[35] In *The Emigrants*, the political potential of the West Indies continues to operate under the sign of imperialism. The imagined construction of the new nation is carried out only through emigration, whose very possibility (or necessity) is the result of a political and economic history that is seldom made reference to in the novel.

The latter sections of the novel are so different from what one would expect in a text about emigration because of the paradoxical way in which the West Indian nation is created in the first section. The labor of creating the West Indian nation comes to a climax right before the ship reaches England. It is celebrated with the party that the emigrants hold on board the ship that is suddenly interrupted by the appearance of England on the horizon. At this point, the "new home" that had been built on the ship has to give way to another, much more uncertain home. As soon as the emigrants leave the ship, everything that they have accomplished in terms of building a community is slowly undone. This is perhaps Lamming's point. The freedom that Dickson feels is absent in the Caribbean is not to be achieved through emigration, but only through the formulation of a new space called "The West Indies." The problem, of course, is that it seems that this new space is both realizable only through emigration and yet made *unrealizable* through emigration as well, composed only to be inevitably decomposed. And this introduces another possible reading of the novel: emigration is something that should never have been undertaken in the first place. This is a reading that transforms the existential crises that the characters repeatedly undergo into signs of the loss of the new community that they had just barely established.

It would be easy in the terms of such an interpretation to account for the remarkable formal characteristics of the train ride that the emigrants take from the dock to London (E 110–25). Lamming writes this section of the novel in a manner that suggests the progressive *de*realization of the emigrant self and its attributes in the face of the phenomenological reality of England. The narrative crumbles and instead of a standard page of type, there appear columns of run-on dialogue or stream-of-consciousness notation about the new environment. The voices are mainly those of the emigrants, but sometimes they are also those of British passengers on board the train, who betray in their speech both their ignorance about the emigrants and their own racist attitudes. For the emigrants themselves, the density of sense impressions they encounter in England seems almost too much to bear — tea served without milk; pints of bitter instead of shots of rum; the enormous dimensions of the train; the darkness and cold of April; the factories glimpsed through the windows, fabled birthplaces of so many of the exotic British products that appear in the West Indies as signs of Britishness. This section grows more and more frantic, ending in complete sensory breakdown, a return to primal fears, and a cry in the dark for a lost home:

> Weak. Frightened. They said it wouldn't
> be so cold. So cold . . . So frightened . . .
> so frightened . . . home . . . go . . . to
> go back . . . home . . . only because . . .
> this like . . . no . . . home . . . other
> reason . . . because . . . like this . . .
> frightened . . . alone . . . the whole place
> . . . goes up up up and over up and over
> curling falling . . . up . . . over to heaven
> . . . down to hell . . . up an' over . . .
> thick . . . sick . . . thick . . . sick . . .
> up . . . cold . . . so . . . frightened . . .
> no . . . don't . . . don't tremble . . . no
> . . . no frightened . . . no . . . alone
> . . . no . . . (E 124)

While the collapse of the self reaches a peak at this transitional moment of enormous change, the existential or phenomenological crises that I alluded to earlier do not originate at the moment when the emigrants decisively leave the West Indies behind and enter England. In fact, as I mentioned earlier, these

moments occur regularly throughout the novel, beginning even before the experiment in nation-building on the ship. The first instance arises in Collis's
reaction to Queenie in Guadeloupe. Looking at Queenie's body, Collis realizes
that he sees it "as an object with its own secret resources that reduced all interest
to a sheer delight in the presence of the object" (E 23). Descriptions of experiences in which a character feels as if he is becoming an object (Dickson in the
house of Tornado and Lillian [E 205], Frederick's preference for the anonymity
of the city instead of the violent singular gaze of an Other [E 171], etc.) or, on the
contrary, turns others into objects under his or her gaze (the "master-slave"
encounter between Dickson and Collis on board the ship [E 31], Collis's vision of
the gross, disembodied fleshiness of Peggy and Frederick [E 217], etc.) are a
reoccurring feature of the novel and take place with apparent disregard to the
larger narrative. It is important to make clear just how abruptly these crises arise
and the degree to which they are described in phenomenological terms. For
example, after all of the discussions about the possibility of a common West
Indies have been carried out on board the ship, two such crises arise before the
emigrants reach England:

> Did it really matter? If each had been turned into a mere object it would not have
> mattered whether there was a place called England. But it was clear from their talk
> that it was a matter of terrible importance . . . The men sprawled on the deck
> heedless of what went on around them. Would it matter if they didn't awake? The
> fact of their sleep seemed a reflection of the accident which would have been their
> failure to awake.
>
> The sun had sunk beneath the cloud and more men had come out. At that moment
> there was a gust of wind and by accident, it would seem, Higgins and Tornado had
> awakened. There seemed no *reason* they shouldn't have remained till they were
> thrown overboard out of the way to become some other substance. (E 83–84)

Higgins was crying and no one knew, but in his resistance, it seemed that he had
become the dormitory itself. He was crying over himself and the others. For in the
dormitory it was as though they were in a cage with the doors flung open, but they
couldn't release themselves. Beyond their enclosure was *no-* THING. Nothing mattered outside the cage, because there was *no-* THING. So they remained within the
cage unaware of what was beyond, without a trace of desire to inhabit what was
beyond. It was unnatural and impossible to escape into something that didn't matter. Absolutely impossible, for within the cage where they were born and would die,

the only tolerable climate of experience was reality which was simply an irreversible instinct to make things matter . . . there beyond the water too large for his view was England rising from beneath her anonymous surface of grey to meet a sample of the men who are called her subjects and whose only certain knowledge said that to be in England was all that mattered. (E 105–7)

What do such passages communicate about the experience of colonialism, emigration, and postcolonial nation-building? The cage that Higgins feels himself to be in acts clearly as a metaphor of the colonial condition. The door to the cage is open, and it is possible to leave it. What makes it *impossible*, however, is the absence of any space *outside* of the cage. All that exists outside of the cage is a void, a space without things, a space that is comprised of nothing (*no-THINGS*). This may be an apt description of the false freedom of "lately emancipated colonials" described earlier by the narrator. The impossibility of leaving the cage is formulated as a logical proposition: escape from the colonial cage can only occur if there is a space of things one might enter. Even after all the deliberations about the possibility of a West Indian identity that could ground a West Indian nation, the only space that "matters," that is, the only space that has matter, appears to be England: England is represented as the inescapable ontological ground of the colonies, so much so that it is only by an extinction of being—to turn into a "mere object"—that England would no longer matter.

As an account of the subjective alienation felt by colonial subjects, their fundamental in-betweeness and dislocation in both the Caribbean and England (and so everywhere), Lamming's text shows the ontological depth of colonialism's impact in much the same way as other postwar texts influenced by phenomenology and existentialism (from Jean-Paul Sartre's *Anti-Semite and Jew* to Aimé Césaire's *Discourse on Colonialism*). But if England "matters" so much, the question that needs to be asked, finally, is *who* it "matters" to in this way? In the passage just discussed, Lamming phrases these philosophical worries in the voice of Higgins: Higgins the optimist, the same Higgins who participated fully in the discussions about West Indian identity on the ship. Yet the form of these worries seems entirely out of place in the character of Higgins. These are rather the worries of intellectuals, both the intellectuals on the ship, Collis and Dickson (the other stand-in for Lamming), and of Lamming himself. For these figures, emigration can always be redescribed as "exile," a movement that is reversible, so that the experiment with nation-building that is conducted on the ship always has the potential to be put to use back in the West Indies. But emigration is not simply exile in a slightly different form; for the vast majority of the emigrants, the experiences described in this novel will not be followed up by the returns to Caribbean space Lamming describes in *Of Age and Innocence* and *Water with Berries*. Collis and Dickson are the characters that are most prone to moments of ontological crisis that strike at the very essence of their identity. By extending these crises to other characters in the novel — to *all* other characters, including the Englishman, Frederick — Lamming tries to generalize these speculations on Being and the loss of Being, making them characteristics not of specific individuals from specific social backgrounds, but of the colonial condition as such. That there is something disingenuous about this process is indicated in the text itself, which notes the differences that continue to exist among the emigrants even in their attempts to produce a common West Indian nation. While Higgins suggests that he and Dickson are essentially similar in their desire to receive certification in England in their respective fields, Dickson is quick to point out the class differences that separate them:

> "I say ah goin' to study cooking just as you study books," Higgins said. "An'tis the same r'ally. We got to get certificates like you before we can get a proper position. In the end you an' me is the same. We all in search o' papers o' qualification.
>
> "I'm not a cook," Dickson said sharply. "I'm a trained teacher with a degree and a diploma in education." He was very firm and very polite. Higgins propped against the ship's side and contemplated the question of papers and qualifications. He understood the difference which Dickson was determined to establish between them, but he had a sense of his importance as a qualified cook. (E 52–53)

In his attempt to create the common space of the nation, a space that would be saturated by a singular national essence, Lamming seems forced to elide important differences of class, race, and gender that exist between individuals as much as between the individual islands of the West Indies. It is the men, after all, who are at the center of the debates on the ship, and though it is strictly speaking nowhere made explicit, it is almost certain that these are all Afro-Caribbean men. There is in *The Emigrants* no equivalent to the children Singh, Lee, and Bob, who in *The Pleasures of Exile* and *Of Age and Innocence* represent the hope for a harmonious racial future for the islands. It is significant as well that the characters of Collis and Dickson seldom participate in the debates over the shape of the West Indian nation: they remain aloof and separate from the others. Nevertheless, it is Dickson's (or Collis's or the narrator's) sense of a freedom yet incompletely established — the freedom of the "lately emancipated colonials" — that in *The*

Emigrants Lamming makes equivalent to the colonial structure of awareness he discusses at length in *The Pleasures of Exile* and that becomes the motivating force for emigration for all the characters in the novel. While it is the attempt to overcome this sickness of Being that is suggested as the prime rationale for emigration, it is likely that most of the emigrants are searching simply (though there is nothing simple about it) for a better set of material circumstances than those that would be available to them if they were to remain in the Caribbean.

In contrast to the ontological consequences of emigration, which are shown here to be merely an *extension* of the already necessarily unstable ontological position of the colonial subject, the novel suggests that it is the creation of a new nation that would provide a form in which a new kind of Being could emerge — a Being that is finally whole and feels a freedom that does not have to be sought abroad. But the form of the nation that is imagined in *The Emigrants*, a form that mirrors the conditions necessary for the production of the West Indies Federation itself, shows that there is an unexpected *equivalence* between the subjects of the new nation and the subjects produced by colonialism. It is here that the repeated ontological crises of the novel become most significant. They arise prior to the trip as well as in its midst; they occur immediately after the emigrants reach England and continue to occur even after they have been living there for years. For Lamming, the new West Indian nation is to be produced through the production of an essential West Indian identity that transcends the particularities of individual islands. The result of this process, however, seems to be subjects who do not experience any greater degree of freedom, but who suffer just as greatly from an ontological sickness as do those colonial subjects who choose to emigrate. *Both* are subjects who lack a certain necessary ontological dimension due to the fact that they are disconnected from any definite place — a place in which, for example, relations of class, gender, and race are significant and meaningful, a place of particular histories and specific social relations. The conditions that Lamming imagines for the new nation do not offer a solution to the problems faced by the alienated colonial self; rather, in the terms laid out here, they do little more than extend or reproduce them: the abstract citizenship required for the creation of a federal nation reproduces the abstraction of the colonial subject in the terms of the vicious ontology of colonialism first outlined by Fanon in *Black Skin, White Masks*.

What this reading of *The Emigrants* highlights is the complex zone of instability in which the project of creating nations comes together with the activities of the writer and intellectual. *The Emigrants* offers an unfaltering exploration of the spaces of this zone and, in so doing, shows just how difficult it is to navigate it. The establishment of a national collectivity in the West Indies has to pass through structures and discourses whose force and logic cannot be undone in any simple way, and certainly not through the desire for such a collectivity alone. As this novel shows, one of the major problems that needs to be addressed is the role and function of the intellectual in the production of this national space. To create the "West Indian" subject that would provide the basis of the freedom that the intellectual seeks — preeminently, in the context of Lamming's comments in *The Pleasures of Exile*, the freedom that would make the Caribbean a space in which it is, in a sense, possible to write *The Living Novel* — seems to require that these subjects be detached from their specific communities and genealogies in order to fit into an abstract category whose definition *even so* remains paradoxically connected to the logic of imperial space. While it is hoped that in this new West Indian space the freedom that eludes the narrator in Trinidad can finally be found, what is produced instead is an empty idea of freedom — freedom as an abstract, ungrounded category, connected to nothing but the subject him or herself.

What *The Emigrants* reveals is the limits of the kind of national literature that Lamming describes later in "The Occasion for Speaking," a national literature that is, finally, not about or for the people, but about the conditions and possibilities of producing literature in the space not yet and perhaps never to be known as "the West Indian nation."

Geographies of Modernity: Naipaul's Caribbean

The West Indian, though provincial, is perhaps the most cosmopolitan man in the world.
— GEORGE LAMMING [36]

If I have to describe the universal civilization I would say that it is the civilization that both gave the prompting and the idea of the literary vocation; and also gave me the means to fulfill that prompting; the civilization that enabled me to make that journey from the periphery to the center; the civilization that links me not only to this audience but also to that now not-so-young man in Java whose background was as ritualized as my own, and on whom — as on me — the outer world had worked, and given the ambition to write.
— V. S. NAIPAUL [37]

There is perhaps no other figure in world literature whose personal politics has been as closely and repeatedly interrogated as that of V. S. Naipaul. If critics have wondered about Lamming's politics, they are at least willing to concede that his heart is in the right place; with Naipaul, this remains a perpetually open question.[38] More than any other author, Naipaul has painted a grim picture of the colonies. He has characterized postcolonial societies as lacking in culture, history, and politics; as inextricably beset by ethnic and racial conflicts that have only become exacerbated with time; as individualistic, materialistic, greedy polities whose nationhood is only an accident of imperial geography; as places in which it is ridiculous to speak of the existence of truly distinctive national characteristics or of the presence of genuine fellow-feeling; and as irrational, disorganized, corrupt countries swimming in real and metaphorical filth. He has been unapologetic about these characterizations. It is perhaps his use of the term "civilization" (which he uses so easily and with such apparent disregard for its historical resonance as a key term in the justification of the colonial project) as an evaluative term that has produced the most diametrically opposed views on the significance and meaning of Naipaul's work. His literary and nonfiction work is dominated by spaces (the Caribbean, India, Argentina, Pakistan, the Congo, the American South, etc.) in which he sees barbarism ruling in the absence of civilization. His views are taken either as being Eurocentric, a prejudice made all the more lamentable by his unquestionable skill as a writer, or as presenting a brave if unpopular assessment of the true state of affairs in the third world. To put this another way, Naipaul's writing is seen either as the literary equivalent of developmental and modernization theories or as its almost exact opposite — as an important corrective to the overly optimistic characterizations of the postcolonial world offered by other writers and critics.

As with all such binaries, the truth is to be found at neither of the poles nor by simply splitting the difference between them. Since he is, unlike Lamming or Wilson Harris, a reluctant theorist of literature and of his own work, Naipaul's politics can be ascertained only by directly examining his writing. I will focus in this section on Naipaul's *The Middle Passage*.[39] Written in 1960 in the midst of the political experimentation with the West Indies Federation, and appearing in 1962 when this experiment had all but failed, the text is interested explicitly in gauging the prospects for the nation in the Caribbean, even if it never makes direct reference to the project of federation.[40] As much as *The Emigrants* is an attempt to imagine the conditions of possibility for federation, *The Middle Passage* tries to deny the possibility that these conditions might exist. As Naipaul will suggest over and over again, the necessary conditions for the existence of a federation, or any kind of national structure, are absent in the Caribbean.[41] But none of this should be taken as an indication that Naipaul is opposed to the nation. Although of all the writers working in the 1950s and 1960s, Naipaul is the most suspicious of the function of nationalism in the formerly colonized world, he is, nevertheless, as deeply tied to the project of the nation as is Lamming, as well as to the place of literature with respect to the nation. What he sets out to show is not that individual Caribbean nations or even a federation is undesirable, but simply that it is not possible. Naipaul's reasons are similar to those offered by C. L. R. James for the collapse of the federation: the existence of the West Indies as a totality is tied too closely to the spatial imprint left behind by colonialism. What separates the analyses of James and Naipaul is their understanding of the difficulties that exist in the Caribbean that impede the creation of a genuine nationalism. For James, it is a difficulty imposed by historical circumstances that can be eroded with time and effort. Naipaul, on the other hand, turns this diffi- culty into a kind of ontology. Without exaggeration, he sees the structural condi- tions of existence in the Caribbean as having doomed it forever. So, of course, the only solution for those with the wherewithal or resources is to leave the slow, sinking shipwreck of these islands, to travel as he himself has to those "civilized" parts of the world that inspired him to write in the first place.

The Middle Passage (1962) is V. S. Naipaul's fourth book, and the first example of the nonfiction travelogues that he has produced with increasing frequency throughout his career.[42] Though these books are distinct from his novels by virtue of the fact that they record "real" events and processes and are marked by Naipaul's direct commentaries and reflections on politics and history, there are significant continuities of theme and form between Naipaul's novels and his nonfiction works that make them virtually interchangeable.[43] This is perhaps best evidenced in *A Way in the World* (1994), a work in which the operations of novel, memoir, and travelogue finally come together. It is important to note that this intersection of different forms does not produce a "new" form that is neither fiction nor travelogue: even though there is a "character" in the book named "V. S. Naipaul" (that is, if it is taken to be a novel), this book does not represent Naipaul's experimentation with a kind of postmodern self-referentiality. After a lifetime of switching back and forth between one form and another, *A Way in the World* represents a collapse of distinctions that always existed only tenuously in Naipaul's work. What is true of Naipaul's latest work is characteristic of his first experiment with nonfiction writing: *The Middle Passage* is a narrative that is in many ways "fictional." It is even unintentionally announced as such in the origi- nal foreword to the book. Naipaul suggests that he hesitated to write a nonfiction book about the Caribbean because "the novelist works towards conclusions of which he is often unaware; and it is better that he should" (MP 6). One imagines that, like the writing of a novel, a travel narrative is only discovered along the way. But perhaps there is something of a problem in trying to stress the fictionality of *The Middle Passage*. For one gets the sense that the dimensions of the story that Naipaul tells in this book have been determined in advance: the plot set out, the thematics developed, the characters chosen. Before he ever arrives in the Caribbean, he has an outline of the complete book in his suitcase to which the reality of his journey must adhere.

All of Naipaul's writing is characterized by a relentless interrogation of the fate of postcolonial societies. The satiric works written prior to *The Middle Passage* — *The Mystic Masseur* (1957), *The Suffrage of Elvira* (1958) and *A House for Mr. Biswas* (1961) (*Miguel Street*, published in 1962 but actually the first book written by Naipaul, is an exception here) — show characters and societies ill-equipped to deal with their rapid emergence into independence. *The Mystic Masseur* and *The Suffrage of Elvira* examine the politics of rural life in Trinidad following World War II. *The Mystic Masseur* narrates the life of the pundit Ganesh Ramsumair, writer of "the first best-seller in the history of Trinidad publishing"[44] and member of the initial Legislative Council following the achievement of universal suffrage in 1946; in *The Suffrage of Elvira*, Naipaul's subject is the politics of vote-buying in an isolated county in Trinidad during its second "free" elections in 1950. In both these works, as well as in *Mr. Biswas*, the politics of colonial societies is skewered ruthlessly for its irrationality, decrepitude, and, finally, emptiness. No one, neither the politicians nor their supposed constituency, imagines that the political process has anything to do with political representation as opposed to naked self-interest and self-promotion on the part of officials for whom being elected is merely a sign of distinction, a symbolic medal to be pinned on one's chest (as well as a means, of course, to plunder the public coffer). *Mr. Biswas*, with its obvious structuring narrative of a search for both a physical and symbolic "home," has usually been seen as a more generous, less critical work. Gordon Rohlehr, for example, suggests that *"A House for Mr. Biswas is more profound than anything else Naipaul has written because, for the first time, he is able to feel his own history not merely as squalid farce, but as adventure in sensibility."*[45] Though this has become an accepted reading, it is also a deceptive one. The disdain for the culture of letters in Trinidad — or, rather, the relentless exposure of the lack of any such culture — that Naipaul exhibits in his narrative about the autodidact, self-published Ganesh, is repeated virtually unchanged in *Mr. Biswas*. The homes that Biswas manages to secure for himself are always illusory and impermanent, solid enough when seen in the darkness, but nothing more than squalid rat-traps when viewed in the light of day. In the context of these earlier works, Naipaul's first nonfiction book reveals the logic behind his aggressive, dismissive characterization of politics and culture in the space of the Caribbean. What is both lacking and all-too present is modernity. Of all the preselected narrative "tools" through which Naipaul narrates his journey through the Caribbean, it is the measuring stick of modernity—a concept whose meaning is at no point very clearly articulated in the text—that forms the basis of his inquiry into the possibilities of the nation in the Caribbean.

As the subtitle of *The Middle Passage* indicates, Naipaul's travelogue offers "impressions of five societies—British, French, and Dutch—in the West Indies and South America." The "five societies" that are divided among these three spheres of colonial influence are Trinidad, British Guiana, Surinam, Martinique, and Jamaica. His explorations of the first two societies—Trinidad and Guiana—occupies well over half of the book; by comparison, his remaining explorations are perfunctory. One senses this is in part because what Naipaul experiences in the other parts of the Caribbean is for him simply "more of the same": his examination of these first two societies effectively exhausts his critique of the Caribbean. Indeed, when Naipaul leaves Trinidad and Guiana behind, he suddenly develops a much more positive attitude toward the latent possibilities of the remaining colonies, as if he has discharged his wrath entirely over the course of his first two journeys. For instance, what he sees as wholly absent in the British Caribbean, Naipaul finds immediately upon arriving in Surinam: "Nationalism in Surinam, feeding on no racial or economic resentments, is the profoundest anti-colonial movement in the West Indies" (MP 181). When he returns to the British Caribbean, visiting Jamaica at the end of the book, Naipaul remarks again on the comparative failure of nationalism in the West Indies. "Nationalism in Surinam, a movement of intellectuals, rejects the culture of Europe," Naipaul writes. "Ras Tafarianism in Jamaica is nothing more than a proletarian extension of this attitude, which it carries to its crazy and logical limit" (MP 240).

There is a tension that runs throughout *The Middle Passage*, one that is particularly prevalent in the sections on Trinidad and Guiana. As a "travel book," one imagines that the main function of *The Middle Passage* is to mark out and characterize the particularities and unique features of each of these societies—if not in the exoticizing, stereotypical manner of European travel guides, then with the critical insight of a cultural "insider." This task is rendered all but impossible or at least insensible in the epigraph that begins the book, which outlines the fundamental logic that drives Naipaul's investigation. The epigraph is drawn from James Anthony Froude's notoriously racist account of the West Indies: The West Indies "were valued only for the wealth which they yielded, and society there has never assumed any particularly noble aspect . . . The natural graces of life do not show themselves under such conditions. There has been no saint in the West Indies since Las Casas, no hero unless philonegro enthusiasm can make one out of Toussaint. There are no people there in the true sense of the word, with a character and a purpose of their own."[46] Not only are there no people in the West Indies that can be characterized or described: Naipaul also suggests that there is no history in the West Indies. He writes that "the history of the islands can never be satisfactorily told . . . history is built on achievement and creation; and nothing was created in the West Indies" (MP 29). What then is the task of Naipaul's book? What is it that draws him back to the West Indies to write this book — a book funded by the government of Trinidad and Tobago and written at the behest of Eric Williams (MP 6)? If he is not writing about the people or their history, what is it that he proposes to write about?

The Middle Passage performs what can only be described as a "negative anthropology": instead of paying attention to the mode of existence of a people, it tries to reveal the conditions that would suggest that these people *do not* exist. In doing so, Naipaul perhaps unintentionally raises the question of what it in fact means to fully "exist" as a people. This question is the fundamental one that is posed underneath Naipaul's travels in Trinidad and Guiana; these societies are measured repeatedly against an ideal sign of human "existence" — the civilized West — and are found to be wanting. The question of what it means to exist is never posed directly but is articulated in terms of Naipaul's reflection on the nature of Trinidadian modernity, the prospect of a Caribbean nation or Caribbean nations, and, not surprisingly, in terms of the place and function of literature in the islands.

Modernity is the theme of almost the entire section on Trinidad and of *The Middle Passage* as a whole. It is evoked immediately in the opening paragraph of the chapter that details Naipaul's return home. Seeing Trinidad for the first time after an absence of many years, Naipaul gazes at the car-clogged streets, shoddy concrete houses, and neon signs of Port of Spain, and comes to an immediate opinion about the island that never changes over the course of his stay there: "Ambition . . . not matched with skill, and the effect was Trinidadian; vigorous, with a slightly flawed modernity" (MP 42). Trinidad has a problem, and its problem is that its modernity is damaged, even if (here at least) only ever so slightly. While the initial impression might therefore be of only a slight difference or deviance in Trinidad's modernity from some other, unnamed model, Naipaul's subsequent references to Trinidadian modernity suggest that it is entirely false, an imitative modernity that has rendered the society sterile and unimaginative. Modernity in Trinidad is described by Naipaul as "a constant alertness, a willingness to change, a readiness to accept anything which films, magazines and comic strips appear to indicate as American" (MP 48); postcolonial modernity thus turns out to be the name for that "extreme susceptibility of people who are unsure of themselves, and having no taste or style of their own, are eager for instruction" (MP 50). Much of Naipaul's description of the problems with modernity in Trinidad stems from an assessment of the thorough penetration of Trinidadian society by American culture. And though Naipaul clearly feels that American popular culture is irredeemable, it is the Trinidadian "pretence of being American" (MP 70) rather than a modernity expressed or embodied by American cultural products that he finds most disturbing.

For Naipaul, the presence of modernity is a positive societal attribute, but only, he suggests, when it develops "organically" out of the soil of the country. "The main, degrading fact of the colonial society," Naipaul writes, is "that it never required efficiency, it never required quality, and these things, because unrequired, became undesirable" (MP 62). Naipaul associates modernity at least in part with a rationalized, capitalist society, and with the cosmopolitan, non-parochial attitude he believes naturally accompanies it. Insofar as Naipaul sees modernity as in some ways another name for the culture of capitalism, it does not seem as if it would be difficult to import modernity to Trinidad just as easily as American cultural products have been imported to the islands. After all, the rabidly consuming Trinidadian subjects that Naipaul describes, easily impressed by advertising, swayed by the lure of foreign products, seduced by the glamour of commodity consumption, and so on, are in no way specific to the island or to the West Indies more generally. But it is because Naipaul also has a different sense of what modernity entails than just the existence of consumerism that he is able to speak of it as "flawed" in Trinidad. He oscillates throughout this chapter between the position that Trinidad's problem is that it has no "proper" modernity and the position that Trinidad's problem is that it is *too* modern. This is an oscillation that is resolved, finally, only through the production of a very strange conception of modernity: that there is no modernity *as such*, only a global collection of various "modernities" (which is right), some of which are genuine, some of which are false and imitative (which is wrong).

It is only through this conception of modernity that Naipaul is able to articulate one of the few positive things he says about Trinidadian society. There is a way in which "the Trinidadian is cosmopolitan" (MP 83). For Naipaul, the Trinidadian is "adaptable; he is cynical; having no rigid social conventions of his own, he is amused by the conventions of others. He is a natural anarchist, who has never been able to take the eminent at their own valuation. He is a natural eccentric, if by eccentricity is meant the expression of one's own personality, unhampered by fear of ridicule or the discipline of a class . . . Everything that makes the Trinidadian an unreliable, exploitable citizen makes him a quick, civilized person whose values are always human ones, whose standards are only those of wit and style" (MP 83). Almost immediately, however, Naipaul suggests that "as the Trinidadian becomes a more reliable and efficient citizen, he will cease to be what he is" (MP 83). The contrasting and unstable meanings that Naipaul has assigned to the term "modernity" come crashing together here. The cosmopolitan Trinidadian is, in a sense, a modern citizen; what marks him as a Trinidadian, however, can only disappear as modernity encroaches. In other words, what Naipaul suggests is that *the Trinidadian will lose his characteristic modernity in the on-rush of modernity* — this second sense of modernity now characterized as "all the modern apparatus of the modern society for joylessness, for the killing of the community spirit and the shutting up of people in their separate prisons of similar ambitions and tastes and selfishness" (MP 83).

What makes it possible for Naipaul to articulate both of these positions at the same time — modernity as Trinidad's saving grace as well as its biggest problem — has a great deal to do with Naipaul's understanding of the significance and function of literature, both its general function as well as its role in Trinidad in particular. Though there is much in Naipaul's writing that is difficult to pin down definitively, Naipaul's relationship to literature is absolutely clear: he is a champion of an unapologetically bourgeois notion of literature. This is a sense of literature that elevates it to a position of unique prominence with respect to its ability to represent and comment on society at large. This is one of the reasons that Naipaul is the Caribbean writer least troubled by the prospect of his self-imposed exile from the islands: it is a writer that he wanted to be, and so he went to the only place that it was possible for him to pursue this calling with any degree of seriousness, London. In his comments in *The Middle Passage* on the necessary function of the West Indian writer a sense of his vision of literature's function emerges, and it is very clearly an idea of literature that is linked to the idea of "civilization" itself, as he describes it in the epigraph to this section. It is a vision comprised of irreconcilable positions. He suggests that "living in a borrowed culture, the West Indian, more than most, needs writers to tell him who he is and where he stands" (MP 73). The West Indian writer needs to speak the truth about the West Indian condition and the particularity of the West Indian herself. Naipaul claims that this has never happened. This is largely due, he suggests, to the inability of the West Indian writer to escape from the racial divisions that plague the islands. In a sense, Naipaul suggests that *there is no literature* in the West Indies: what is written under the "sign" of literature "has little to do with literature and much to do with the race war" (MP 74). The literature of the West Indies is at its best didactic and "propagandist" (MP 75), since "the Trinidadian expects his novels, like his advertisements, to have a detergent purpose" (MP 74). In short, for Naipaul the problem with literature in the West Indies is that it is *too* particular. It arises out of the specific circumstances of the gulf between the races in the Caribbean, and so lacks what one assumes is the sign of real literature: "universal appeal." It is in this sense that Naipaul's paradoxical construction of modernity reoccurs in his prescriptions for West Indian literature, in the form of the need to write the universal in terms of the particular, but only so long as the particular does not intrude on the universal.

One last point needs to be made before bringing all of this to a conclusion. Not surprisingly, Naipaul also expresses the view that "Nationalism was impossible in Trinidad" (MP 78). Nationalism requires some sense of communal bonding, some idea around which the nation can be imagined. In the Caribbean, one imagines this to be an anti-imperialist sentiment of the kind described by Partha Chatterjee as foundational to all postcolonial nationalism.[47] Naipaul demurs: "there was no profound anti-imperialist feelings" (MP 45). Not only is there no anti-imperialist feeling, he claims that there is no communal feeling *whatsoever* in the islands: "Everyone was an individual, fighting for his place in the community. Yet there was no community. We were of various races, religions, sets and cliques; and we had somehow found ourselves on the same small island. Nothing bound us together except this common residence. There was no nationalist feeling; there could be none" (MP 45).

As a result of its negative view of the possibilities of the West Indian nation, *The Middle Passage* might seem to occupy the opposite pole from the work of

Lamming. Yet each writer figures the relationship of literature to the nation in a similar way: both react to the same conditions of possibility of literary nationalism in the West Indies. For both writers, the nation, with all that this implies (a universal culture, a "proper" modernity, etc.), represents the existence of a "real" people in the West Indies, a real people with a real history. It is not surprising that Naipaul finds that the nation is not a form that can be attained in the Caribbean. What Naipaul expresses in *The Middle Passage* is not just another example of his relentless negativity when it comes to the prospects of postcolonial societies, which he has always viewed as damaged "beyond belief." Rather, this conclusion stems, it seems to me, from the impossible conditions that Naipaul sets out for a "true" nation in the West Indies: West Indian society has to have its own unique identity and traditions and is to be criticized insofar as it does not; it must also be able to fully participate in the larger, modern world and is to be criticized to the extent that it remains particularistic. In some sense, what Naipaul insists on attributing to the deep structural conditions of the West Indies alone (again, like Lamming, he insists on its "unique" status even among other postcolonial nations) is in fact the problem faced by all societies in modernity: how to be modern while retaining the particular practices and habits that define a unique mode of communal life. It is a difficult problem. What should be asked here, however, is *why* Naipaul insists on the necessity of modernity in the West Indies. What is it, precisely, that the West Indies lacks in the absence of a real nationalism and a real modernity? And why does it matter so much to Naipaul? The answers to these questions are to be found in the epigraph to this section: the real problem, I would suggest, is not that the people are ontologically incomplete, but (once again) that in the absence of "civilization" there is no possibility of writing in the Caribbean. The theme of exile and its connection to literature thus returns, this time buried somewhat under the trope of an ethnographic investigation of the conditions for existence in the West Indies in general.

The reading of *The Middle Passage* that I have offered here has focused more or less on the substantive critical comments that Naipaul makes about literature, modernity, and the nation. In doing so, it has failed to discuss or to characterize what makes up most of the book: the narrative of Naipaul's peripatetic journeys through five Caribbean and South American countries. Naipaul wanders: sometimes alone, sometimes with friends (like the Jagans in Guyana), and sometimes with guides that he meets along the way. He complains a great deal: his coffee arrives at his table too slow; the people are philistine and boring; there are endless red laterite roads to be driven along, with not much to see or do; there is rampant political apathy everywhere; in general, things are worse than he expected, which means, of course, that they are exactly as he expected them to be—*worse* is an adjective that for Naipaul has managed to turn into a noun. When he crosses the border from Guyana into Brazil to visit the modernist city of Boa Vista, this too is found wanting. With the exception of the roads, all of it sounds much like what Naipaul would have experienced on a trip anywhere in Britain outside of London. Yet what needs to be emphasized when thinking about Naipaul's wanderings through the Caribbean in 1960 is not, it seems to me, what he sees and writes down, but the conditions of possibility of the trip itself—and by this I mean the brute historical facts, the "occasion" that led him to return to the Caribbean after a decade in England. The context for this trip is nothing less than federation itself, and in the context of federation there is a willful and unmistakable politics at work in this text. When Eric Williams invited Naipaul, the acclaimed author of *A House for Mr. Biswas*, to come home to write a book on the Caribbean, he was looking for a text that might offer support to the nascent federation. Naipaul produced a very different kind of text from what was expected. But perhaps this difference is not so remarkable as the places that Naipaul visits—not just one island in the West Indies, but *all* of the major islands, and, specifically, the ones most deeply engaged in the debates over the form that the federation was to take; and he visits not just the British Caribbean, but the French and Dutch Caribbean as well. It is as if Naipaul was intent on exhausting the possibility of nationalism *in the entire region*, that is, not only of the West Indies Federation, but of a larger federation that may have eventually included not only the former colonies of Britain, but the whole of the Caribbean. Were this to happen, it would disrupt the lingering remnants of the colonial system—the system that meant that "it was only our Britishness, our belonging to the British Empire, which gave us any identity" (MP 45). And in these deliberations, size *does* matter. When Naipaul suggests that "nothing was created in the British West Indies," it is because "the size of the islands called for nothing else" (MP 27). Federation would overcome the limited spaces of the individual islands, adding to it the vast bush of Guyana that Naipaul concedes to Brazil,[48] as well as a space of identity even greater than physical space. This possibility has to be denied by Naipaul at all costs: even when there are obvious signs of a West Indian nationalism, he has to affirm that there is no such thing. His understanding of literature depends on it; for the existence of the nation would mean that even those novels with "detergent purpose" might suddenly be placed alongside his own so carefully cultivated style of writing, as equals in the world of literary production, elevating the barbaric to the civilized and rendering the civilized barbarous.

Federation No More: *Beyond a Boundary*

Cricket had always been more than a game in Trinidad. In a society which demanded no skills and offered no rewards to merit, cricket was the only activity which permitted a man to grow to his full stature and to be measured against international standards . . . The cricketer was our only hero-figure. And that is why cricket is played in the West Indies with such panache; that is why, for a long time to come, the West Indians will not be able to play as a team. The individual performance was what mattered.   — V. S. NAIPAUL [49]

What do they know of cricket who only cricket know?

With my excellent batting record, good bowling and fielding, admittedly wide knowledge and fanatical keenness, it was clear that I would play for one of the first-class clubs. The question was: which one? This, apparently simple, plunged me into a social and moral crisis which had a profound effect on my whole future life.
                    — C. L. R. JAMES [50]

Cricket gives . . . the sense of having hijacked the game from its English habitus into the colonies, at the level of language, body, and agency as well as competition, finance, and spectacle.   — ARJUN APPADURAI [51]

C. L. R. James is perhaps the most prominent intellectual to emerge out of the English Caribbean.[52] In addition to being one of the most important writers in the region — his early novel *Minty Alley* (1936) paving the way for all subsequent literary production in the West Indies — he is the figure (along with Eric Williams) most commonly associated with the cause of Caribbean self-government and nationhood. His early essay, "The Case for West-Indian Self-Government" (1933) — a chapter of James's pioneering political work, *The Life of Captain Cipriani* (1932), that was later reprinted in pamphlet form — was an extremely influential text throughout the Caribbean for the anticolonial movements that developed both before and after World War II. After spending over two decades in the United States and in England working on a variety of socialist and revolutionary causes, James was drawn back to the Caribbean by the promise of self-government that he had long advocated. In Trinidad from 1958 to 1962, James was the secretary of the Federal Labour Party, the governing party of the West Indies Federation, and a frequent contributor to *The Nation,* the newspaper of the People's National Movement led by Williams, and though he was interested in the achievement of political independence for Trinidad, it was the hope of a new nation born out of the union of the individual islands that fueled James's political activities and critical writing of this period.

The failure of the West Indies Federation therefore came as an enormous blow to James and led almost directly to his return to England at the end of 1962. Writing in 1958, James claimed that *"Federation is the means and the only means whereby the West Indies and British Guiana can accomplish the transition from colonialism to national independence, can create the basis of a new nation; and by reorganizing the economic system and the national life give us our place in the modern century."*[53] It was clear for James that only a federation of the islands held open the possibility of a genuine movement beyond colonialism through the creation of entirely new political and economic structures that had no relationship to colonial government. James saw that the islands on their own were too small in terms of both population and resources to create true nations: nations that could compete in the international system of nations, nations that differed in terms of their "form" (the nature of political institutions) and their "content" (the identity of the new rulers) from the colonial past. "Without federation," James writes, "the consequences for these islands would be dreadful."[54] So it is not surprising that James spent much of his four years in the Caribbean speaking and writing tirelessly on behalf of federation.[55] Nor does his perseverance for this cause come as a surprise. As a last ditch argument for West Indian Federation when all seemed lost, James published at his own expense a pamphlet of letters exchanged between himself and Kwame Nkrumah, the president of Ghana. Nkrumah puts forward an argument to the people of the West Indies that is clearly James's own, but which he no doubt thought would have more impact being spoken in the voice of a successful leader of a West African revolution.[56] Nkrumah writes in a letter dated June 8, 1962, that "I hope that these leaders will realize that it is not yet too late to save the islands from disintegration in the separate and competitive existence which will result from their failure to federate now."[57] He makes the reasons for federation even grander than simply that it would save the Caribbean from political anarchy. The success of the West Indies Federation would establish a precedent for the decolonizing efforts everywhere: "The establishment of a powerful West Indian nation would substantially assist the effort we are making in Africa to redeem Africa's reputation in world affairs and to re-establish the personality of the African and people of African descent everywhere."[58]

While he was in the West Indies working on behalf of federation, James wrote a number of his most important books and essays, including *Modern Politics, Party Politics in the West Indies* (which includes his famous essay on "The Mighty Sparrow") and what is perhaps his definitive statement on Caribbean literature, "The Artist in the Caribbean." The essential themes of "The Artist in the Caribbean" were repeated by James throughout this period, finding their way, for instance, into the middle of his "Lecture of Federation," the concluding remarks appended in 1962 to the original version of "The Mighty Sparrow," and his elegant 1964 eulogy for federation, "A National Purpose for Caribbean Peoples."[59] James's essay is a meditation on the significance of the artist — and he means in particular, the writer — for the nation. He is willing to claim on behalf of Caribbean writers the mantle of the best writers of English language in the world. What disturbs him, however, is that these writers (he cites Lamming, Naipaul, and Vic Reid) are nevertheless not "great artists": "the product of a long and deeply rooted national tradition" who appear "at a moment of transition in national life with results which are recognized as having significance for the whole civilized world."[60] In part, this is due to the fact that all of these writers live abroad and write not for a national audience, but for a foreign audience; James argues that they must then "come home" in order to do what only great artists can: the artist "exercises an influence on the national consciousness which is incalculable. He is created by it but he himself illuminates and amplifies it, bringing the past up to date and charting the future."[61]

But James claims that the Caribbean writer is also circumscribed with respect to the nation in other ways than by the fact of exile. As proficient and skilled as Caribbean writers might be, they are nevertheless not utilizing a "national form" that has a "national audience." The literary forms in which Caribbean writers write are foreign forms that neither enjoy mass popularity nor have been domesticated and transformed into something particularly "of" the Caribbean. To find this kind of "artist" with the impact that the great artist can have on the formation of the nation, James suggests that one must instead turn to an analysis and examination of two forms that *are* national forms. The first of these is calypso; the great artist of calypso is the Mighty Sparrow. The second is cricket; the great artist of cricket is Garfield Sobers. At first, the choice of cricket seems to be an odd one, since like the novel it is also a "borrowed" form. James clarifies: this is "a medium which though transported was so well established that it has created a Caribbean tradition of its own."[62]

In this context, it is not surprising that the period from 1958 to 1962 marks another important point of development in James's intellectual career:

> Once in a blue moon, i.e., once in a lifetime, a writer is handed on a plate a gift from heaven. I was handed mine in 1958. I had just completed a draft of this book up to the end of the previous chapter [Chapter 17] when I returned to the West Indies in April 1958, after twenty-six years of absence . . . immediately I was immersed up to the eyes in "The Case for West Indian Self-Government"; and a little later, in the most furious cricket campaign I have ever known, to break the discriminations of sixty years and have a black man, in this case Frank Worrell, appointed captain of a West Indies team . . . The intimate connection between cricket and West Indian social and political life was established so that all except the willfully perverse could see. It seemed as if I were just taking up again what I had occupied myself with in the months before I left in 1932, except that what was then idea and aspiration was now out in the open and public property.

The book that James makes reference to is his celebrated analysis of cricket (and personal and political memoir), *Beyond a Boundary*, which was completed during the years in which he returned to the Caribbean to work on behalf of the federation; the book was first published in 1963, shortly after his return to England after the federation's failure. In addition to writing political columns for *The Nation* while he was in Trinidad, James also resumed writing a sports column on cricket. What James suggests here in the opening paragraph of the final section of *Beyond a Boundary*, "Vox Populi," is the sudden emergence in the midst of federation of the logic of the entire book he had long been working on: the intimate relationship between sports and national politics in the Caribbean, that had become by the time of federation a visible part of the politics of the region. In the Caribbean, cricket emerges as the site of national politics, a physical space in which the fate of the nation is symbolically displayed in a fashion that is close to everyone's daily existence and in a form that is clearly understood by all: "I was told of an expatriate who arrived in Trinidad to take up an important post which the people thought should be filled by a local candidate. Such a storm arose that the expatriate had to be sent away. In 1959 British Guiana was thrown into turmoil and strikes over a similar issue and the Governor had to retreat. In cricket these sentiments are at their most acute because everyone can see and can judge" (BB 233).

In "Vox Populi," James's specific task is to explore the reasons for the violence that broke out in a 1960 match between the West Indies "national" team and a club team from England. He convincingly argues that it evolved out of a long-standing racial dispute over the captaincy of the team. A less experienced white player was made captain instead of Frank Worrell, one of the great cricketers of his era, who was of African descent. When this incident is placed alongside other racial disputes involving the captaincy of teams in the West Indies (from George Headly to J. K. Holt), a map of the intricate, dialectic relationship between cricket and the politics of the nation emerges:

> What do they know of cricket who only cricket know? West Indians crowding to Tests bring with them the whole past history and future hopes of the islands. English people, for example, have a conception of themselves breathed from birth. Drake and mighty Nelson, Shakespeare, Waterloo, the Charge of the Light Brigade, the few who did so much for so many, the success of parliamentary democracy, those and such as those constitute a national tradition. Underdeveloped countries have to go back centuries to rebuild one. We of the West Indies have none at all, none that we know of. To such people the three W's, Ram and Val wrecking English batting, help to fill a huge gap in their consciousness and in their needs. In one of the sheds on the Port of Spain wharf is painted a sign: 365 Garfield Sobers. If the old Maple–Shannon–Queen's Park type of rivalry was now insignificant, a nationalist jealousy had taken its place. (BB 233)[63]

Beyond a Boundary displays James's undoubted love and intimate knowledge of the game of cricket. But the book represents more than simply the musings of an intellectual enthusiast on a subject of relatively minor importance in comparison to his philosophical, literary, political, and critical output. For James, cricket is fundamental to an understanding of the politics of the West Indies. In the words of Neil Lazarus, "James identifies cricket as a privileged site for the playing out and imaginary resolution of social antagonisms in the colonial and postcolonial West Indies."[64] What is thus displayed in *Beyond a Boundary* is an enormously sophisticated example of what might now be referred to as "cultural studies"[65] — the serious study of what has for too long been seen as "unofficial" or "low" culture, an exploration of the people's culture that does not assume the disinterested pose of an anthropological treatise or ethnographic monograph. In the game of cricket, James sees culture and politics fused together in the vernacular of the people. In addition to stressing the importance of cricket as a national idiom, *Beyond a Boundary* can be seen as representing for James himself a massive "un-learning" of all the ways in which he had previously presumed to read the political signs and symptoms of Caribbean culture. The literary, on which intellectuals such as James had placed so much import, is pushed to the margins, while what was marginal emerges as central to the imagination of the nation and intellectual life. He writes near the beginning of *Beyond a Boundary* in a passage that was added to the manuscript during federation:

> If you had asked me then, or for many years afterward, where cricket stood in my activities as a whole, I would have without hesitation placed it at the bottom of the list, if I had listed it at all. I believe and hope to prove that cricket and football were the greatest cultural influences in nineteenth-century Britain, leaving far behind Tennyson's poems, Beardsley's drawings and concerts of the Philharmonic Society. These filled space in print but not in minds . . . To my house on personal subscription came a mass of periodicals from abroad. I have to give the list. Not only *The Cricketer,* but the *Times Literary Supplement,* the *Times Educational Supplement,* the *Observer,* the *Sunday Times,* the *Criterion,* the *London Mercury,* the *Musical Review,* the *Gramophone,* the *Nouvelle Revue Française,* the *Mercure de France,* for some time the *Nation* and the *New Republic,* the editions of the *Evening Standard* when Arnold Bennett wrote in it, and the *Daily Telegraph* with Rebecca West. I read them, filed most of them, I read and even bought many of the books they discussed. I had a circle of friends (most of them white) with whom I exchanged ideas, books, records, and manuscripts. We published local magazines and gave lectures or wrote articles on Wordsworth, the English Drama, and Poetry as Criticism of Life. We lived according to the tenets of Matthew Arnold, spreading sweetness and light and the best that has been thought and said in the world. We met all visiting literary celebrities as a matter of course. Never losing sight of my plan to go abroad and write, I studied and practised assiduously the art of fiction: Dostoevsky, Tolstoy, Tchekov, Flaubert, Maupassant and the Goncourt brothers . . . What ultimately vitiated all this was that it involved me with the people around me only in the most abstract way. I spoke. My audience listened and thought it was fine and that I was a learned man . . . What now stands out a mile is that I was publicly involved only in cricket and soccer. I played both of them, but the playing was only the frame. I was a sports journalist. The conflicts and rivalries which arose out of the conditions I have described gripped me . . . Our community was small. I fought the good fight with all my might. I was in the toils of greater forces than I knew. Cricket had plunged me into politics long before I was aware of it. When I did turn to politics I did not have too much to learn. (BB 65)

After *Beyond a Boundary*, what can it mean to write nationalist literature in the Caribbean — literature that speaks of the nation, that tries to bring the nation into existence? *Beyond a Boundary* announces James's refusal to play the game of the third-world literary intellectual who believes in the importance of literature for the purposes of national revolution — literature, and nothing but. At the end of the experiment with federation, James's book on cricket convincingly announces the end of a certain form of literary politics: a form practiced and advocated by Lamming, practiced and decried by Naipaul. For James, it was clear that literature neither had the impact on the formation of the nation that Lamming thought that it necessarily must, nor did it speak to the people, much less of them. In comparison with the discourses of literature, cricket succeeded wildly in the West Indies as a discourse of the broader nationalism that federation promised but was unable to produce. Though competition between the Test Squads of the various countries within the English Caribbean remains fierce, one of the most powerful forces for the national union of the islands remains the enormously powerful emotional attachment to the joint West Indian team. As Neil Lazarus has written, what James came to realize is that "cricket is not only *also* culture, that is, one cultural form among several, but culture itself. It was not only the rare cricket critic who, watching Sobers send a good length ball skimming to cover boundary, felt himself to be in the presence of a national cultural treasure. Rather, this was the experience of the West Indian crowd as a whole."[66] It is at this point, in this medium, that the intellectual and the people share a common insight into the national body that requires the production of no manifestos or the elaboration of difficult epistemologies to bring them together.

The works that I have looked at in this chapter highlight the paradoxes of modernity and the nation in the Caribbean in the decades following World War II. One of the central issues in creating a national space is the condition of subalternity outlined in different ways by Lamming and Naipaul. Though it seems to offer a potential way out of this condition, literature also complicates it further, raising the necessary and important issue of the function of literary writing in the postcolony and the problematic relationship of the intellectual to the public. Put in another way, the problem that these texts outline is what Jameson describes in "Third-World Literature" as the problem of cultural revolution. By ending with James's *Beyond a Boundary*, I do not mean to suggest that a solution can be found in popular culture that cannot be found in literature. It is too simple to suggest that the problems of creating a Caribbean collectivity dissolve by turning to the practices and activities of the masses. James doesn't presume to stabilize the zone of instability that Lamming and Naipaul work in and through. Rather, by revealing some of the forces and discourses that produced, for instance, the knot of problems that led to exile, James pushes things in different and potentially more politically fruitful directions for both the Caribbean and the literature in and of the region.

CHAPTER THREE

The Novel after the Nation

Nigeria after Biafra

> At this point we leave Africa, not to mention it again. — G. W. F. HEGEL

> In Africa, the native literature of the last twenty years is not a national litera-
> ture but a Negro literature. — FRANTZ FANON

The Black Man's Burden: The Nation in Africa

Basil Davidson, the preeminent contemporary historian of Africa, has described the nation as "the black man's burden."[1] His discussion of the development of nations and nationalisms in Africa in the twentieth century follows what
has become an entirely familiar way of characterizing recent African history:
revolutionary, nationalist hopes give way to the disappointments and disillusion-
ment of the corrupt postindependence state that Fanon simultaneously describes
and prophesizes in *The Wretched of the Earth*. The succession of one corrupt
regime by another has been a persistent pattern that has defined the politics of
almost the entire continent and shows little sign of changing or abating. The
recent hope of yet another political rebirth in Africa that followed the removal of
the Mobutu regime in the Congo by the forces of Laurent Khabila have faded
away entirely as the bad political business of the country continues as usual;
Africa remains today in a precipitous political state, despite (or perhaps because
of) the supposedly newfound confidence of foreign investors to resume the plunder of African resources following the trip to the continent by U.S. President Bill
Clinton in 1998 and by U.S. Treasury Secretary Paul O'Neill and rock star Bono

in 2002. Overall, the almost half-century of national and nationalist politics that has framed all of these developments has been an unmitigated disaster. In Davidson's words, "If the postcolonial nation-state had become a shackle on progress . . . the prime reason could appear in little doubt. The state was not liberating and protective of its citizens, no matter what its propaganda claimed: on the contrary, its gross effect was constricting and exploitative, or else had simply failed to operate in any social sense at all."[2]

All nations are invented through an investment in various discursive and in-stitutional operations that together manage convincingly (more or less) to pro-duce the geographic coincidence of state power with cultural, ethnic, linguistic, and political boundaries. As Craig Calhoun reminds us, the nation is a discursive structure as much as it is a political one: nationalism is "the production of a cultural understanding and rhetoric which leads people throughout the world to think and frame their aspirations in terms of the idea of the nation and national identity."[3] The central insight into the phenomenon of the nation that is shared by all of the recent critical writing on the subject has been that all nations must be seen as essentially arbitrary configurations of culture and power, which the phe-nomenon of nationalism tries to obscure and make timeless and natural. While it is true that all nations across the globe are in this sense arbitrary, there is perhaps nowhere in the world where the nation has been as arbitrary a political form as in Africa. By this I mean that it is difficult to pretend that the political boundaries within present-day Africa even minimally cohere to any long-standing ethnic, linguistic, or cultural divisions, beyond the fact, that is, that all are the residue of the political and economic struggles of competing European imperial powers. For example, it seems at times that what gives coherence to a nation such as Nigeria, which has enormous ethnic and linguistic variations within its bounda-ries,[4] is *only* its history as a colony of a particular imperial power, which has left it with a different European language from that of some of its West African neigh-bors and with borders defined and established prior to its independence in 1960 that it has insisted on clinging to through all manner of political strife. Any initiative that would try to create the imaginative or discursive structure of the nation in an effort to link together all of the peoples of Nigeria would seem to be imperiled from the very start: what the Ibo, Hausa, and Yoruba peoples share, at least with respect to the geographic borders of the country called "Nigeria," is the experience of British colonialism and, perhaps, all of the efforts devised since to hold the nation together. It is no doubt for this reason that in Nigeria as well as everywhere else in Africa, with the notable exception of the *participação popular* that arose out of the Portuguese anticolonial movements, most of the nation-building on the continent has been "top-down"—an imperative of the rulers rather than the ruled.[5]

One outcome of this "imposed" nationalism has been the stifling of other forms of political affiliation that existed in the African precolonial past. "'Mass participation,'" Davidson writes, "however variously mediated by this or that structure of representation and control, was at the heart of all those African societies which had proved stable and progressive before the destructive impact of the overseas slave trade and colonial dispossession had made itself felt."[6] In addition to struggling with the dubious legacy of African nationalism, one of the central intellectual and cultural challenges that has faced postcolonial Africa has been the need to establish categories and concepts that are expressive of African difference—categories that neither hypothesize African Otherness through a simple negation of European definitions of humanity and culture (the old criticism of nativism), nor embrace the messy modernity of the nation-form imported from Europe. It is for valorizing the former through the production of the setting of African literature as "a landscape of elephants, beggars, calabashes, serpents, pumpkins, baskets, towncriers, iron bells, slit drums, iron masks, hares, snakes, squirrels . . . a landscape portrayed with native eyes to which aeroplanes naturally appear as iron birds"[7] that the two best-known Nigerian writers, Wole Soyinka and Chinua Achebe, have harshly criticized proponents of negritude. Both these writers are critical not only of negritude's fascination with the African past, but also of what they see as the false internationalism of negritude's diasporic politics. They criticize this internationalism in much the same way as Fanon, who took negritudinists to task for failing to see that "every culture is first and foremost national and that the problems that kept Richard Wright or Langston Hughes on the alert were fundamentally different from those that might confront Léopold Senghor or Jomo Kenyatta."[8] Through the events of Biafra and all the coups, countercoups, and endlessly proclaimed democratic transition programs, Soyinka and Achebe have remained vocal supporters of the Nigerian *nation*, believing that it is above all else the nation that provides a political form that will enable a renewed postcolonial polity to exist. For each writer, the issue of the nation figures prominently in their understanding of the necessity and the form that African writing takes; for both writers, African literature must be *nationalist* literature before it can be anything else.

In the context of the past half-century of African history, it is tempting to see the nationalism of Achebe and Soyinka as simply a problematic residue, perhaps of their European education and their common (though not exactly similar) liberal humanist understanding of international politics.[9] However critical they might be of negritude, the necessity of the nation cannot help but appear as exactly that which negritude sought to exorcise: the affirmation of the inevitability of Western concepts and Western modernity. This is, of course, far too simple and reductive. It is easy enough to see each writer's early attention to the discourse of nationalism (as exhibited in Achebe's early novels and in Soyinka's dramatic celebration of the birth of the new nation, *A Dance of the Forests* [1960]) as part of the wider cultural and political discourses that accompanied decolonization. This explanation is itself limited in another way, since it fails to pay adequate attention to the complicated intersection of the concept of the nation with that of the literary in Nigeria. In other words, what it fails to address is the way in which it is precisely a certain conception of the "literariness" of literary writing that makes it an object for the nation and vice versa; and it is here, rather than in the particularities of biography or the vagueness of context, that an answer must be found. Rather than repeat the analysis of the previous chapter, in this chapter I will look at a different but related dimension of the problem of literature and the nation in the postcolony. I will examine the views of Achebe and Soyinka on the nation, literature, and their interrelation, by focusing on how these change (or fail to change) as a consequence of the tragic collapse of nationalist hopes in the bloodbath of the Biafran conflict. In other words, what this chapter will address is the question of what happens to nationalist literature *after* the nation, as a way of throwing into relief the connections that Achebe and Soyinka make between the novel and the nation. The two works that I will look at especially closely are the post-Biafran novels of Soyinka and Achebe — the only novels that either of them have written since 1966: Achebe's *The Anthills of the Savannah* (1987) and Soyinka's *Season of Anomy* (1973). What is remarkable about these works and both authors' subsequent critical writing is how little their commitment to the nation has wavered over the years. One of the main reasons, it seems to me, that the outcome of the Biafran conflict does not point for either writer to the impossibility of the Nigerian nation and the need for different modes of political life, is that they read Biafra to some degree as a sign of an *aesthetic* failure: the failure of the novel to accomplish the task that only it can carry out. In their shared antipathy toward nativism and their insistence on the inevitability of modernity, the nation becomes an inviolable principle of political life. As a result, these post-Biafran novels are curious artifacts that symbolically consume themselves and willingly stage the erosion of their own political effectivity. Since Achebe and Soyinka are unwilling to give up on the idea of the nation, it seems that the novel must be sacrificed on the altar of Nigerian nation-building.

Before proceeding any further, it is necessary to review at least the bare outline of the causes of the Nigerian Civil War. The Federation of Nigeria gained independence from Britain in 1960. A federal system of highly autonomous regions divided primarily along ethnic lines (Northern Region: Hausa-Fulani; Western: Yoruba; Eastern: Ibo) was established with the aim of making the country of Nigeria a workable whole. This close association of region and political party with ethnicity (one of the problems faced by many federations around the world) generated immediate difficulties for the new country: given the structure of the federal government, each election would inevitably result in one political party — and therefore one region and ethnic group — being effectively excluded from government (forming neither the official opposition or the government itself). The inevitable ethnic tensions produced as a result were further heightened by the ethnic composition of the military: the officer corps were primarily Ibo, while the enlisted men were drawn mainly from the north.

A military coup led by Ibo officers in January 1966 constituted the last straw for the north and led to the eruption of violence against Ibo living in the north. A countercoup led by northern elements of the army led to the brief restoration of the federal system under the leadership of General Yakuba Gowon. This countercoup led to a mass exodus of Ibo from the north to the Eastern Region, and to the secession of the Eastern Region early in 1967 as the independent "Republic of Biafra." An incursion by Biafran troops into the Western Region in an effort to capture Lagos led to all-out war on Biafra by the remaining regions of the federation; a blockade of Biafra by both land and sea contributed to the death of up to two million Biafran civilians, mainly by starvation, before the surrender of Biafra in January 1970. Only now is Nigeria beginning to emerge from this dark period that has effectively constituted the entire short history of the nation.[10]

In part because of his more extensive body of critical writing prior to the Nigerian crisis, and because his views on the function and purpose of writing in Africa were so influential across postcolonial space, I begin with a discussion of Achebe. Though it might seem that in this chapter I violate the rough periodizing boundaries that I established earlier, what will become clear is that these novels are in many respects belated, responding to a logic of nationalist literature that was established well before their actual publication dates.

The Ambiguity of the Political:
Achebe's *Anthills of the Savannah*

It is the story that outlives the sound of war-drums and the exploits of brave
fighters. It is the story, not the others, that saves our progeny from blundering like
blind beggars into the spikes of the cactus fence. The story is our escort; without it,
we are blind.

— CHINUA ACHEBE [11]

In me grows a tiny feeling against dichotomies (strong-weak; big-small; happy-
unhappy; ideal–not ideal). It is so only because people cannot think more than two
things. More does not fit into a sparrow's brain. But the healthiest thing is simply:
maneuver.

— BERTOLT BRECHT [12]

If it is not entirely correct to characterize Chinua Achebe as a writer who has had
little difficulty in clearly delineating his politics — and, furthermore, the place of
writing and the function of the writer within this politics — it is nonetheless
certain that over a career of almost four decades his political positions have been
characterized by a relative lack of ambiguity. For a writer of fiction, and of
predominantly realist fiction, ambiguity of any sort would appear to be a virtue.
The world, especially the world of postcolonial African societies, is extraordinarily complex (an enormous understatement, to be sure), and any fiction that
would presume to capture the dizzying heterogeneity of this world, the nearly
sublime movement of forces and agents with, against, and through one another
must be careful to avoid the adoption of easy positions and the mobilization of
simple polemics. The success of Achebe's novels is largely due to the fact that
they *do* manage to present a fully formed African present in just this way, an
"ambiguous" Africa composed of multiple, equivocal voices. The sole exception
to this fictional richness, however, may be found in the comparatively definitive,
*un*ambiguous character of the political options Achebe makes available to African
societies in their struggle to define themselves in the aftermath of colonialism.
Yet if an ambiguity of the political has not been a characteristic of Achebe's earlier
work (and here I am thinking as much of his critical writings as of his novels),
Anthills of the Savannah is a novel that exhibits fully and forcefully the complexities of African politics and, after Biafra, of the political more generally.

It is impossible to pass over the twenty-one year silence that ends with the
publication of *Anthills of the Savannah* without speculating on the problems that

Achebe may have encountered in attempting to produce a novel-length work during this period. Given the more ambitious literary form of *Anthills* as compared with his earlier work, this silence would seem at least partially to be the outcome of serious reflection on Achebe's part on the appropriate form to describe a world in which, suddenly, the greatest hopes for African independence came so quickly to an end. More significantly, however, this silence seems to have grown out of a necessary, difficult reconceptualization of the role of the African writer or intellectual in bringing about positive change in a society characterized by widespread corruption and political inertia. (For example, the two chief political candidates in the first election in Nigeria's Second Republic in 1979 — Obafemi Awolowo and Nnamdi Azikiwe — had been leading candidates in the elections of the First Republic in 1960. *Plus ça change . . .*) The changes in Achebe's thought represented by *Anthills*, both in its theme and its form, show a willingness on his part to consider for the first time the difficulties of politics in Nigeria *as* difficulties; solutions to these difficulties will have to come later, if indeed, solutions to the troubles with Nigeria, and Africa more generally, are to be found at all. In *Anthills*, the political is shown to be as complex and heterogeneous as the rest of human experience, fraught with impossible choices, insoluble antinomies, and frustrating, intransigent paradoxes that are less conceptual — which would mean that intellectuals could somehow then think or write their way out of them — than material and historical.

This represents a fairly dramatic shift in Achebe's own view of politics. These politics are comprised of a fairly consistent set of positions, from *Things Fall Apart* (1958) to *The Trouble with Nigeria* (1983), and are of two essential modes, divided thematically and chronologically but intimately related nonetheless. The first, as reflected in the essays collected in *Morning Yet on Creation Day* (1975) and *Hopes and Impediments* (1983) and in *Things Fall Apart* and *No Longer at Ease* (1960), is to challenge colonial readings of the African novel that would, for example, find the latter's significance only in its universal character (i.e., its potential for "speaking" to Europeans and Americans as well as Africans) and to create an autonomous space for the critical assessment and artistic development of African writing independent of Western aesthetic or linguistic categories. Achebe repeatedly denounces the idea "that before I write about any problem I must first verify whether they have it too in New York and London and Paris"[13] — the reductio ad absurdum of the colonial critic's demand for universality in the African novel. With respect to the autonomy of the African novel, Achebe makes a simple plea: "don't fence me in."[14] His well-known defense of the use of non-African languages in African writing,[15] for example, reflects Achebe's fervent desire for the African novel to become whatever it wishes to become, independent of artificial, externally imposed criteria as to what "properly" constitutes such a novel: "My answer to the question *Can an African ever learn English well enough to be able to use it effectively in creative writing?* is certainly yes. If on the other hand you ask: *Can he learn to use it like a native speaker?* I should say, I hope not. It is neither necessary nor desirable for him to do so. The price a world language must be prepared to pay is submission to many different kinds of use. The African writer should aim to use English in a way that brings out his message best without altering the language to the extent that its value as a medium of international exchange will be lost."[16]

If this first dimension of his politics can be described as predominantly a reaction to a *colonial* situation that aims above all else to restore to Africans a positive self-image and belief in their abilities that colonialism did so much to erode, the second aspect of Achebe's politics can be characterized as a reaction to a *postcolonial* situation. This second dimension of Achebe's politics is less concerned with the politics of writing or aesthetics more generally, which, whether from the side of the artist or the audience, formed the basis of his earlier preoccupations, than with politics per se. It represents an attempt on Achebe's part to make sense of the African political or social situation following independence and Biafra. The colonial powers have departed, and yet the whole continent seems more awry than ever, oscillating between supposedly democratic and antidemocratic military regimes, both of which are enormously inefficient and monstrously corrupt. Achebe tries to make sense of the failure of African independence, and of Nigerian independence in particular, by exploring the psychology of corruption and the conditions that lead to a situation in which power and privilege are flagrantly abused in such a way that the majority of people nevertheless refuse to rise up and challenge the abuses of their leaders (the problem of contemporary ideology in a nutshell). He is chiefly concerned with examining the way in which the people, insofar as they have values and expectations that mirror the sickened and diseased values of their rulers, are complicit in the material despair and political demagoguery characteristic of African nations. The novel that represents this attempt most fully is *A Man of the People* (1966), which exhibits a noticeable thematic shift from his first three novels. While *Things Fall Apart*, *No Longer at Ease*, and *Arrow of God* explore the relationship of an earlier generation of Africans to the colonial situation and the extent of their complicity in (neo)colonialism, *Man* represents a very direct confrontation with postcolo-

nial politics and the "corroding effect of privilege."[17] The critical work that
details the failure of leadership and the indiscipline and corruption of Nigerian
society is *The Trouble with Nigeria*, which in many ways represents a systematiza-
tion of the problems first expressed in *A Man of the People*.[18]

What connects these two politics in Achebe's work is both the ease with which
he assumes that problems or potential problems in the African polity can be
identified, and the corresponding ease with which solutions to these problems
are proposed. At its base, Achebe's politics is straightforward and moralistic: the
enemy can be identified, the character of his activity evaluated as good or bad,
revolutionary or reactionary, and the appropriate measures then taken. There is,
in other words, an epistemological simplicity to his understanding of the political: politics is simply what takes place between powerful figures in specific build-
ings in the capital of a country. Even if Achebe appears to realize that the "political" exists as much in the habits and practices of groups and individuals as in the
chambers of power, a fact suggested by his consideration of the manner in which
corruption pervades the entire body of the Nigerian polity in *The Trouble with
Nigeria*, his is nonetheless a politics that has what Michel Foucault described as a
"juridico-discursive" understanding of power in which change occurs by cutting
off the head of the king.[19] This is nowhere so clear as in the opening lines of *The
Trouble with Nigeria*. Achebe writes: "The trouble with Nigeria is simply and
squarely a failure of leadership. There is nothing basically wrong with the Nigerian character. There is nothing wrong with the Nigerian land or climate or
water or air or anything else. The Nigerian problem is the unwillingness or
inability of its leaders to rise to the responsibility, to the challenge of personal
example which are the hallmarks of true leadership . . . I am saying that Nigeria
can change today if she discovers leaders who have the will, the ability, and the
vision. Such people are rare in any time or place. But it is the duty of enlightened
citizens to lead the way in their discovery and to create an atmosphere conducive
to their emergence."[20]

For Achebe, the problems of Nigerian society (tribalism, an absence of patri-
otism, social injustice, indiscipline, corruption, etc.) originate at the top of the
political order and work their way down. Leaders must be understood as role
models for the rest of the society. If the rulers of the country are undisciplined
and corrupt one can hardly expect those not in positions of power to act any
better. An end to the troubles with Nigeria must then come through the election
or elevation to power of more enlightened rulers than those currently in power,
Platonic philosopher kings who would lend substance to positions of leadership

and defeat the cynicism of the people that Achebe describes in *A Man of the People:* "Tell them that this man had used his position to enrich himself and they would ask you — as my father did — if you thought a sensible man would spit out the juicy morsel that good fortune placed in his mouth."[21]

If the writer of fiction is to be involved in politics — and it is clear that for Achebe she must be if she is not to be "completely irrelevant"[22] given the character of contemporary African societies — it is thus clear what her role must be. In Africa, literature should be about "right and just causes";[23] fiction is what "helps us locate again the line between the heroic and the cowardly when it seems most shadowy and elusive."[24] Fiction serves, then, an almost journalistic function or at least the political function that journalism would ideally serve if allowed free expression in Nigeria. The role of the writer of fiction is to clarify the problems of African society, to make the sometimes opaque maneuverings of power and prestige a little more transparent. For Achebe, it is this characteristic more than any other that separates the African novel from its (comparatively) highly aestheticized Western equivalents. Given the pervasive problems facing African nations, Achebe suggests that the African writer "cannot expect to be excused from the task of re-education and regeneration that must be done." This might mean that Achebe's writing, along with that of other African writers, is often something, he admits, more like "applied art as distinct from pure," more didactic than an example of "art for art's sake" (a characteristic modernism that he tends to associate with first-world writing in general). This is a fact that does not seem to bother him in the least: "But who cares? Art is important, but so is education of the kind I have in mind."[25] If the form of the African novel is polemical and didactic, more concerned with functionality than with the development of a pure aesthetic, it is a form that is necessary given the state of contemporary Africa. A journalistic, didactic novel is more likely to have a definitive political impact than one that aims primarily at some form of aesthetic transgression. And this perhaps explains why Achebe is able to detect even in Amos Tutuola's *The Palm-Wine Drinkard* a preoccupation with a primarily moral set of questions.[26]

If Achebe's writing prior to *Anthills* can be characterized by a politics in which the intellectual or writer plays a necessarily prominent role in the political transformation of African societies — due both to her analytic function in diagnosing the character of the nation's social sickness and in presenting it to the public, *and* as the cure (in the form of a new leadership) for the same sickness — *Anthills* represents a shift from this politics. "Reversal" suggests a typical intellectual maneuver, for example, from an elite politics to a democratic one, from thoughts about the halls of the mighty to the quotidian existence lived out by the masses in the fields and streets. And while *Anthills* might appear to be characterized by just this sort of reversal, a shift in which Achebe begins to imagine the possibility or even the necessity of political agency originating from the masses rather than from a newly enlightened elite, it is less a reversal that takes place than a complete *abandonment* of a politics that operates through those dichotomies toward which Brecht expressed such suspicion. It is in this abandonment of any straightforward notion of the political, a withdrawal from an epistemologically simple politics that posited easy political answers, that an "ambiguity" of the political arises in *Anthills.* This is an abandonment that is both brave and problematic: brave, because it opens up the possibility for politics in Africa to move beyond the stagnant, cyclical corruption characteristic of both right- and left-wing regimes; problematic, potentially dangerous, because it displaces the political so greatly from its known parameters and paradigmatic expressions that it appears at times to offer no real possibility for any movement or determinate political agency whatsoever.

Anthills of the Savannah is the story of three men who have known each other from their days together at Lord Lugard College, a school named after the British colonialist responsible for bringing Nigeria together as a unitary state in 1914, which in the novel is the institution primarily responsible for the reproduction of the indigenous elite. They have subsequently become powerful political figures in Kangan, the fictional West African country in which the novel is set. As in Lamming's *The Emigrants* and Soyinka's *Season of Anomy*, this shift from a specifically Nigerian (and Ibo) setting to an imagined space is significant. Sam, who went on to study at the British military college Sandhurst, has by the beginning of the novel become the country's military dictator; Chris Oriko is the Minister of Information in the government headed by Sam; and Ikem Osodi is the editor of the *Gazette*, the most important newspaper in Bassa, Kangan's capital. The narrative centers mainly on Chris and Ikem and their gradual fall from political grace as tensions in the government mount over the situation in Abazon, a province of Kangan affected by severe drought. Significantly, although the novel begins as a story about these three men, the other main character in the novel turns out not to be Sam, who with the exception of the first few chapters of the book lingers mostly in the background, but Beatrice, Chris's lover and an old friend of Ikem's. As will become clear given the importance of Beatrice to the politics of the novel, the movement of Sam to the narrative periphery of the novel itself indicates Achebe's political shift in *Anthills*. The tale of the dictator makes way for a woman's story—a clear sign of the shift in Achebe's views from the period in which he began writing the novel (after the publication of *A Man of the People* in 1966) to its completion in 1987.

The novel rearticulates a number of the themes that arise in Achebe's *The Trouble with Nigeria*. As summarized in Ikem's one-verse hymn, *Anthills* also stresses the way in which the greatest political threat is not nakedly displayed power, but the way in which the dispositions of the powerful can infiltrate themselves into those of the powerless:

> The worst threat from men of hell
> May not be their actions cruel
> Far worse that we learn their way
> And behave more fierce than they. (AS 43)

But while the political problem here might once again appear to be that of leadership or its lack, the solution offered to this problem in *Trouble* (i.e., the need for a new set of leaders) is rejected in *Anthills* as unlikely to furnish any real solution. As the initial chapter, which describes a meeting between Sam and his sycophantic cabinet, makes abundantly clear, even a government begun with the best intentions has the potential to devolve into a dictatorship in which, among others things, flattery comes to assume the place of real debate (AS 2) and the moral force of governing is displaced by internal struggles over power. What Kangan might in fact need to set the country aright is a leader who would be less of an "actor" than Sam, whom Ikem describes as having "no sense of moral commitment whatsoever" (AS 50). As Chris sarcastically puts it: "What this country really needs is a ruthless dictator . . . and we will all laugh in loud excess because we know—bless our hearts—that we shall never be favoured with such an undeserved blessing as a ruthless dictator" (AS 3). A disciplined leader that would be willing to stand by a set of consistently crafted and articulated policies, regardless of whether these policies originate from the right or the left, is not something that the citizens of Kangan can truly hope for, given the history of the leaders they have had to endure. In any case, simply waiting for the right leader to appear does not really constitute a politics likely to result in positive change. If in *Trouble* Achebe berates the educated elite for betraying the "high destiny" (AS 2) of Nigeria through their refusal to take on the challenge of genuine political reform, in *Anthills* it quickly becomes apparent that the problem, and therefore the solution, lies elsewhere, outside and beyond the dangerous play of the elite.

Anthills opens up the possibility of another solution. Much of the narrative concerns the gradual education of the elite figures of the novel — Ikem, Chris, and Beatrice as well — about the importance and dignity of the ordinary citizens of Kangan. The elite are separated from the rest of the citizens of Kangan not only by status and power, but physically: all three of the central figures live inside the "safe" confines of the government living compound and so occupy the "alien climate" (AS 9) of the chambers of power. Chris and Ikem in particular manage to learn, if too late, losing their lives in the process of this education, that "this world belongs to the people of the world not to any little caucus, no matter how talented" (AS 232). Political change will have to involve the people in some other way than simply as a reflection of an elite with a different, more democratic set of dispositions. For it is only if the people are themselves involved in change that political change can be taken to be substantive and permanent, a systemic or structural change rather than a mere shift in personalities. In essence, this is the same solution proposed by Basil Davidson to the problem of the nation in Africa: a transformation from the ground up rather than from the top down.

Exactly how the "people" are to be involved in political change and what the role of the intellectual is in precipitating this change are questions explored by Achebe in an extremely complex manner. There is no easy shift from the corruption of a Europeanized African elite to the supposed (political) authenticity of the African masses. In this respect, in *Anthills* Achebe astutely preserves and builds upon the insights of *A Man of the People*. In this earlier novel, the political fall of Chief the Honourable Nanga has nothing to do with the effort of Odili and Max on behalf of the Common People's Convention to educate the populace about the scope of Nanga's corruption. It is not a lack of knowledge that prevents the people from casting Nanga out of office, but the existence of an all-pervasive political culture in which Nanga's actions are simply understood to be consistent with the actions of those in power. Odili says of his father: "He took the view (without expressing it in so many words) that the mainspring of political action was personal gain."[27] The people of Odili's home village briefly consider lending him their support only when they realize that having one of their own in a position of power might result in substantial economic benefits for the village. While the people cannot thus be entrusted with the expression of their own political views, it is nevertheless clear in *Man* that it is equally dangerous to allow intellectuals to speak on their behalf. Odili's political motives, for example, arise less from his own desire to improve his country's situation than from his desire to exact revenge on Nanga for having personally humiliated him. A third, intermediary path between these two possibilities—between becoming the "man" and allowing the "people" to speak—seems difficult to imagine. If Achebe no longer believes the intellectual to be the one who, in the words of Michel Foucault, speaks "the truth to those who had yet to see it, in the name of those who were forbidden to speak the truth,"[28] nor assumes that the multitude is capable of a politics of its own that would be any better than that practiced by the elite, it is unclear what form a postcolonial African politics might take.

Much of *Anthills* constitutes a direct meditation on this difficult question. This is particularly true with respect to the character of Ikem, who, as one of the chief sources of the news in Kangan, one of it most popular and influential writers, and political spokesperson for his homeland of Abazon, may be seen at times as standing in for Achebe himself.[29] There are three pivotal scenes in the novel involving Ikem in which he more or less directly questions his previous, Marxist revolutionary stance, and begins to articulate a set of concepts and problems that form a more adequate political theorization of the problems with democracy in Africa; Chris undergoes this same transformation from the ideologically opposite side—both, then, moving toward some political middle ground. In these scenes (AS 96–101; AS 136–42; Ikem's speech, AS 152–61), which heavily overlap in terms of the themes and issues addressed, Ikem reconsiders the place of women in politics, the relationship of the intellectual to the masses, and considers the possibility that reform might finally be more feasible and workable than the idea of a cataclysmic class revolution, even if this means that only a very slow narrative of political progress can be imagined.

The first impression given in the novel about Ikem's relationship to and treatment of women is highly unfavorable. The second scene in which Ikem appears (he appears earlier as an aggressive and confrontational driver on the streets of Bassa) begins with him sending home his working-class lover, Elewa, under the pretense of not wanting her to stay the night in the government compound and so appear as a "loose" woman. In reality, having already made love to her, he wishes to have the remainder of the evening to himself, during which time he might (for example) once again contemplate aesthetically his neighbor's abuse of his wife: there is for him "an extraordinarily surrealistic quality about the whole thing that is almost satisfyingly cathartic" (AS 34). Having just seen an example of Ikem's behavior, we aren't surprised when Beatrice confesses to Chris that Ikem, "the great revolutionary," "doesn't say much to any girl. He doesn't think they have enough brains" (AS 65).[30] The largest flaw in Ikem's thinking, as Beatrice has repeatedly told him over the years, "is that he has no clear role for women in his political thinking and he doesn't seem to be able to understand it" (AS 91). Expanding the role for women in politics and seeing their absence from the political as a critical sign of all that is wrong in Africa become important in *Anthills* for both Ikem and Achebe.

Whether it is due to his suspension as editor of the *Gazette* or to the accumulated force of Beatrice's charges, Ikem's thinking undergoes a dramatic change in the novel. After he has been relieved of his editorial duties, Ikem appears at Beatrice's house with what he describes as a "strange love-letter" (AS 97) in which he reconsiders the role of women in African politics and society. This is not, however, all that he rethinks: his political shift is larger, more general, involving a full-fledged contemplation of "the nature of oppression—how flexible it must learn to be, how many faces it must learn to wear if it is to succeed again and again" (AS 97). All the issues that Ikem rethinks throughout the novel are shown in this first scene to be interrelated in important ways. On the subject of women, Ikem relates two traditional ideas concerning women that have worked to isolate them from the political. In the Old Testament as well as in Kanganian creation stories, women are first made the subjects of men because "She caused Man to fall" (AS 97)—a crime for which "she" must pay in perpetuity. The New Testament overturns this "candid chauvinism" through the figure of Mary, as does the Kanganian idea of women as *Nneka*, "Mother is Supreme" (AS 98). Here again, however, women are displaced from practical, earthly affairs, and placed on a pedestal, made irrelevant and disconnected from the concerns of the polity. What is the new role for women that Ikem imagines will overturn these sexist roles? Ikem answers: "I don't know. I should have never presumed to know. *You* have to tell us. We never asked you before" (AS 98).

The move to give to subaltern or oppressed groups the power to determine for themselves what their roles (political and otherwise) will be in the future together with the simultaneous renunciation of this power by those who once presumed to speak "the truth to those who had yet to see it" are familiar (if mainly symbolic) political strategies. Achebe wishes to reempower the oppressed; the rest of Ikem's speech to Beatrice complicates immensely the means by which such empowerment might take place. It is not simply a matter of a chivalrous renunciation on the part of the intellectual of his power to speak for others. Nor is it simply a matter of easily determining the crimes committed from (as it were) "above" and returning to the oppressed a freedom that is simple, monologic, and negative in form. Women are, Ikem says, the largest group of oppressed people in the world. He notes, however, that there are innumerable other groups that are oppressed, a

vast heterogeneous assembly of the powerless. "There is no universal conglomerate of the oppressed" (AS 99); "the oppressed inhabit each their own peculiar
hell" (AS 99). This introduces a practical, political difficulty. Political theories, as
well as political movements, have relied on large-scale abstractions and totalizing
generalizations in order to link the oppressed together under labels such as the
"working class" or the "proletariat." If each group of the oppressed or even if
each oppressed individual must be considered in his or her singularity, this requires a radical reconceptualization of the political, the invention of a political
that has not yet been thought, composed of an infinitely heterogeneous notion of
the modalities of both freedom and oppression.

While Achebe does not explain what this would amount to, he does make
some suggestions as to what it might look like. For example, such a politics would
have to be able to accept the perpetual presence of what Ikem calls the "stubborn
antibody called surprise" (AS 99). It would need to have a new understanding of
contradiction. Contradiction would no longer be avoided as a "deadly disease"
(AS 100) but would be cultivated as "the very stuff of life" that "can spark off the
fires of invention" (AS 100). This means as well that the attitude toward change
that such a politics would possess would not be revolutionary, but reformist, a
gradual rearrangement and shifting of society "around what it is, its core of
reality; not around an intellectual abstraction" (AS 100). The result would be a
politics that could make sense of the complexity of the world (and particularly its
radical contingency) without resorting to ideologically charged stereotypes. As
Ikem puts it near the end of his "love-letter": "Those who would see no blot of
villainy in the beloved oppressed nor grant the faintest glimmer of humanity to
the hated oppressor are partisans, patriots and party-liners. In the grand finale of
things there will be a mansion also for them where they will be received and
lodged in comfort by the single-minded demigods of their devotion. But it will
not be in the complex and paradoxical cavern of Mother Idoto" (AS 100–101).

The complex and paradoxical politics that Ikem's letter to Beatrice introduces
has obvious implications for his own role (and that of Achebe's as well) as a writer
and intellectual. Ikem realizes that he "had always felt a yearning without very
clear definition, to connect his essence with earth and earth's people" (AS 140–
41). He realizes as well that this separation from the mass is not a gap that can be
bridged in anything but a false way, through invocations of the "people's name"
and under the rubric of "public affairs" (AS 141) when the people are in fact
absent and the "public" simply acts as a convenient euphemism for the sphere of
"closed transactions of soldiers-turned-politicians" (AS 141). Ikem is what he is

and can make connections outside of his social position as an intellectual only in slow, careful, halting ways: "There seems no way to become like the poor except by faking. What I know, I know for good or ill. So for good or ill I shall remain myself; but with this deliberate readiness now to help, and be helped. Like those complex, multivalent atoms in Biochemistry books I have arms that reach out in all directions—a helping hand, a hand signaling for help. With one I shall touch the earth and leave another free to wave the skies" (AS 142).

The image that is presented here is compelling: the individual as an atom with numerous valences, each of which enable it to conjoin with substances different from itself to form entirely new compounds whose properties would be radically unlike the individual elements that comprise it. But this is only a metaphor: it does not explain the process by which such a radical transformation is to be brought about. It may in fact be the case that a politics of the sort imagined by Ikem can proceed only through metaphors. The metaphors presented in this passage are powerful ones. One hand reaches out to aid others, while the other calls for help: the intellectual is no longer the singular source of aid for the oppressed, but requires help to rise out of his own oppression. This shatters the myth of self-genesis or auto-poesis: everyone is implicated in everybody else's existence. There is a necessity to think materially (earth), but also to combine this thought with a potential utopian overcoming of the limits of materiality (the immateriality of the skies). Nevertheless, it is clear in *Anthills* that Achebe does not wish to be left simply with a metaphoric politics of this kind. Even if the shifts in Ikem's political outlook represent a necessary complication of the politics appropriate to the seemingly intransigent problems of postcolonial Africa, Achebe does not want to leave the political field complicated, ambiguous, indeterminate, and indeterminable. Whatever else this reformulated politics might be, it is not a vision that wishes to promote a new, theoretically justified quietism. As Ikem says, "None of this is a valid excuse for political inactivity or apathy. Indeed, to understand it is an absolute necessity for meaningful action, the knowledge of it being the only protective inoculation we can have against false hopes and virulent epidemics of gullibility" (AS 100). The question remains, however, if politics is centered neither in the people nor in the activities of the elite, what is the location of the political? Is it even correct any longer to speak of location, a place of agency, in this way?

Achebe's answer to this question is as intriguing as it is problematic. In locating a third site for politics he follows a somewhat predictable course, though the fact that it is predictable does not make it uninteresting nor lessen the possibility that this course might in fact represent the source of a renewed politics. A typical maneuver: if the political is no longer functioning, look to renew it in something thus far (or even perpetually) "outside" of the political. Better yet, make this "outside" the cause of the original failure, so that its reintegration creates a genuine, undeformed, "whole" politics for the first time. In *Anthills* this "outside" is found in women, as exemplified in particular by Beatrice and, to a lesser degree, Elewa.

Chapter Seven begins with a surprise: "For weeks and months after I had definitively taken on the challenge of bringing together as many broken pieces of this tragic history as I could lay my hands on I still could not find a way to begin. Anything I tried to put down sounded wrong—either too abrupt, too indelicate or too obvious—to my middle ear" (AS 82). The narrative voice belongs to Beatrice. In the passages in which Chris and Ikem appear as first-person narrators they are described as "witnesses" (AS 1, 34). This suggests at first that the story of *Anthills* belongs to them. The paragraph that opens Chapter Seven makes it clear, however, that the story of the novel—of the education and death of Chris and Ikem—is in fact Beatrice's: Chris and Ikem's accounts are included in this story in the form of something like additional source material, an effort to include multiple voices. With respect to Chris and Ikem, this has the effect of focusing attention on the negative connotations of "witness": someone connected to the events that have taken place, though not in a direct way, whose view of these events must be seen as partial, subjective, and individualized. This does not mean that Beatrice's story represents an objective view of the events that transpire in *Anthills*. Indeed, she is intimately aware of the power of stories and of the storyteller, and problematizes this power in ways that Chris and even Ikem never manage to. Beatrice is aware that for Chris and Ikem "the story of this country . . . is the story of the three of you" (AS 66). She, on the other hand, is unwilling to conflate her personal story with that of the nation's, or even to write her story at all if it can only be written at the expense of a larger, more encompassing narrative: "I didn't set out to write my autobiography and I don't want to do so. Who am I that I should inflict my story on the world?" (AS 87). It is significant that *Anthills* is a woman's story not only because this represents a first in Achebe's oeuvre, but also because it acts as an explicit criticism of the univocality, the singularity of masculine narratives expressed in writing and in politics. The humility with which Beatrice approaches writing is for Achebe a characteristic that belongs not to her alone, but to women more generally, and for Achebe the cultivation of this kind of humility is what is necessary for a renewed politics.

In case we might miss the way in which Achebe intends Beatrice to "stand in" for women more generally, he christens her with the name Nwayibuife ("A female is also something" [AS 87]). In *Anthills*, a female is not just "something" but comes to assume the most important role in renewing the political. The humility characteristic of Beatrice the writer also makes possible the reformulation of a new community on the ashes of the old at the end of the novel. Just as she is able to write the story of Kangan with the awareness that there are other stories to be written, the baptism of Elewa's daughter, Amaechina (*"May-the-path-never-close"* [AS 222]) in the final scene of the novel exhibits an ability to rethink the tragic dichotomies dividing the Kanganian polity. Significantly, the formation of a community of "a small band of near-strangers that was to prove stronger than kindred or mere friendship" (AS 218) is made possible not only through the rejection of divisions based on kinship, ethnicity, tradition, and religion, but also through the confusion of sexual roles and identities. Elewa's girl is christened with a boy's name, with the hope, perhaps, that she may in the future assume a man's (political) function as well. Amaechina is named not by her father, Ikem (as is tradition), but out of a necessity as spiritual as it is material (Ikem has been killed), by all those gathered (AS 225). This is an act that puts an end simultaneously to traditional gender roles and to the persistence of a sad irony of Kanganian naming: "call it *The-one-who-walks-into-abundance* or *The-one-who-comes-to-eat* or such like and then blithely hand it back to its mother to begin a wretched trudge through life" (AS 217). It also constitutes the institution of an "authorless" community, a community in which power in dispersed and diffuse because all share in the activity of naming, and all are both father and mother to the children of the community.

This is a surprisingly hopeful ending to an otherwise pessimistic novel, an ending that is somewhat jarring, and perhaps even somewhat inappropriate. The formation of a utopian Kanganian community at the end of the novel implies a solution to the difficult political dilemmas that Achebe explores in the rest of the novel that is too easy. Both in the conclusion of the novel and in the figure of Beatrice as the imputed writer of the story, the answer to the question "What is to be done?" is to leave the reconceptualization of the political to women. Women have thus far remained outside of the political, which seems for Achebe to mean that vis-à-vis the political they occupy a position that has not yet been claimed by the systemic corruption endemic to the rest of (male) Kanganian society. This immediately brings to mind yet another of Beatrice's criticisms of Ikem: "Here's a man, who has written a full-length novel and a play on the Women's War of 1929 which stopped the British administration cold in its tracks, being accused of giving no clear political role to women. But the way I see it is that giving women today the same role which traditional society gave them of intervening only when everything else has failed is not enough, you know, like the women in the Sembene film who pick up the spears abandoned by their defeated menfolk. It is not enough that women should be the court of last resort because the last resort is a damn sight too far and too late!" (AS 91–92).

If it is at times difficult to see Achebe as doing something other than using women as a "court of last resort" in this way, a more balanced reading of the novel would make it apparent that the feminine in *Anthills* acts as a general figure that implicates more than simply women. There are other scenes of resistance to dominant modes of political thought in *Anthills* than those in which the character of Beatrice appears. The people, even if they can at times act like a "mass" in the most degenerate and pejorative sense of this term (as in Ikem's description of the public execution), can also manage to resist being turned into passive objects of political power. When a soldier refuses to kill a young trader in the Gelegele market because " 'If I kill you I kill dog' " (AS 48), it is reinterpreted by the trader in a humorous way that challenges the power of the soldier: " 'Does he mean that after killing me he will go and kill a dog?' " (AS 48). For Achebe, there remains in the people a resistance that is not simply linked up with some sense of their authenticity, a "core" that "is in perfect health" (AS 141), but with "an artless integrity, a stubborn sense of community which can enable Elewa to establish so spontaneously with the driver a teasing affectionateness beyond the powers of Ikem" (AS 142). This is a spontaneity and a stubbornness that Beatrice herself must learn. Beatrice, who treats her maid Agatha quite harshly (AS 93), realizes that if "*it is now up to you women to tell us what has to be done*" (AS 184) that Agatha is a woman who has to be listened to and respected as much as an elite woman such as herself. Just as there is "no universal conglomerate of the oppressed," there is not simply the category of "woman" alone, but particular women who are the product of particular configurations of race, class, kinship relations, and so on. It is this set of configurations, insofar as they differ from the *habitus* of elite institutions like Lord Lugard College that reproduce the ruling elite in clockwork fashion, that Achebe wishes to draw into politics in order to produce a more differentiated political culture. Women are the focus of *Anthills* with respect to this attempt only because it is along the axis of gender perhaps even more than class that African politics has remained monological, unable to move beyond the limited set of degraded concepts that structure political life.

There is nonetheless something troubling about the "solution" the novel offers to the stagnation of post-Biafra Nigeria. It relies too heavily on a fact of Ikem's implicit editorial policy at the *Gazette:* "Our best weapon against them [the rulers] is not to marshal facts, of which they are truly managers, but passion" (AS 38). Passion draws the small community at the end of the novel together through a refusal to stick to the "facts" that have impeded the formation of genuinely pluralistic communities in Africa. The ending of the novel may simply reflect the desired alternative to present-day African society, highlighting the divisions within the culture that need to be broken down in order for such a community to come into existence. What is troublesome, however, is the absence of a sense of how the political culture of Kangan is to be changed in such a way that the pluralistic openness of those gathered together at the end of the novel — an openness that in the novel all of them *already* possess, making the creation of the new community no great feat — is to be made a feature of the polity more generally; this is, after all, the hard question with which much of the novel is concerned. The assertion of "passion" — of something "outside" the field of politics as defined by the ruling elite — seems too easy. There *is* a potential answer to this question suggested by the novel, but it is one that is equally unsatisfactory. As Neil ten Kortenaar points out "the overt message is that Chris and Ikem must learn the importance of ordinary citizens, but the novel itself focuses more upon the manner in which they learn this lesson than upon the people they must learn about."[31] In this light *Anthills* suddenly appears as a continuation of *The Trouble with Nigeria:* a critique of the elite, directed at the elite, staged through the typicality of elite figures who occupy key nodes of the political structure, which is meant to encourage them, in the manner of Chris and Ikem, to change their politics and their political outlook. This would also mean that all of the attempts to encourage the inclusion of different voices in the political in *Anthills*, insofar as they are contained by this discourse of the elite, can be taken as only partial successes confined to the political logic that already exists.

What should be emphasized, however, is that *none* of the problems or solutions in *Anthills* can be taken as prescriptive. If in "The Novelist as Teacher" the task of the writer was a pedagogic one, one of the most important features of *Anthills* is the way in which the role of the writer is reconceptualized in a manner that makes this function problematic. Indeed, the opposite view of the task of the writer is expressed. Ideally, the writer does not express views to the masses eager to listen to his wisdom. Rather, "a novelist must listen to his characters who after all are created to wear the shoe and point the writer where it pinches" (AS 97). Ikem makes the implications of this shift more explicit in his speech to the university students: "A writer wants to ask questions. These damn fellows want him to give answers" (AS 157–58). The function of the writer or intellectual in *Anthills* becomes a more modest one, that of a Socratic gadfly: "As the saying goes, the unexamined life is not worth living . . . As a writer I aspire only to widen the scope of that self-examination" (AS 158); the political aims of the novel itself must be seen more modestly, as doing something different from fulfilling a pragmatic, educative function.

It is finally in this light that *Anthills* must be viewed. With this novel, Achebe manages to point to the extremely complicated nature of the political in Africa, creating a new conceptual framework for politics where an older model had subsisted even in his own work; simultaneously, he places his own work into the field of movements and maneuvers of this new politics. If the intellectual has become suspect in his (and here the male pronoun is not an accident) role as the (universal) voice for those unable to speak for themselves, this suspicion must of necessity extend to Achebe's text as well. It, too, must remain as partial and incomplete as every other claim on the political. *Anthills* admirably manages to maintain such an incompleteness, not only thematically, in terms of content, but in terms of form as well. The fact that Achebe, unlike so many other postcolonial writers, has remained formally committed to a more-or-less realist style is not insignificant. Achebe does not attempt in *Anthills* to affect, by means of an analogy that has become all too common, a transgression of the political by means of an aesthetic transgression. Nor does he try to map the new systems of political relations that he introduces through a shift in form, a "mapping" which might be seen as a feature of those texts described variously as postmodern, metafictional, or magical realist. These latter formal modes, which attempt at least in part to break up or challenge narrative modes linked to totalizing systems of thought — Western metaphysics, colonialism, and the like — have at their basis a vision no less totalizing in its ambition: to *reflect* (or express) at the level of form an epistemological shift that has taken place elsewhere. As but one example: since power is now imagined as capillary and diffuse, the imperious voice of the third-person, realist narrator must also be made diffuse. This represents a curious kind of inverted realism that challenges the artificial mimetic claims of an earlier realism (i.e., its claim to accurately depict the world "as it is") by drawing attention to the way in which it itself mimetically "succeeds" where realism had failed. It is with reference to these hidden ambitions of postmodern fiction that Achebe's novel, which offers up a story, an account of events *without* an accompanying formal, epistemological machinery that would highlight this fact again and again, presents a realism that is partial, contingent, and historical, especially with reference to some of the now dominant forms associated with the postcolonial novel.

But it is important to point out that the more modest role for the intellectual *and* for literature that emerges in *Anthills*—a consequence of what I have described as Achebe's growing sense of the ambiguity of the political—has its origins in a site that the novel never sees fit to name. It is the necessity of a *national* politics, a politics for all of Kangan, that produces a sense of the limits of the intellectual and of the function of literature after Biafra. Once the political begins to fragment in the way that Ikem describes, becoming finally radically individualized, the pedagogic task of the African writer becomes much reduced. It is possible to see the new community that is formed around the birth of Amaechina as the symbolic birth of a new political formation. Yet it is clear that for Achebe this community is meant to be taken not as a sign of something that needs to be formed in place of the nation, but rather, as a sign of the renewal of the nation. The new community formed at the end is the nation represented in miniature, not a self-sufficient community in its own right, composed of all of the diverse and previously divisive elements of the federal body of the nation. Indeed, it is possible to reread all of Achebe's moves to dissolve the power of the intellectual as an argument on behalf of the nation. In place of the singular intellectual, Achebe celebrates the authentic national "passion" of the people that manages to survive against all odds. The dominance of the political by men gives way to women, which is nothing less than a reinvigoration of one of the oldest tropes of nationhood: the national "mother" or motherland whose autobiography doesn't have to be written precisely because it forms the basis of all autobiography.

Spreading the Word: Soyinka's *Season of Anomy*

What sort of nation is this? We grasp only too painfully what the nation can be, what it deserves to be. If Ken Saro-Wiwa's death-cry does prove, in the end, to have sounded the death-knell of that nation, it would be an act of divine justice richly deserved.
                                                                   — WOLE SOYINKA[32]

He laid aside the book he had been reading. "I like your Mao . . . a man of simple truths and a large experimental farm."
                                                                   — WOLE SOYINKA[33]

The relationship of the novel to the nation after the nation that runs through *Anthills* in a subterranean manner is brought to the surface in Wole Soyinka's second novel. Of all the work that makes up Soyinka's enormous literary output, *Season of Anomy* is perhaps the one that has had the least amount of critical attention paid to it.[34] This is due in part to the fact that Soyinka is known more as a poet and playwright than as a novelist. Derek Wright, for example, is content to characterize Soyinka's fiction as little more than "poet's novels, given to dense metaphoric overloading and massive rhetorical redundancies," which contain "some of the most inept features of Soyinka's writing."[35]

Even so, Soyinka's first novel, *The Interpreters* (1965),[36] has long occupied a fairly prominent place in African fiction alongside other novels that detail the reactions of a younger, foreign-educated intellectual class to the disorder and corruption they find in the new African nation-states upon their return, novels such as Achebe's *Man of the People* and Ayi Kwei Armah's *The Beautyful Ones Are Not Yet Born* (1969). While it is possible to glimpse already in *The Interpreters* the political conditions that would eventually result in the Biafran War, by comparison to *Season of Anomy* the novel is nevertheless surprisingly apolitical, which is perhaps one reason that it has remained a more palatable and popular work. The main characters of the novel are shown to be in open revolt against the close-minded, imitative colonial mentality that persists among the new African elite of the country even after independence. But this revolt is staged as much as a spiritual, generational revolt as a political one, an indication that this is a work that is still framed by an interest in cultural nationalism as opposed to the problems of the nation-state.[37] This can be seen, for example, in what has become a set-piece of postcolonial fiction: the diplomatic dinner party, which brings together academics, journalists, important foreigners, politicians, and their henchman — the whole of the postcolonial elite. The party functions as a way of playing out in a dramatically compressed setting all of the political tensions that exist among the elites of the country. In *The Interpreters*, these multiple set-pieces are staged mainly around the refusal of Mrs. Oguazor, the white British wife of Professor Oguazor, to play by the confining social rules of the new elite. She is a constant embarrassment to her husband, who fears that she threatens his academic career through her social ineptitude; she is as a result adopted into the group of friends around whom the story revolves — Sagoe, Sekoni, Lasunwon, Bandele, Egbo and Kola — as a symbolic expression of their own impatience and dissatisfactions with their society and with the preoccupations of social climbers like Oguazor.

By comparison, the party scene in *Season of Anomy* is one of enormous political tension and drama, a turning point in the novel, and a scene from which it never manages to recover: in many ways, by the party scene, barely twenty pages into the novel, the novel is already over. At this party, the pleasantries lie entirely on the surface: lives are at stake; the future of both the nation and the main character, Ofeyi, will be determined by the way in which the events at the chairman's party unfold. Prior to the party, the novel offers a vision of political hope, one, it is true, that has already been thwarted, but that retains at least a potential for progressive politics. After the party, the novel descends into a Dante-esque journey through successively more gruesome levels of hell, which in overwhelming and graphic detail show the way these hopes have been decisively crushed by the assault of the military on the people it is supposed to protect. The party constitutes the moment in which the struggle that Ofeyi has waged against the vicious cartel is revealed. So in addition to representing a turning point for national hopes, it is in this scene that the viability of a certain kind of (what turns out to be a) literary politics becomes evident. This is roughly the politics that Soyinka describes in his 1965 essay, "The Writer in an African State," in which he urges African writers to wake up from their "opium dreams of metaphysical abstraction"[38] in order to deal with the realities of African society. Just as for Achebe, for Soyinka the writer has a pedagogic role to perform in her society: "the African writer must have the courage to determine what alone can be salvaged from the recurrent cycle of human stupidity."[39]

Season of Anomy constitutes Soyinka's most explicit literary reaction to the failure of the Biafran revolution.[40] Written "between the lines of Paul Radin's *Primitive Religion* and [Soyinka's] *Idanre*"[41] while he was imprisoned from 1967 to 1969 during the Nigerian civil war,[42] it is a work that not only considers the possibility of the Nigerian nation in the aftermath of Biafra, but one that undertakes an inquiry into the relationship between literature and the Nigerian nation. *Season* probes the conditions that might yet create a genuine nation and the ways in which literature — or at least something symbolically akin to it — might influence or produce these conditions. It is thus a kind of literary "thought experiment" (a *roman a thèse*) that measures the distance between Utopia and the reality of a corrupt state that, while never directly named (like Achebe's Kangan, it is an invented nation), is Nigeria after Biafra.

As if establishing a philosophical proposition that the rest of the novel will test, *Season* begins by first establishing the existence of this Utopia: "A quaint anomaly, had long governed and policed itself, was so singly-knit that it obtained a tax assessment for the whole populace and paid it before the departure of the pith-helmeted assessor, in cash, held all property in common, literally, to the last scrap of thread on the clothing of each citizen — such an anachronism gave much patronizing amusement to the cosmopolitan sentiment of a profit-hungry society. A definitive guffaw from the radical centres of debate headed by Ilosa, dismissed Aiyéró as the prime example of unscientific communalism, primitive and embarrassingly sentimental" (SA 236).

These opening sentences of *Season* are as explicit as Soyinka ever becomes on the topic of Aiyéró. For the most part, Aiyéró functions more as an abstract concept than as a living place: it is an empty container for the concept of the perfect society, rather than a society whose practices are described in near ethnographic detail (like the utopias of old). To Aiyéró comes Ofeyi, the promotions man for the Cocoa Corporation to which the country "owes its prosperity" (SA 277). Part of Ofeyi's work is to convince farmers to expand their production of cocoa so that the military-political-industrial cartel that controls that country can reap the benefits of its export. A growing part of his job is also to create an internal market for the domestic consumption of "cocoa-wix" and "cocoa-bix," which he describes as "cocoa-flavored sawdust" (SA 292), so that the cartel can recoup domestically even the small amounts of money it pays to farmers for the production of cocoa. Ofeyi's position is a deeply compromised one, and so it is not surprising that his experience in Aiyéró is transformative. The "pocket Utopia" captures his imagination and he can no longer carry out his cynical work for the corporation. He is particularly intrigued by the fact that although the youth of Aiyéró are encouraged to travel and study abroad in order to experience other ways of life, "they all returned. The neon cities could not lure them away" (SA 237).

Aiyéró is an exemplary community in many ways. It is not a utopia that has managed to survive by means of its relative isolation from the world. Indeed, it is strikingly cosmopolitan and progressive in its outlook, constantly engaged in and with the outside world, but without suffering any of the usual consequences of such interaction: the gradual erosion of their own particular values and the substitution of other, foreign ways of life. How or why this is possible is something that Ahime, Aiyéró's "leader," claims not to know, nor is it something that Ofeyi is able to discover. If the discovery of a utopian community was not enough, it is this characteristic of Aiyéró's people, who are able to be somehow simultaneously "local" and "global," that makes the narrative and the political project of the novel possible. It is also what renders it somewhat suspect, especially when these features of Aiyéró are symbolically transferred to Ofeyi: before his first trip to the community is over, Ahime suggests that Ofeyi become his successor in Aiyéró, which would allow him to sever his ties with the corporation and begin over again in a place that is relatively immune from the cynical politics that have infected the rest of the country.

Though Ofeyi declines, the transfer of the properties and attributes of Aiyéró has nevertheless taken place symbolically. By the time of his second visit to Aiyéró on behalf of the corporation, he has come up with an idea by which the utopian conditions of Aiyéró might be transferred to the nation at large:

> The idea that came from his first encounter with the commune was only one of many that sought to retrieve his occupation from its shallow world of jingles and the greater debasement of exploitation by the Cartel. The pattern could be reversed, the trick of conversion applied equally to the Cartel's technical facilities not merely to effect restitution to many but to create a new generation for the future. A new plantation within the communal, labouring, sharing entity — seed through nursery to the mature plant and fructification — Ofeyi envisioned the parallel progress of the new idea, the birth of the new man from the same germ as the cocoa seed, the Aiyéró ideal disseminated with the same powerful propaganda machine of the Cartel throughout the land, taking hold of undirected youth and filling the vacuum of their transitional heritage with virile shoot. (SA 253)

Ofeyi's plan is to transform the nation into a larger version of Aiyéró through the subversive, counterhegemonic use of the very same marketing mechanisms by which the cartel has tried to extend its interests into every corner of the nation. As shown by their desire to market cocoa-wix even to the unimportant, supposedly backward community of Aiyéró, the corporation intends to saturate the whole of national space with its message to produce and consume cocoa. Just as efficiently, the assumption that Ofeyi (and Soyinka) make is that a different message can be communicated to the nation by means of the same mechanisms. This is an assumption that masks another one: that the essence of Aiyéró lies in an "idea" that can be disseminated into the body politic like a virus, rather than in the actual material practices of this communal society (which are in any case never fully described). Ofeyi's project is ambitious, and it fails almost immediately. The Aiyéró work songs that Ofeyi transforms into jingles and the advertising images he captures of collective labor in the "experimental" farm he asks the corporation to establish in Aiyéró, trigger an immediate response from the cartel: sensing a problem, the corporation forces Ofeyi to take a study leave abroad or face dire personal consequences at home for his subversive activities.

It is obvious enough here that Ofeyi's situation is that of the third-world writer, especially the writer who would hope to be able to politically transform his or her society. What is perhaps less obvious, though even more striking, is the assumption that is made about the appropriate *scale* of the writer's project. At one point, Ahime says that "it was good to know that our ways have always been the dream of mankind all through the ages and among people so far apart" (SA 246). The conditions of life represented by Aiyéró are universally desirable. Yet the space into which the Aiyéró "idea" is to be expanded seems of necessity, or naturally, to be that of the nation. This is not merely because this is the space saturated by the marketing mechanisms of the corporation, so that when these mechanisms are turned against themselves it is necessarily in the same nation-space that Aiyéró is conceptually reproduced. There is rather something else at work here that makes it possible to move from the limits of Aiyéró to the larger space of the nation with apparently little worry that the practices that make one space possible may not be so easily reproducible in the other, or even that it is precisely the limited space of Aiyéró that produces a utopian formulation in the first place, and that this can only be lost or destroyed if an attempt is made to multiply it effects.

What is assumed throughout *Season* in the structure of Ofeyi's first and subsequent projects is that it is only at the scale of the nation that "real" politics occurs. Writing must then also situate itself as a national project of some kind if it is seen to have any political import. How this is to be done, or (given the failure of Ofeyi's initial project) whether it can be done at all, is the question that is taken up repeatedly in the remainder of the novel, even if the answer each time appears to be the same. Indeed, the failure of Ofeyi's initial project suggests that an answer has already been decided in advance: the nation is the appropriate political level to which the utopian project must finally aspire; if the nation cannot be produced in this way, then the problem must lie in the means that have been used to spread the word about the Aiyéró idea—for Ofeyi, the language of advertising, for Soyinka, the language of the novel.

Ofeyi hatches a new plan upon returning from his study leave, which seems initially to be different in form from the first: "It was this, or leave the entire initiative to other, more drastic, means. The goals were clear enough, the dream a new concept of labouring hands across artificial frontiers, the concrete, affective presence of Aiyéró throughout the land, undermining the Cartel's superstructure of robbery, indignities and murder, ending the new phase of slavery" (SA 257). Yet what seems to be a more material way of spreading the beliefs of Aiyéró throughout the land is in fact simply a different mode of transmission that circumvents the need to use the corporation's mechanisms. In the dispersal of the people of Aiyéró across the nation, it is in fact the abstract "idea" that they embody that has been planted in the national soil. The embodiment of the idea becomes important later on in terms of the pathos and despair generated through desciptions of the cartel's assault on the Aiyéró people, but as Maduakor points out, for a book that is putatively about the masses and their slaughter by the forces of the military, neither is ever present to any degree in the novel except as an abstract part of the plans hatched by Ofeyi and then as the dead bodies that he sees lying in the streets in the second half of the novel.[43] For these reasons, it quickly becomes clear that this second plan is essentially the same as the first, especially when at the party we are alerted to the fact that the cartel is again troubled by the kinds of jingles and print advertising that Ofeyi has been producing. This time around, Ofeyi's ads are much more difficult for the cartel to make sense of, more subliminal and allegorical, and thus more successful. Even so, the cartel is quickly on to him again, only this time they have decided that their response will be more decisive. At the opening of the second section of the novel, the chairman of the Cocoa Corporation reflects on one of Ofeyi's songs that is being played by the band at his party:

> In the beginning, there was nectar and
> ambrosia
> A golden pod contained them . . .

But the Chairman was no longer riled. He could afford to smile his benediction of the orchestra . . . do carry on, carry on fools. It's not who begins it but who ends it. And we will. We will.

> Favoured of gods they made the cosmos
> rosier
> The gods wiped the dribble from their
> beard
> And snores of thunder soon were heard
> For the elixir also bred divine amnesia

Ta-ra-ra-ra-. ta-. ta — ta———. The Chairman even supplied the coda in his head. It was different at the beginning when he raged at the perfidy. Now he could even afford to be amused. He ran his hand over his chin as if to treat his fingers to the rich dribble of nectar before it vanished into mere imagination. Damned weeping jeremiads. Envy-ridden flea-bitten social dregs! As for Ofeyi — it was clear, he had learned nothing. The Corporation had wasted money on him. He had returned truly incorrigible. (SA 266)

The centerpiece of Ofeyi's new marketing scheme is the Cocoa Queen Iriyise, who appears in all of his ads and who is famed for her personal appearances in which she arises (like Aphrodite) from the half-shell of a giant cocoa bean. As a prelude to Iriyise's appearance during each of the performances, sculpted images of microbes, weeds, and viruses — all of the various threats to the cocoa plant — float, suspended from balloons, out of something Ofeyi refers to as "Pandora's Box." For the performance at the chairman's party, which is attended by other influential members of the cartel, Ofeyi has added a surprise to "Pandora's Box." After the microbes and weeds have floated away,

> four familiar faces, puppet-forms, suspended also from balloons, faces whose identities none, not even of those present, dared claim to recognize — Ofeyi had counted on this — faces whose names were whispered with dread even in the hardiest sanctuaries of the underworld. These, the real powers of the cartel unfurled with linked arms as the balloons flew higher and the strings were unraveled . . . Other eyes which had followed the marionettes found themselves face to face with a spectacle which began by astounding, then, as memories were awakened, ended with a cold apprehensiveness. There was no one present who did not remember the morning when the country had woken to the knowledge that their destiny had been taken in charge by the once-invisible men of the gun. (SA 280–81)

This deliberate symbolic attack on the cartel has a predictable outcome. Fleeing the agents of the cartel, Ofeyi has to go permanently into hiding to escape their long grasp. Once again, his attempt to transform the country is put to an end. But the cartel does not stop at simply removing Ofeyi from his position as their marketing manager. Long suspecting Ofeyi's larger plan, the cartel takes swift and decisive military action against the people of Aiyéró, who had been introduced into communities around the country, and in particular, against the Aiyéró-dominated Shage dam project at Cross-river. At the same moment that the agents of the cartel begin spilling blood across the nation in an unprecedented wave of violence, Ofeyi reflects that "inwardly he took pleasure from the knowledge that Aiyéró, once the comic Utopia, had become a moral thorn in the complacent skin of the national body" (SA 320). A moment later, Ahime informs him about the viciousness of the cartel's response, and Ofeyi's hopes turn to despair.

As if the images of bloodletting and the repeated discovery of all manner of grisly scenes (slaughtered women with babies still suckling at their breasts, a lake full of floating, bloated corpses, etc.) that dominate the remainder of the book are not enough of a signal of the potential limits of the kind of politics that Ofeyi had engaged in, they are explicitly foregrounded in the frequent encounters that Ofeyi has with "the Dentist." The Dentist is a highly skilled assassin and revolutionary who sees violence as the only way in which anything can be done to change the situation of the country. Ofeyi first meets him by "chance" in an airport lobby while on his study leave (later we learn that he has been keeping an eye on Ofeyi on behalf of Ahime). Immediately after hearing about the tragic results of his experiment with the Aiyéró people, Ofeyi recollects his first encounter with the Dentist and with his philosophy of "extraction before infection" (SA 326). The discussion of their opposing positions in their first encounter establishes the character of all of their many subsequent disagreements:

> He gestured towards the arm-chair. "Whiskey? Oh, I forget. . . ."
>
> "No, it's all right. I am . . . no longer on duty."
>
> Ofeyi glanced at the suitcase. "Yes . . . to quote a title from the world of fiction — mission accompli?"
>
> The youth smiled apologetically. "I'm afraid I'm not familiar with the world of fiction. In fact, I rather despise it." (SA 335–36)

> "Nothing can be achieved by isolated acts, we have to organize."
>
> It drew a mere grunt of partial agreement. "Of course. But one cannot ignore the real incorrigible enemies who are impervious to education. The kind that hunted us down as soon as they came to power, the fat bourgeoisie who immediately began to suck up to them and lick their boots in public!" (SA 338)

> "And afterwards," Ofeyi demanded. "What do you envisage?"
>
> "Envisage?" His tone rose in protest. "Why do you want me to envisage anything? Is that my field? I thought it was yours."
>
> "Surely, when you — eliminate, you have in mind something to follow, something to replace what you eliminate. Otherwise your action is negative and futile."
>
> The Dentist sighed. "Why do you people, you intellectuals or whatever you call yourselves impose on us burdens to which we lay no claim." (SA 345)

In the debates between Ofeyi and the Dentist, Ofeyi claims the position of the writer for his own: instead of intervening "directly" in the revolution, the writer (or the intellectual more generally) plays an important task in organizing and educating the populace, bringing about the massive shift in consciousness that forms the necessary precondition for the new nation. The Dentist is willing to concede that this is an important role. At the same time, these debates are staged in such a way that in the context of what has just happened to the people of Aiyéró, Ofeyi seems more of a hindrance than a help to the national cause. In a sense, he is responsible for what has happened in the country, a fact with which the Dentist directly confronts him: "That is why our people die. Because you paced in silence at the incubation of a monstrosity, preoccupied with a study of the phenomenon" (SA 368). Against such accusations, Ofeyi's self-rationalizations, which do in fact capture the *anomy* that grips the nation, nevertheless seem weak indeed: "The offensive outcrop was only a willful, incidental warning. The real death that the people were called upon to die was the death from under, the long creeping paralysis of flesh and spirit that seized upon them as the poison tuber might spread through the bowels of earth. Those noisy individual deaths were merely incidents. The real extermination went on below" (SA 363).

For a novel that is about the situation of post-Biafran Nigeria, Soyinka's multiple and relentless assaults on the (figure of the) intellectual in *Season of Anomy* are an unexpected theme. In many ways, Ofeyi is criticized as much as the cartel itself; this is perhaps why the cartel, the people, and Aiyéró seem at times to function as abstractions through which Ofeyi's politics and its outcome can be explored and mapped, and thereby lauded, questioned, challenged, or criticized. There are many other elements of the novel and of the symbolism that Soyinka employs that I have not touched on here: for example, the overt symbolism of the journey through hell, suggested by the use of the Orpheus-Eurydice (Ofeyi-Iriyise) myth in structuring Ofeyi's passage through the various chambers of the Temoko prison to find Iriyise, by the explicit reference to Dante in the words that are inscribed at the entrance to the prison ("abandon hope all who enter"), by the angelic figure of Taiila, and so on. But the danger in spending too much critical energy explaining these elements is that it inevitably begins to push to one side what is in fact the fundamental conflict in *Season of Anomy*. It is not, it seems to me, a conflict between the violent methods employed by the Dentist and the more evolutionary, nonviolent solutions proposed by Ofeyi — the novelistic staging of a debate on revolutionary method. Nor is it about the internalization of this conflict in the character of Ofeyi, for whom, after all, the Dentist is in many ways nothing more than a figure that represents another way of doing things to which he finds himself also attracted (which is made clear in Ofeyi's rescue of Semi-Dozen from the mob that has surrounded his house). The conflict has to be seen as taking place on a slightly different level where one can ask what makes it possible to deploy the contents in this manner. What needs to be explained about *Season of Anomy*, a novel in which perhaps too much is made explicit, is why a novel about the implosion of the nation through a divisive civil war takes the form of an attack on the writer and on the practice of writing.

Season of Anomy repeatedly rehearses the conditions of its own impossibility:

the impossibility of the novel after Biafra. It goes over the same terrain again and again, as if trying to make sure that there is nothing left behind that might form the basis for a new novelistic project. For it is the novel in particular (rather than literature and literary writing in general) that for both Achebe and Soyinka comes to an "end" after the nation. What imperils the novel is not some kind of aesthetic blockage, some inability of the novel to deal adequately with the terrors of the war, or a sense that another form could better represent its causes and consequences. In fact, the novel would seem to be a singularly appropriate form by which the extent of war's impact on the nation might be captured. Even though *Season of Anomy* tends toward abstraction, its description of the death and damage left by the cartel's attack is not something that could be easily shown in a play, as evidenced by the fablelike character of Soyinka's other literary work on Biafra, *Madmen and Specialists*. What we have here instead is an act of displacement. Biafra signals in a very real way the failure of the nation in Nigeria, but since this cannot be admitted, it appears symptomatically in the other term of nationalist literature as the failure of a certain form of national *literary* politics.

For if something has to end as a result of Biafra, it cannot be the nation. It is the nation that seems to represent and coalesce for Achebe and Soyinka the very possibility of politics in Africa. The nation avoids both of the problems that they identify with negritude: it is neither contextless, immersed in the international space of the African diaspora, nor requires the excavation and resurrection of precolonial forms of politics. The nation is a modern form and African countries are modern entities. To get a sense of this commitment to the nation in *Season*, one need only remember that there is something for Soyinka that is distasteful about Aiyéró when taken on its own: "It is rather like those white monks who have stayed within their citadels of stone, shut off from the real world of evil, offering candle-puffs of piety on behalf of the hideous hunger of the living world and even, presumptuously, of the hunger of the dead" (SA 259). A utopic formation that exists only in a single place, a specific community, an isolated region is irrelevant to the larger world. For Aiyéró to be anything other than "a quaint anomaly," the space it occupies must be able to be made co-extensive with the nation-space. This does not happen in *Season*, and neither did such an all-embracing (though by no means utopic) idea of the nation manage to fuse together the Nigerian federation. Regardless, the necessity of this expansion appears to be an inviolable principle for Soyinka, which leaves only two culprits to blame for the failure of the national project: the forces of the cartel/Nigerian military government, and the politics of the intellectual and of the novel.

To get a sense of Soyinka's continued commitment to the Nigerian nation, one need only turn to his most recent work. For what is perhaps the most surprising feature of *The Open Sore of a Continent* — which is his most explicit examination of the meaning and significance of the nation to date — is not the level of political corruption and moral decrepitude that he describes in the Nigerian body politic, but that he has continued to remain a committed nationalist even after everything that has happened in Nigeria. Although each attempt at democratic reform has been squashed by successive military regimes (and the status of the current democratically elected government is shaky at best), the question of what would yet make Nigeria a "nation" is the central issue that Soyinka takes up in this book. The events that prompted the writing of the book concern the removal of the interim government of Moshood Abiola by General Sani Abacha in November 1993 and the subsequent persecution and imprisonment of the Ogoni writer and political activist, Ken Saro-Wiwa, by Abacha's government. Soyinka's analysis of these events, and of the historical and social conditions in Nigeria that have perpetuated the iron-fisted rule of the military, are enormously valuable, especially with respect to subsequent events in Nigerian politics: Saro-Wiwa's execution in November 1995 in the face of enormous international opposition and the reinstitution of a date for new democratic elections in Nigeria in 1999 in the wake of Abacha's *and* Abiola's deaths. What frames Soyinka's discussion of these empirical events is an epistemological and ontological inquiry, the question of "When *is* a nation?"[44] This question is posed over and over again, taking a slightly different form each time (these are but some examples):

> We shall come later to what we believe the international community can do to save the nation, not so much from itself as from the internal expropriators of the national weal. We must advance to the complementary questions: Save it for what? Or, as what? As a nation? As nations? As a satellite or satellites of other nations' arrangements? (OSC 19)
>
> What more defines a nation? Or indeed, what yardsticks? What does the claim "I belong to this nation" mean to the individual, and when did it begin to mean anything? . . . When, and this is what is demanded, when are all the conditions present that make a nation? Can they be upheld by objective tests? Or is a nation simply a condition of the collective mind? Or will? A coerced state, the objective manifestation of an individual will? A passive, unquestioned habit of cohabitation? Or a rigorous conclusion that derives from history? (OSC 19–20)

> When is a nation? Could one of the conditions in resolving this sometimes
> emotive issue be the articulated or demonstrable decision by the polity that actually
> makes up the nation? (OSC 22)

> The Nigerian geographical entity was indeed upheld, but was the *nation?*
> (OSC 28)

There is one question that is never asked: *why* the nation. As he shows in his
analysis of both Nigeria and other national situations, Soyinka is well aware of
the real and epistemic violence that has been carried out in the name of the
nation. Even so, he continues to envision the nation as something other than and
separate from those situations in which "the national ideal becomes, for instance,
conflated with notions of racial purity or other forms of extreme nationalism"
(OSC 116). The criterion for a genuine nationalism that he finally decides upon
is one that works on behalf of "the lowest common denominator, the human
unit" (OSC 117). For Soyinka, this was the promise contained in the vote on
behalf of Abiola, who garnered for the first time in Nigerian history a significant
majority of votes from almost every region of the country. Soyinka claims that,
"Nothing can erase the basic quality of the event: this was a *national* triumph, and
the championing of its integrity must remain a national undertaking" (OSC 48).

But there is an odd sleight of hand in this book. The Abiola election is taken as
an answer to the (more or less) theoretical questions that he poses throughout the
book. For Soyinka, by voting for Abiola the Nigerian *people* as a collectivity cast
their vote for the *nation*. They were certainly voting to improve their situation
after years of military rule; it is only in terms of Soyinka's undertheorized sense of
the nation as that government or state whose interests are "with" the people that
it is possible to leap to the conclusion that now, finally, with the election of Abiola
the Nigeria nation is born. All of the ominous examples of nationalism that he
describes so well (as, for example, "mostly a gambling space for the opportunism
and adventurism of power" [OSC 121]) become by contrast merely aberrant
examples of some true national essence never really described. The connection
between space and politics that is assumed in the construction of the entity called
Nigeria is itself never interrogated (why this space? why not a smaller space or a
larger one? etc.).

It is possible to treat Soyinka's insistence on the nation in Nigeria as either
wishful thinking or as a theoretical error, a failure to learn the lessons of *Season
of Anomy*. One of the difficulties inherent in the form of the Nigerian nation
remains the multiple ethnicities and other divisions of identity (rural-urban,

for instance) that complicate national politics. In *The Open Sore of a Continent*, Soyinka takes the vote for Abiola as a resolution of these multiple divisions, so that where there was once people with regional and ethnic loyalties, there are now only individual Nigerian *citizens*. But perhaps it is this hope that the nation names: the promise of a collectivity like Aiyéró that is an expression of a uniquely African response to modernity. Of course, this isn't all that it names. As is shown by the questions that Soyinka poses in both *The Open Sore of a Continent* and *Season of Anomy* — questions reminiscent of the ones that Fanon poses at the end of "On National Culture" — the concept of the nation is implicated in too many other discourses to be identified simply with utopian longings: the violence of identity over difference, the space of empire, the mode by which a specific collectivity is interpellated into the international system of nation-states, the determinations of modernity itself.

And once again, the nation also names the problematic of the third-world writer. In the wake of the bloody conflict over the Nigerian federation, the connection between the activity of writing literature and producing a collectivity — between literature and the nation — is taken up as an explicit question by both Achebe and Soyinka. In their post-Biafran novels, both writers explore with great insight and intensity the zone of instability within which they must of necessity work. In this conscious exploration of the problems and possibilities of literature as a means of creating a genuine collectivity, the limits and possibilities of intellectual activity are exposed in fascinating detail. The delineation of these limits is not to suggest that there is no role for the intellectual or writer. Rather, it is a way of understanding the accumulation and concentration of forces and discourses that make up this zone that permits a more thorough understanding of the problem of cultural revolution in Nigeria. Achebe's and Soyinka's continued commitment to the nation is in this respect not a mistake, the expression of a troubling belief in a political form that both know to be fraught with problems. On the contrary, it is the apparent impossibility of the nation that produces the demand for its possibility — the persistence of a belief in the possibilities of the kind of collectivity that the election of Abiola promises.

CHAPTER FOUR

The Persistence of the Nation
Literature and Criticism in Canada

Many were born in Canada, and living unlived lives they died
of course but died truncated, stunted, never at
home in native space and not yet
citizens of a human body of kind. And it is Canada
that specialized in this deprivation . . .
And what can we do here now, for at last we have no notion
of what we might have come to be in America, alternative, and how make
    public
a presence which is not sold out utterly to the modern? utterly? to the
savage inflictions of what is for real, it pays off, it is only
accidentally less than human?　　　　　　　　　　　— DENNIS LEE

On the morning, afternoon and evening of July 1, all Canada became, for
the time-being, a single assemblage, swayed by a common emotion, within
the sound of a single voice. Thus has modern science for the first time realized in the great nation-state of modern days, that condition which existed
in the little city-states of ancient times and which was considered by the wisdom of the ancients as indispensable to free and democratic government—
that all the citizens should be able to hear for themselves the living voice. To
them it was the voice of a single orator—a Demosthenes or a Cicero—
speaking on public questions in the Athenian Assembly or in the Roman
Forum. Hitherto to most Canadians, Ottawa has seemed far off, a mere
name to hundreds or thousands of our people, but henceforth all Canadians
will stand within the sound of the carillon and within hearing of the speak-
ers on Parliament Hill. May we not predict that as a result of this carrying of
the living voice throughout the length of the Dominion, there will be
aroused a more general interest in public affairs, and an increased devotion
of the individual citizen to the commonweal?

　　　　— PRIME MINISTER WILLIAM LYON MACKENZIE KING

The Nation in Canadian Literary Criticism

In the decades following World War II, the Canadian federal government began an ambitious series of programs whose intention was to identify, foster, protect, and develop Canadian culture in order to assert and maintain Canadian political sovereignty. The period from 1950 to 1970 witnessed the implementation and completion of a number of projects that manifested symbolically the newfound confidence and national identity of a country that had been officially independent from Britain since 1867 but had remained in many ways "a pure colony, colonial in psychology as well as in mercantile economics."[1] As with the nineteenth-century project of a national railway (completed in 1885), which physically linked together all of the far-flung parts of Canada in order to preserve Canadian sovereignty against the threat of American expansion in the West, many of these projects involved the technological bridging and unification of Canadian space. In 1952, federally funded national television broadcasting began; 1960 saw the establishment of passenger jet service between Vancouver and Toronto; and in 1962, the Trans-Canada highway was opened, and Canada's first communications satellite, Alouette I, launched. Given the physical size of Canada, technology has always played an important part in the creation and consequent development of the Canadian nation. Maurice Charland has in fact suggested that the rhetoric of Canadian nationalism has always been that of a technological nationalism that "ties Canadian identity, not to its people, but to their mediation through technology."[2] While technology has never ceased to be an important element of Canadian nationalism, the establishment of programs that dealt explicitly with Canadian culture in the period following World War II indicated that the government also felt a need to produce what might be seen as a more "organic" nationalism, a sense of national identity mediated and produced by culture rather than (or in addition to) technology.[3]

The program for postwar governmental involvement in Canadian culture was established by the influential 1951 Report on National Development in the Arts, Letters and Sciences, more commonly known as the Massey Report after its chairman, Vincent Massey.[4] In his penetrating historical study of the work of the commission, Paul Litt has written that "The commission was interested not just in culture in Canada, but in Canadian culture. As the commissioners themselves put it, their work was 'concerned with nothing less than the spiritual foundation of our national life.' They operated on the premise that their enterprise deserved the support of all patriotic citizens because culture was what bound Canadians together and distinguished them from other nationalities. It followed that the Canadian state had an obligation to support the cultural activities which legitimized its very existence."[5]

It is this paradoxical formulation of the intimate connection between culture and nation, and thus of the responsibilities of the nation toward culture, that fueled the government-sponsored cultural programs that grew out of the Massey Report. Culture was what gave the nation its life; a distinctive Canadian culture therefore provided the raison d'être of the Canadian nation. But the need on the part of the nation to intervene and provide funding for cultural production suggested a reverse logic: it was the nation-state that gave life to Canadian culture in order to give legitimacy to itself. The first programs established on the basis of the report's finding revealed another ambiguity. In 1951, the National Ballet of Canada was founded; the National Library of Canada was founded in 1953; and in 1957, the Canada Council, the body that would have the single greatest impact on cultural development in Canada, was established to disperse funds to worthy artistic, cultural, and academic groups. As even these few examples suggest, from the beginning of state-supported culture in Canada it is possible to see a confusion between the two senses of the term culture that Raymond Williams has identified: culture as "a noun of 'inner' process, specialized to its presumed agencies in 'intellectual life' and 'the arts' " and culture as "a noun of general process, specialized to its presumed configurations in 'whole ways of life.' "[6] The cultural programs instituted by the Canadian government primarily funded intellectual activities and the arts in a broad sense, because these were seen to reflect, express, or in some other way embody a whole Canadian way of life, even if few Canadians have the opportunity to enjoy the National Ballet or to ever make use of the National Library.[7]

The influence of the Massey Report and of the Canada Council on literary production in Canada was considerable. As late as 1984, B. W. Powe was able to write that he knew "no novelist, poet or essayist, no university or writer's program, who has not had support from the omnipresent Council or its provincial counterparts."[8] Government support of individual writers, journals, presses, and conferences made possible the "explosion" of Canadian writing in the 1960s and 1970s:

> Writers were sought for Writers-in-Residence programs at Universities; credit
> courses were introduced; teachers were hired and given CANLIT books: *Course Count-*

down: A Quantitative Study of Canadian Literature in the Nation's Secondary Schools, Something for Nothing: An Experimental Book Exposure Programme, and *CanLit Teacher's Crash Course Kit;* magazines with titles like *Delta, Descant,* and *Exile* flourished; new names were heralded, like Hodgkins, Ondaatje and Musgrave; trade magazines like *Books in Canada* and *Quill and Quire* enlarged in circulation and importance; small publishers expanded, like Talonbooks (British Columbia), NeWest (Alberta), Oberon, Coach House, Anansi (Ontario), Fiddlehead (New Brunswick); the Writers' Union, the union des ecrivans québécois and the League of Canadian Poets was formed . . . institutional support grew in influence, from the CBC (radio especially, with shows like "Anthology"), to the separate Provincial Arts Councils . . . and awards—awards *galore,* The Governor General's Award, the Seal Books $50,000 First Novel Award . . . the Books in Canada First Novel Award, the Gerald Lampert and Pat Lowther Memorial Awards for poetry, to name a few out of dozens.[9]

Government funding was just as important to the enterprise of literary criticism. Financial support from the Canada Council (and later the Social Sciences and Humanities Research Council of Canada) was essential to the operation of university presses and to the organization of virtually every major academic conference and association in Canada. Robert Lecker has argued that, through its direct support for the New Canadian Library paperback series, which first made "classic" and contemporary Canadian texts widely available to high school and university students, and through its substantial support for the production of the very first *Literary History of Canada* (1965), the federal government invented *ex nihilo* the canon of Canadian literary texts that would occupy much of the literary critical energies of this period and that would define the field of Canadian literature in the decades to follow.[10]

It should not come as a surprise that, in the context of the concerted effort to support not just "culture in Canada" but "Canadian culture," Canadian literary criticism during this period would come to be underwritten by what Lecker has called a "national-referential aesthetic" (MR 4). Especially as expressed in the work of the "thematic critics," a term most commonly identified with the critical writing of Margaret Atwood, John Moss, and D. G. Jones, the literary analysis of Canadian texts was for a period dominated by a desire to locate what was essentially or particularly *Canadian* about Canadian literature.[11] Just as the Massey Report emphasized the need to support the culture on which the nation depended, so, too, Canadian literary critics focused on those features of Canadian literary texts that could be the basis for a specifically and identifiably Canadian mode of writing. It was agreed that such characteristics could only be seen as elements of the text's *theme*, since, as Northrop Frye pointed out, "what the Canadian writer finds in his experience and environment may be new, but it will be new only as content: the form of his expression of it can take shape only from what he has read, not from what he has experienced;"[12] formally, literature in Canada mimicked European and American models. For Atwood, this was the theme of "survival," for Moss the "garrison mentality" first identified by Frye in his conclusion to the *Literary History of Canada*, and for Jones the perpetual search for "national identity" itself. The unspoken assumption of this kind of criticism was that the writing produced in the nation must of necessity thematize the conditions of possibility of the nation itself; in this sense, Canadian literary criticism has long been dominated by a much simpler version of the "national allegory" that Fredric Jameson has ascribed to third-world texts in general.[13] This led these critics to valorize literary texts that expressed nationalist ideas and themes; other texts, especially experimental texts, were seen as exceptions to general national literary characteristics or were, through the expenditure of enormous amount of critical labor, domesticated and rendered into nationalist objects, as Donna Pennee has shown in her analysis of the critical reception of Sheila Watson's *The Double Hook*, which has been identified as the first Canadian modernist novel.[14]

The search for thematic similarities that underlie literary production in Canada—that produce, in other words, the particular "Canadianness" of Canadian texts—has since the early seventies been energetically challenged from a number of different perspectives. In what has been called a "seminal attack,"[15] Frank Davey has criticized thematic criticism for its failure to "do what the criticism of other national literatures has done: explain and illuminate the work on its own terms, without any recourse to cultural rationalizations or apologies."[16] An emphasis on the formal, literary qualities of the text, as opposed to the supposedly "extraliterary" factors of history and nation, has also been the basis of calls for more theoretically motivated readings of Canadian literature, as exemplified in the collection *Future Indicative*, and in the work of critics such as Barbara Godard, Sylvia Söderlind, Barry Cameron, and Michael Dixon.[17] More recently, postcolonial critics such as Diana Brydon have criticized thematic criticism for effacing the connections and parallels between Canadian writing and writing in other regions and nations that have similarly labored under the legacy of colonialism.[18] Finally, critics who have wanted to emphasize the multiplicity of "Canadas" that the identification of a singular national identity would obliterate have criticized the emphasis in thematic criticism on a static notion of national identity that fails to take into account the work of immigrant, ethnic, Native, and women writers.[19]

Out of these various challenges to the supposed hegemony of thematic criticism — a hegemony that has, at least in part, been invented by its critics in order to give additional urgency and weight to their criticisms[20] — has emerged a widely accepted periodizing schema for Canadian literary criticism and (since these are closely connected in Canada) for Canadian literature as well. It is a periodizing schema that mirrors the one offered by Said for postcolonial literature in general. There is, first, a nationalist phase of Canadian literature and criticism: a crude, perhaps necessary phase of cultural self-assertion that is now seen as definitively superseded. In its place, there is a more savvy, self-confident criticism that does not see the need to produce in the field of literature a national culture consonant with the demands of the Canadian state. For example, in his examination of sixteen novels written after 1967, the year of the Canadian centennial, Frank Davey suggests that they announce collectively "the arrival of the post-national state — a state invisible to its own citizens, indistinguishable from its fellows, maintained by invisible political forces, and significant mainly through its position within the grid of world-class postcard cities."[21] In addition to worries about a complicity with the governmental agenda to create a national culture, there is then another reason for leaving the "national-referential aesthetic" behind. Since the community that was once named "Canada" has been dissipated by various globalizing or modernizing forces, there no longer exists *any* national referent to which the national-referential aesthetic might connect.

For Davey, this has consequences not simply for the study of contemporary novels of the "post-national" period but also for the interpretation of *all* the texts of Canadian literary history. Davey suggests that nationalist readings of Canadian literary texts, which purport to be opposed to the abstract, universal ideology of humanist or formalist readings, also constitute an ideology that has diverted attention away from "the political dimensions of literature."[22] He writes that "all nationalist readings of Canadian literature are in a general sense 'political'. All attempt to construct links between the literary text and the cultural one, to show the literary as contributing in some way to the formation of the cultural."[23] Nevertheless, he suggests that the national framework of such readings produces a politics that is totalizing, unambiguous, and homogenizing — exactly, in other words, what nationalism rejects in humanist readings. Nationalist readings fail to observe that gender, class, region, ethnicity, and economic structures can mark texts as decisively as can nation or "world culture," that the codes of literature are shared, and produced in concert, with the other written and unwritten texts of a society, that a writer's choice of codes, or positions in relation to these codes, can again be influenced by matters of gender, class, region, ethnicity, and economic practices, and that the usual relationship between codes, as between regions, classes, genders, ethnic affiliations, and economic practices, is one of contestation and/or dominance. This contestation is frequently more intense *within* a society than it is between it and other societies — in fact, such an intensity of internal conflict is probably the distinguishing feature of a separate society.[24]

It is thus possible to revisit the texts of the *pre*-postnational period in order to capture what the thematic critics missed: all of the complex, myriad, heterogeneous internal conflicts of Canadian society that nationalist readings have indiscriminately blurred together through various critical metaphors of national unity, however unflattering: "victim," "Wacousta," "butterfly," "garrison mentality," "bush garden," and so on.

What is apparent even in the attempt to write a "post-national" criticism is the degree to which Canadian literary criticism nevertheless continues to depend on the nation. There is, first of all, a continued reliance on the nation as the defining element of the field of literary texts from which Davey draws his examples. The sixteen novels that he examines, chosen carefully it seems to represent different regions and constituencies within the nation, are all *Canadian* novels, organized and selected on the basis of their national origin and as representatives of various aspects of the national "mosaic." Davey is right: gender, class, region, ethnicity, and economic structures can mark texts as decisively as the nation, which raises the question of why the nation nevertheless remains the overall framework within which he addresses these features. This is a problem as well of Davey's earlier call for an end to nationalist criticism in *Surviving the Paraphrase*. There, too, Davey suggests that Canadian literature should be analyzed along axes other than that of the nation. The only difference is that the emphasis is formal rather than political: the need to examine the literary text itself rather than those "extraliterary" factors attended to by the "bad sociology" of nationalist criticism.[25] What he proposes as an alternative are formal studies not of literature per se, but of *Canadian* literature, without ever challenging or questioning the nationalist assumptions implicit in the division of literatures into national, natural kinds.

This might seem to be little more than definitional or epistemological hairsplitting on my part. Isn't it possible, after all, to simply choose to examine Canadian texts without necessarily affirming the priority of the nation in them (to read them, that is, without emphasizing the ways in which they express or affirm the nation)? It is possible for an individual critic to decide to do so and to simply pay attention to other elements of the text. This is, however, a deeply ideological choice, a decision to adopt theoretical blinders regarding the conditions of possibility of writing and reading a "minor literature" like Canada's. For no matter how forcefully it is denied, it appears that inevitably the question of the national basis of Canadian literary works anxiously reemerges. The nation appears a necessary and unavoidable element that defines the boundaries of this particular literary critical field of study: without the nation, the field of Canadian literary criticism is all but unintelligible. In "Thematic Criticism, Literary Nationalism, and the Critic's New Clothes," T. D. Maclulich has argued that "Canadian literature is inevitably a subject in which political and literary considerations overlap."[26] If the context of a literary work is removed, the situation in which its meaning is perhaps most meaningful, "hybrid literary-political categories such as Canadian literature become meaningless."[27] In other words, "some form of literary nationalism provides the only logical justification for treating Canadian literature as a separate field of study."[28] The study of Canadian literature as a separate field of study, Maclulich suggests elsewhere, "is linked with a conviction of our cultural divergence from the United States."[29] If this conviction is abandoned, then so, too, should the study of Canadian literature as a distinct branch of contemporary world literature, for, in strictly literary terms, there are far more similarities than differences between Canadian and American literary texts.[30]

There is a second way in which the nation persists even in Davey's attempt to articulate a postnational criticism. What Davey wants to attack—the "national-referential aesthetic" that has defined so much Canadian criticism—nevertheless remains central to his account of postcentennial Canadian literature. Though he introduces what might appear to be a more theoretically sophisticated reading strategy based on poststructuralist theory, the primary mediating term between the literary text and the social or political "text" remains the nation. A postnational criticism arises out of the novels that he reads because these novels indicate that, *within* the boundaries of the nation which these texts are assumed to reflect, the nation has vanished: "Specific novels may argue for a humanist Canada, a more feminist Canada, a more sophisticated and worldly Canada, an individualist Canada, a Canada more responsive to the values of its aboriginal citizens, but collectively they suggest a world and a nation in which social structures

no longer link regions or communities, political process is doubted, and individual alienation has become normal . . . *Caprice*'s twentieth-century narrator
laments a community of difference that has vanished: 'We are all Europeans
now.' "[31] And yet there nevertheless remains as direct a connection between novel
and nation as in the work of the thematic critics, the main difference being that
what the novels after 1967 reveal are not characteristic qualities of Canadian
culture and the nation, but rather that the nation has disappeared. In other
words, novels continue to be seen as mimetically reflecting the national situation,
even if what they reflect is that the "national-ity" of this situation has been placed
in jeopardy, if not dissipated entirely.

   It is under these circumstances that Davey suggests that a criticism based on
a national-referential aesthetic makes little sense, for other realities are now at
work: especially after NAFTA, whatever real or imagined borders may have been
placed around the Canadian nation and culture have been dissolved or have become radically porous. Another way of putting this is to suggest that in the present, Canadians are not just Europeans — they are the world. To follow through to
the conclusion that Davey's work points to, it seems that the price of being able to
view with greater clarity the conflicts internal to the Canadian nation (race,
class, gender, etc.), that the discourse of literary nationalism hides, is the end
of the nation itself, in which case it is not clear in what sense these conflicts
remain "internal" or are simply (more or less) local manifestations of global
processes that don't necessarily need to be affirmed as "Canadian" phenomena.
Postnational criticism begins from an assumption that the nation has come to an
end, that ideas of community and difference have totally collapsed, and that
globalization of the world has generated a homogenous world culture in which
national cultural differences exist only as the subjects of theme-parks, travel
books, dissertations, and utopian longing. It also suggests, perhaps inadvertently,
that the Canadian nation once really did exist, that the idea of the nation once had
enough currency to connect across regions or communities to create a national
body whose disappearance can now be lamented.

   This chapter will constitute an examination of the meanings and uses of the
nation in Canadian literature and literary criticism after World War II. As in the
literatures of Nigeria and the Caribbean, the period following World War II
witnessed an explosion in the production of Canadian literary texts. It should
already be clear that the reasons for this explosion are much different from either
of the previous cases that I have examined in this study. The greater material
resources of the Canadian state made it possible for the government to actively

support and encourage the rapid growth of Canadian literature and literary criticism as a matter of government policy. Elleke Boehmer writes that in postcolonial literatures, "it was seen as the writer's role to reinterpret the world, to grasp the initiative in cultural self-definition."[32] In Canada, the active role of the state in using culture for its own "war of position" had the effect of taking on the writer's role as its own. There have thus always been worries that the aims of a nationalist literature in Canada have been co-opted from the outset, that any idea of the nation produced by or through literature merely meets the demands and desires of the nation-state. The utopian hopefulness that accompanied literary nationalism in other parts of the Commonwealth is for the most part not echoed in Canada. Instead, there is a sense that the possibility of a Canadian nation is by the middle of the century already somehow an anachronistic notion. Furthermore, unlike the Caribbean or Nigeria, the national question in Canada during this period does not primarily concern its position within the British Empire — a fact that has too often been glossed over in attempts to add Canada to the field of postcolonial studies. The main concern of the Massey Commission was to produce Canadian culture in opposition to the spread of mass, popular culture from the United States into Canada. Literary nationalism in the postwar period is directed toward an identification of the unique national characteristics of the Canadian nation either in opposition to the United States or to what the United States represents: the embodiment of the values of modernity in national form. This is not to say that there are no longer any references to Canada's colonial inheritance from Britain or that the political and cultural threat of the United States was not articulated during earlier periods of literary history. Indeed, Canadian culture and writing is still situated by many writers and critics during this period as being located "between" Britain and America.[33] Nevertheless, it is the threat of American cultural dominance — of neoimperialism and cultural imperialism rather than colonialism and imperialism — that is the most important stimulus for literary and critical examinations of the Canadian nation; neocolonialism is the starting point of literary and critical inquiry in Canada, not a fact whose gradual emergence produces a rethinking of the possibilities of literary nationalism, which is characteristic of the texts that I looked at in the West Indies and Nigeria.[34]

Unlike earlier chapters, the bulk of this one will not focus on readings of specific and exemplary literary texts, but on an examination of the nation as it has circulated within Canadian literary criticism since the 1950s. There are a number of reasons for the shift in this chapter from literature to criticism. The most important of these is that it is in the discourse of literary criticism rather than in the literary texts of this period that literary nationalism is seen to be a particularly pressing concern. It is the discourse of Canadian literary criticism that seems to require the production of a homogenous national space. By comparison, in his overview of Canadian fiction since the 1960s, Leslie Monkman writes that:

> What has not been acknowledged is the extent to which many of the most acclaimed English-Canadian novels of the sixties to eighties link their thematic concerns and narrative strategies to an interrogation of the revived nationalism that sup- ported their publication and dissemination. Despite the speedy designation of his 1959 novel, *The Apprenticeship of Duddy Kravitz* as a "Canadian classic," Mordecai Richler would continue to take delight over the next three decades in puncturing the absurdities of flag-waving nationalism . . . Less obviously, two of the most honoured novels of the era, Margaret Atwood's *Surfacing* and Margaret Laurence's *The Diviners,* raised related issues while Rudy Wiebe's *The Temptations of Big Bear* and the fiction of Alice Munro subverted the governing clichés of both national- ism and regionalism, its inevitable concomitant in Canadian political and cultural discourse.[35]

There is *nowhere* in Canadian fiction after World War II a national literature that aspires to write the nation into existence. English-Canadian literary texts of this period inevitably examine and articulate the differences (with varying de- grees of success) that exist *within* the boundaries of the nation, paying especially careful attention to the internal colonization of Native peoples and the Qué- bécois. While they do articulate worries about American cultural imperialism, even what are thought to be classics of English-Canadian nationalist literature, such as Atwood's *Surfacing* (1972) and Hugh MacLennan's *Two Solitudes* (1945) or David Godfrey's *Death Goes Better With Coca-Cola* (1969) and Ray Smith's *Cape Breton Is the Thought Control Centre of Canada* (1969), cast a surprisingly critical eye on the prospects of a unified, national body, and pay as much attention to the coexistence of multiple Canadas as Leonard Cohen's *Beautiful Losers* (1965) — a difficult text exploding with seemingly incommensurable modes of political, so- cial, and cultural signification that deconstructs every concept around which the Canadian nation might be preserved. MacLennan's novel in particular exhibits the problem of trying to create the nation through the novel in the dissonance between the politics articulated in its first two sections in contrast to the last two. The marriage of anglophone Janet Methuen with the francophone Paul Tallard on the eve of World War II — a heavy-handed, symbolic union of the nation's "two founding races" — makes almost no sense in the context of earlier events in the novel. *Two Solitudes* begins as a remarkably insightful examination of the effects of encroaching modernity on the lives of Québécois inhabitants of the village of Saint-Marc. The position of the rural French in Québec in relation to the English-dominated business classes in Montreal is shown by MacLennan to be an explicitly colonial one. Paul's father, Anthase Tallard, a man caught between the worlds of tradition and progress, religion and secularism, French and English, is destroyed spiritually and financially by his decision to embrace the forces of modernity (through his involvement in the construction of a hydroelectric project in Saint-Marc and his support for francophone conscription in World War I). It is hard to reconcile this with Paul's eagerness to join the war effort on behalf of the Canadian nation, and with MacLennan's ecstatic evocation of the birth of the nation in the paragraph that concludes the novel: "And almost grudgingly, out of the instinct to do what was necessary, the country took the first irrevocable steps toward becoming herself, knowing against her will that she was not unique but like all the others, alone with history, with science, with the future."[36]

I need to make some caveats here regarding the claim of an enormous gap between the actual content of Canadian literary texts and the ways in which they were interpreted during this period — a rather undialectical assertion of a difference between literature and criticism that seems as if it can only be read (as subsequent critics like Davey have) as an enormous category mistake on the part of the Canadian critical enterprise. I am not claiming that there are no examples of Canadian literature from 1945 to 1970 that can be read or interpreted as nationalist texts. Such a sweeping claim inevitably invites a flood of counterexamples, whether in the form of explicit examples of attempts to found the nation within the text or as examples of sophisticated readings of texts that draw out their nationalist orientations (any text can be read as an allegory of its national context). Indeed, if by Canadian texts we mean here to include the work of Québécois writers of this period, it would not be difficult to read the entire period, from Paul Émile Borduas's *Refus Global* (1948) to the Parti Pris in the sixties, as one long exercise in nationalist writing, to which, as a negative formation, English-Canadian literary nationalism constitutes a response.[37]

If we are to limit our investigation to English-Canadian literature it is difficult to see the impulse to read literature in terms of its nationalist orientations as anything other than an imperative of literary criticism rather than as a determinate feature of the literature itself. It is, of course, difficult to separate these elements, especially in the Canadian situation, where a relatively small literary community has ensured that literature and criticism overlap to a considerable degree. Many of the best literary critics in Canada have also been important writers: Louis Dudek, A. J. M. Smith, Dennis Lee, Michael Ondaatje, and Margaret Atwood are but a few who have occupied both roles. Nevertheless, in Canada the concept of the nation is articulated differently within literary criticism than within literature, which is a point of difference from the other postcolonial zones that I have examined in this book. One way of formulating this difference might be to suggest that if in Nigeria and the Caribbean the nation emerged as a strategy of *writing*, in Canada it can be seen as emerging preeminently as a strategy of *reading*, which in and of itself reflects significant material differences regarding the social status of literature that renders problematic any simple extension of the mantle of postcolonialism to Canada. In the absence of a Canadian literature whose intent it was to produce the national "imagined community," it is hard not to see literary criticism as a kind of symptomatic substitute: yet another example of the technologies by which Canadian space has been sewn together—the high cultural equivalent of the Canadian National Railway.

Instead of offering a historical overview of the development of literary criticism in Canada since the 1950s,[38] what I will concentrate on is a careful, detailed analysis of a recent attempt to make sense of the legacy of literary nationalism in an effort to produce a criticism that surpasses it: Robert Lecker's *Making It Real*. In this book, Lecker considers the consequences of the rapid construction of the Canadian canon in the period following World War II and the central place of literary nationalism in producing this canon. By tracing out the central argument of Lecker's book, what I am interested in examining is the paradoxical reemergence of a literary nationalism very similar to that of the thematic critics in his very attempt to move beyond the nation as a defining feature of Canadian literary criticism. As critics such as Davey and Tracy Ware have pointed out, Lecker's characterization of the development of Canadian literary criticism is partial, partisan, and limited.[39] Nevertheless, Lecker's text is a particularly useful one to examine because it brings together all of the vexed questions of the nation in Canadian literature and literary criticism since World War II. In doing so, it (perhaps inadvertently) reveals the logic of literary nationalism that underlies all of these positions and explains the gap between literature and criticism in Canada. What Lecker's book shows is, as I have already suggested in my assessment of Frank Davey, that the nation is an indissoluble figure of Canadian literary criticism. But the persistence of the nation is not necessarily something to be lamented. It does not indicate that Canada remains in a state of literary or cultural immaturity, consigned forever to the first phase of literary development as outlined by Said and the authors of *The Empire Strikes Back*. I want to suggest instead that the persistence of the nation has to be seen as stubbornly holding open the possibility of a political project that has almost disappeared, however difficult and futile this project might seem to be. Against the realities of atomized subjects and the dispersed communities that emerge out of in Davey's postnational readings, the nation in Canadian literary criticism continually reaffirms the connection between literature and politics. It does so, of course, in an ambiguous way, affirming the political at one level by arguing for the autonomy of Canadian space against (American) modernity in the form of what Marshall McLuhan referred to as a "counter-environment,"[40] while at the same time, reinforcing the leveling out of all differences in an effort to produce a singular Canadian nation for Canadian literature. It is with the latter that the modern nation has inevitably been identified, as a form opposed to difference in its desire to produce manageable, rationalized citizens. But in a minor country like Canada, consigned by history, geography, and demography to the margins of the West even as it remains a part of it, the nation has to be seen as part of a dialectic that tries to preserve difference even as it destroys it.

Before turning to a direct examination of Lecker and his attempt to exorcise the demon of nationalism from Canadian literary criticism, it is important, I believe, to consider the intellectual climate out of which thematic criticism developed. George Grant and Northrop Frye have often been identified as two of the intellectual forefathers of thematic criticism. This might suggest that Grant and Frye were cultural nationalists, whose work in social and literary criticism respectively inspired the critical search for literary tropes and figures of national identity. I want to argue for a different understanding of these seminal figures in Canadian intellectual life. It seems strange to me that the work of Grant and Frye have been used to provide theoretical frameworks for the analysis of Canadian identity, both within literary criticism and outside of it. If anything, what the work of these thinkers suggests is that the question of Canadian identity — the cultural identity of the nation — arises at a time when such a question no longer has any meaning, let alone any answer. While other countries have some possibility of forming nations late into the twentieth century, both Grant and Frye suggest that Canada has none: it is too much a product of modernity to be able to create meaningful structures in opposition to it; whatever possibilities may once have existed for Canada to be a nation have long since melted into air. If there is a division between literature and criticism in Canada over the issue of the nation, there emerges here another division that needs to be addressed: Grant and Frye's common insistence on the impossibility of the Canadian nation versus the thematic critics's insistence on the necessity of a nationalist criticism. It is difficult to see how thematic criticism's faith in the possibility of a Canadian identity expressed through literature could have originated out of the work of these grim thinkers; it is only by addressing this question, however, that the form in which the nation has circulated in Canadian literature and criticism can be clearly understood.

Doomed by Modernity: Grant's Canada

In power and precise knowledge, Europe still, even today, outweighs the rest of the world. Or rather, it is not so much Europe that excels, but the European Spirit, and America is its formidable creation.   — PAUL VALÉRY[41]

In the period following World War II, a period which saw the United States definitively achieve its position as a cultural, economic, and political superpower, questions regarding the continued viability of the Canadian nation extended into virtually every form of governmental and intellectual discourse. In addition to the cultural programs instituted as a result of the findings of the Massey Report, a number of programs promoting Canadian economic nationalism were also instituted during this period as a consequence of the 1957 Royal Commission on Canada's Economic Prospects.[42] At the same time, the repeated political crises of the Cold War continually raised questions about Canadian political independence vis-à-vis the United States, since Canada was rarely able to make foreign policy decisions contrary to those advocated by the United States.

The intellectual anxieties of this whole period in Canadian history find their most cogent theoretical expression in the work of the philosopher George Grant. The poet and critic Dennis Lee has written that "Grant's analysis of 'Canadian Fate and Imperialism' . . . was the first that made any contact whatsoever with my tenuous sense of living here — the first that seemed to be speaking the words of our civil condition."[43] Along with Harold Innis and Marshall McLuhan, the other great theorists of the Canadian condition, Grant was among the first to take seriously the idea that Canada had become in the postwar period, little more than a de facto colony of the United States. Grant articulated the differences that existed between the social and political cultures of Canada and the United States at a time when there was a good deal of worry that no such substantive differences existed. He identified these differences as growing out of each country's separate place in the stream of (the history of) political philosophy. The political culture of Canada, embodying the values of a conservative tradition extending back to Edmund Burke, stood in stark opposition to the Jeffersonian liberalism of the United States. By lending to claims concerning Canada's colonial status both a vocabulary and an intellectual respectability, Grant's work became the theoretical basis for a number of literary projects in the late 1960s and 1970s whose intent was to articulate the distinctiveness of Canadian national culture, whether through the writing of literature or through criticism of this literature. It is for this reason that Powe has suggested Grant was the "spiritual leader"[44] of the thematic critics. Even if his direct influence on literary culture cannot always be pinned down, it is nevertheless clear that Grant, along with Northrop Frye, established the broad intellectual framework within which the fate of the Canadian nation was analyzed and assessed in the decades following World War II.

Having said this, it is nevertheless surprising that Grant's work should form the basis for the project of Canadian nationalism. For by the time Grant wrote *Lament for a Nation: The Defeat of Canadian Nationalism* in 1965, he had all but concluded that the possibility of a Canadian nation was already lost to the past, if such a possibility had indeed ever existed at all.[45] Grant writes that "the crucial years were those of the early 'forties . . . Once it was decided that Canada was to be a branch-plant society of American capitalism, the issue of Canadian nationalism had been settled" (LN 40–41). Grant makes explicit the link that he sees between economics and culture: "Branch-plant economies have branch-plant cultures" (LN 41). And while this does get to the heart of Grant's claims, it also over-simplifies what is a complicated account of the position of Canada with respect to modernity. Part Jacques Ellul, part Martin Heidegger,[46] *Lament for a Nation* traces out the conditions of impossibility of creating a nation late in the twentieth century. *Lament for a Nation* is not intended to be a diagnostic text that would help committed nationalists isolate the problems with forging a contemporary Canadian nation. On the contrary, it is a text that analyzes the rather unfortunate condition of being a Canadian in the late twentieth century.

It is in this sense that Grant's text constitutes a "lament" rather than a series of practical proposals. Throughout the book, he insists on seeing the disappearance of the Canadian nation as "a matter of necessity" (LN 5) or "fate." Although he criticizes the Canadian political, economic, and bureaucratic elite for their failure to take action to preserve Canadian values and interests and for their failure to even understand what these values consist of, it is clear that for Grant the collapse of Canada "stems from the very character of the modern era" (LN 53). The lament that Grant engages in is directed toward the past, to what Canada was and what it could have been: a different, more just version of the North American experiment. It is a lament that is "a celebration of memory" for what is already gone, as made glaring and empirically evident by the events that form the occasion for Grant's text: the Defense Crisis faced by the government of John Diefenbaker in its attempt to forge an independent reaction to American involvement in the Cuban Missile Crisis.[47]

Though the positive identity of the Canadian nation springs largely from the "negative intention" (LN 68) not to be like the American republic — which is to say that Canada has no self-identical sense of identity, which positions it as an exemplary postmodern nation in the eyes of some recent commentators[48] — the characteristics that Grant defines as belonging to Canada have remained an essential part of the self-definition of the Canadian nation and of broader intellectual discourses concerning Canadian national identity. What Canada was, or at the very least, what it promised to be, was "a more ordered and stable society than the liberal experiment in the United States" (LN 4). The chief objection to life in the United States is also one that has since become a familiar part of both popular and academic discussions of Canadian identity. For Grant, the United States embodies the eroding, homogenizing powers of modernity — the universal that opposes and destroys all particularities. It is, specifically, the breeding ground of a capitalist modernity that has become its chief export: a whole "way of life based on the principle that the most important activity is profit-making" (LN 47). Grant suggests that "a distinction between Canada and the United States has been the belief that Canada was predicated on the rights of nations as well as on the rights of individuals" (LN 21–22). How to isolate and separate these different senses of "rights" is not made clear, but in any case it is the dominant image that is important: Canada as a collective nation, the United States as a nation of individuals.

As an alternative version of the New World experiment, one that is less individualistic and so, in a certain sense, less modern, the promise of the Canadian nation is that it might preserve a space that is not limited to the individualist logic of homo economicus. But it is the impossibility of this possibility that Grant laments. "In the mass era," Grant writes, "most human beings are defined in terms of their capacity to consume. All other differences between them, like political traditions, begin to appear unreal and unprogressive" (LN 90). As has become especially apparent since the end of the Cold War, one of the particularly powerful effects of American modernity has been to make capitalism into the end of history; appropriating the dialectical teleology of Marxism, it is capitalism, and all of the social relations that it embodies, that takes on the role of the realized essence of humanity worked out only after a long, historical struggle. It might not be entirely correct to say that there are no other ways of organizing life imaginable. However, capitalist modernity, bolstered by a general faith in the capacities of science, has become the only form of life that can be *pragmatically* envisioned. Every other idea, including the idea of the Canadian nation, is relegated to the dusty stacks of libraries — ideas, but hardly living ones.

There are a number of reasons why Grant believes that the possibilities of Canada as an alternative, essentially nonmodern space on the new continent never came to fruition. The most important of these is the fact that Canada is itself in many ways the historical product of modernity. As he writes in "Canadian Fate and Imperialism," a later essay that recapitulates the fundamental arguments of *Lament for a Nation* in the context of American involvement in Vietnam, "Canada could only continue to be if we could hold some alternative social vision to that of the great republic. Yet such an alternative would have to come out of the same stream — Western culture."[49] Grant locates the source of Canada's strength and independence as a nation in its connection to Britain; as long as this connection existed, Canada occupied an intermediary space between the relentless modernity of the United States and the (supposedly) traditional, organic nationalities of Europe.

This celebration of Canada's ties to Britain has had the effect of making Grant appear an apologist for the British imperial project — of making him seem to choose one empire over another instead of articulating some more genuine form of Canadian political freedom — and has made his arguments against modernity seem little more than a veiled attempt to protect his own position of status in a colonial hierarchy that in the 1960s was being eroded by widespread shifts in Canadian society.[50] It is hard, for example, not to see his worries about the modernizing effects of the Quiet Revolution on the Catholic character of Québécois society in this light. Yet it is a mistake to see Grant as an advocate of the regressive character of life in Québec under Duplessis or to see him as merely interested in protecting the British character of Canada. He suggests, rather, that the alternative that Canada could represent must come from outside of (American) modernity: the dominance in Québec of a hierarchical, religious way of life more attuned to the nineteenth century than the twentieth and the British conservative tradition that Grant appeals to are such alternatives that do not owe their patrimony to modernity. It is important to recognize from the outset that the conservative tradition that Grant is so attracted to *predates* British imperialism; as for imperialism itself, Grant sees it as responsible for modernity, and thus sees Britain as, perhaps unfortunately, "the chief center from which the progressive civilization spread around the world" (CFI 73). In this sense, British imperialism must be seen as a betrayal of British conservatism, rather than an extension of it. Since Canada is one of the products of imperialism, the ideology of "progressive civilization" appeared in Canada from the outset. Yet unlike the citizens of the United States — "the only society on earth that has no traditions from before the age of progress" (CFI 65) — English-speaking Canadians, Grant believes, continued to have "connections with the British Isles, which in the nineteenth century still had ways of life from before the age of progress" (CFI 71). Canada nurtured and maintained values and ways of life predating modernity; and it is here that its possibilities for a different way of life were preserved, though only very precariously, with more promise than possibility, since these links to an older Europe were the product of progressive forces that eventually devour all such ties.

The possibility of maintaining this kernel of resistance based on a slowly fraying connection to an English-speaking community located across an ocean was a slim one indeed. In *Lament for a Nation*, Grant compares Canada in 1965 to Poland, another country located geographically next to a superpower, whose sovereignty and culture had also been severely impinged as a result. Grant writes: "There are clearly two chief differences between ourselves and that nation. First, the Poles have an ancient culture which has shown strength in resisting new change. The new came to Poland not only as something Russian (that is, nationally alien) but also as something Marxist (that is, profoundly alien to a Roman Catholic people). In Canada, outside of Québec, there is no deeply rooted culture, and the new changes come in the form of an ideology (capitalist and liberal) which seems to many a splendid vision of human existence . . . the governments of small capitalist nations do not have the same means to protect themselves as do small Communist nations" (LN 43).

The lack of a deep-rooted culture, a culture predating modernity, combined with the temptations offered by the ideologies of progress, means that the gradual erosion of the possibilities represented by the Canada nation are inevitable. Yet even without a primordial culture to draw on, or one organized around ethnic or linguistic particularities, Grant suggests there are other ways of resisting foreign encroachment. During the period following the American ascension to world dominance, Grant outlines two possible forms of resistance to western imperialism. He calls these "Castroism" and "Gaullism" after each of their respective practitioners. Castroism involves the establishment of "a rigorous socialist state that turns to the Communist empire for support in maintaining itself" (LN 45). Gaullism is the practice of connecting "the nationalist spirit to technological planning and to insist that there are limits to the western 'alliance'" (LN 46).

There are limits to each of these forms of resistance, but what is most important here is the fact that Grant indicates that neither of these methods of resistance can be practiced in Canada. Grant sees Castroism as a potential politics only in situations where industrialization is desired by the majority but is prevented from happening by a capitalist empire (i.e., the United States) and its local representatives. In the period following World War II, there is no analogous situation in Canada, except perhaps in the relationship between rural, agrarian French Canadians and the English-Canadian business and political elites in Montreal prior to the Quiet Revolution. The success of Gaullism depends on the importance of nationalism as a motive among the political and economic elite of the nation. In the Canadian situation, however, Grant argues that the elite have little interest in being nationalist. Grant writes that "most of them made more money by being the representatives of American capitalism and setting up the branch plants" (LN 47). The compromised character of the African national elites that Fanon decries in *The Wretched of the Earth* is thus perhaps even more deep-rooted in Canada. With a history unmarked by a specific transformative "event" such as a definitive moment of decolonization (however artificial or momentary this might prove to be), there is in Canada nothing that could act as a historical marker against which the present state elite (i.e., whether it is worse or better than before decolonization) could be assessed. So it would appear that the possibility of a genuine Canadian nationalism — one that would be more than an expression of American/modern values over a putatively separate and independent geographic space — is blocked from every angle.

It is possible to understand the thrust of Grant's argument without having to discuss his appeal to the traditions of conservative political thought. But with Canadian nationalism being at every turn an impossibility, it is through an explanation of what attracts Grant to the conservative tradition and how he defines this tradition that any sense can be made of even a structural possibility that has now been lost and must be lamented. For it is, finally, in the persistence of something as tenuous as this political tradition that Canada's potential difference from the United States lies. Grant defines traditional conservatism as "the right of the community to restrain freedom in the name of the common good" (LN 64). In Canada, both the French and the English had the "belief that society required a high degree of law, and a respect for a public conception of virtue" (LN 69). This conservatism is "essentially the social doctrine that public order and tradition, in contrast to freedom and experiment, were central to the good life" (LN 71). This is in contrast to the liberalism that Grant sees in the United States, a liberalism whose roots lie in the Enlightenment. The liberal ideology of individual freedom is for Grant essentially the same as that which underlies the scientific ideology of progress and capitalism. Grant writes that "liberalism is the perfect ideology for capitalism. It demolishes those taboos that restrain expansion" (LN 47), including, of course, national boundaries.

Grant feels that it is Canada's connection to Britain that has fostered the persistence of a conservative ethos even next to the most purely liberal country on earth. It is the waning of the East-West connection in Canada, which Grant at least partially attributes to the increasing economic advantage of North-South trade, that he laments: with the passing of this connection so too passes the possibility of an independent country in the northern part of North America. One of the unfortunate side effects of this argument is that it cannot help but seem anachronistic or even racist. Canadians no longer predominantly trace their ethnic heritage back to the British Isles, and, increasingly, there are fewer and fewer whose ethnic or national heritage finds its origins in Europe at all. The global movement of peoples that has transformed Canadian society would no doubt be seen by Grant as a visible sign of a global modernity in which "Canada" has already been lost. It should be pointed out, however, that Grant is ambivalent even about Canada's relationship to Great Britain. "British conservatism," he writes, "was already a spent force at the beginning of the nineteenth century when English-speaking Canadians were making a nation . . . for all the fruitfulness of the British tradition in nineteenth-century Canada, it did not provide any radically different approach to the questions of industrial civilization" (LN 74). Grant begins *Lament for a Nation* by locating the end of Canadian nationalism in the Defense Crisis of 1962–63. By the end of the book, he seems to have argued that any of the conditions that would have made Canadian nationalism possible historically, economically, culturally, or ideologically, had all passed away a long time before. While he criticizes the policies of the Diefenbaker government and the Liberal government of Lester Pearson that followed, there is little that either of these governments could have done to change the Canadian situation. What limits the possibility of the Canadian nation is something more general: a modernity whose ideological temptations seem impossible to resist for a nation without ancient roots.

The problem that Grant identifies in *Lament for a Nation*, a problem that appears to be intractable, is the difficulty in modernity of attempting to maintain meaningful traditions and significant cultural differences while also desiring the material benefits associated with "progress." Especially in his discussion of Québec, it is clear that Grant understands the ideological and material power of "progress," which has a tendency to make all nationalisms appear illogical, reactionary, and dangerous. For Grant, Québéçois society has a much deeper tradition than its English-Canadian counterpart. Its Catholicism, for example, has meant that it is necessarily conservative: in Québec, "virtue must be prior to freedom" (LN 76). The dilemma faced by French Canada is that faced by all indigenous cultures around the world: "Nationalism can only be asserted successfully by an identification with technological advance; but technological advance entails the disappearance of those indigenous differences that give substance to nationalism" (LN 76). The government headed by Duplessis attempted to solve this dilemma by openly welcoming American capital while simultaneously turning matters of education and culture over to the church: a division between the spiritual and the material is a common response to the colonial situation. The result, however, was the production of new classes "ultimately more hostile to Catholicism than to capitalism" (LN 77). This is apparent in the problems faced by the avowedly nationalist governments of the Parti Québécois under René Levesque. To undo the prominence of the church that kept Québec underdeveloped, the state assumed the position formerly held by the church in matters of education and was committed to modernizing education in Québec in order to produce a French managerial elite that would wrest financial control away from English Canadians and Americans. But here, too, "The dilemma remains. French Canadians must modernize their educational system if they are to have more than a peon's place in their own industrialization. Yet to modernize their education is to renounce their particularity. At the heart of modern liberal education lies the desire to homogenize the world. Today's natural and social sciences were consciously produced as instruments to this end" (LN 79). It does not therefore seem possible to be both modern *and* antimodern; for Grant, one lives the other's death, and if local customs and practices remain, they are insignificant by comparison to the more general and dominant logic of capitalist modernity. As he writes, "the impossibility of conservatism in our era is the impossibility of Canada. As Canadians we attempted a ridiculous task in trying to build a conservative nation in the age of progress, on a continent we share with the most dynamic nation on earth. The current of modern history was against us" (LN 68).

Lament for a Nation is a rant, and as with all rants its claims are not always well-thought out or clearly articulated. In particular, Grant seems to move back and forth between the theoretical and empirical levels he deploys here. On the one hand, the text is a reaction to the increasing control and foreign ownership of the Canadian economy by Americans, which had the real effect of reducing Canadian political sovereignty in the 1950s and 1960s. It is also an assessment of the paths not taken by Canadian businessmen and politicians in defending Canadian political and social values against the encroachment of American ones, with particular reference to the experience of the Diefenbaker years, and a severe criticism of the abandonment of nationalist principles by an economic elite for whom the eradication of borders constitutes a financial advantage. On the other hand, there is a sense in which all of this more or less empirical analysis is moot. The problem is not that certain Canadian politicians or members of the business elite have played their hand poorly or have been tempted by the material luxuries promised by the American way of life, but that, given Canada's marginal position vis-à-vis the United States and the West more generally, everything that happened was inevitable, part of an historical teleology in which all resistance dissolves in the acid-bath of progress.

Grant's movement from volunteerism to determinism is not an unprecedented one; it exists, for example, in Marx's own writings on capitalism, as concretized by the theories of Mao on the one hand and Althusser on the other. What is perhaps more problematic is how much is not expressed here. For example, Grant gestures at the deficiencies of modernity and the preferability of tradition without ever being explicit about either. The conservative model that he prefers — one in which there would be great emphasis on the community at the expense of individual rights and freedoms — is asserted more than argued for, with the United States occupying the role of a figure that can be filled with almost any content, any sense of what is wrong with the world. It could be argued just as well that there are a great many problems with and limitations of an emphasis on the community over the individual. Québec under Duplessis may have represented a more organic community than that of the society south of the border. At the same time, the impulse behind the Quiet Revolution in Québec was not merely an uncritical acceptance of the values of modernity, but a reaction to an extremely paternalistic and class-divided social order. What is lacking in Grant's assessment of Canada's possibilities as a nation is the profound ambivalence of modernity, which is both a destroyer of tradition and a liberating force from some of the restrictive aspects of tradition.

What would count, for Grant, as the difference that makes a difference in defining the Canadian nation? It is not the preservation of "charming residual customs" (LN 21), but something more fundamental: a radically different way of organizing life and society than that which has become the global, Americanized norm. Anything less for Grant constitutes a failure to be genuinely different. Unless the nation embodies an utterly unique mode of life, it would seem that the "nation" simply becomes a way of geographically dividing the riches of the earth among sets of elites. The rhetoric that continues to persist in Canadian public life about the defining characteristics of the nation rests on the difference of its institutions from those of the United States. In particular, it is common to assert that in Canada there just *is* the sort of social democratic or even socialist tradition that values the collective over the individual. The facts would suggest that this is mainly a rhetoric that has helped to preserve the favorable conditions experienced by the Canadian elite: the amount of social spending in Canada as a portion of GDP is closer to the United States than to nations like Sweden or Denmark; and Canada as a nation has as great a division of wealth as any country in the industrialized world.[51] Grant himself is clear on the fact that institutional difference between the two countries is very minor: "Our parliamentary and judicial institutions may be preferable to the American system, but there is no deep division of principle. Certainly none of the differences between the two sets of institutions are sufficiently important to provide the basis for an alternative culture on the northern half of this continent" (LN 74).

Frye's Modern Century

I remember glancing through Herbert Marcuse's book, *One Dimensional Man,* and wondering what he would have made of the modern world if he had to live in a one-dimensional country.
                                                            — NORTHROP FRYE[52]

The logic of Grant's lament, a lament over the inevitable loss produced by modernity, would seem to eviscerate the Canadian nation as a viable, positive project around which to muster one's forces. In Grant's analysis, nationalism in Canada is a spent force, an impossible project. If Grant occupies the position of "spiritual forefather" to thematic criticism, this might suggest that the nation would not occupy an important position in Canadian literary criticism. And yet the very opposite has been the case. In Canadian literary criticism, the nation has become the concept around which every other consideration revolves and to which every discussion turns. As we shall see with Lecker's criticisms later in this chapter, in literary critical readings of Canadian texts the necessity of locating or identifying unique national characteristics originates from a much more prosaic reading of the relationship between text and context that does not always raise larger questions about Canada's relationship to modernity in the way that Grant does. There seems to be an enormous amnesia about the radical conclusions suggested by Grant's work, or, at the very least, it is perhaps Grant's volunteerism that has been emphasized to the detriment of his more deterministic proclamations.

This same kind of misreading has been at work in the interpretation of the other figure who has exercised an enormous influence on the course of Canadian literary criticism in the period following World War II, Northrop Frye. Lecker has written that "the publication of the *Literary History of Canada*, in 1965, was a signal event that transformed the making of Canadian literary history and permanently altered the country's critical and creative landscapes" (MR 191). Frye's conclusion to this volume, which "introduced an influential theory about the evolution of Canadian literature and about the shifting modes of representing this evolution" (MR 191), has in turn been its most important and most widely-read section; it has been the source of critical projects that take their inspiration from it and those that position themselves in direct opposition to it. In either case, it has become an unavoidable text, the Urtext for the critical analysis of Canadian literature. What I want to argue briefly here, before moving on to my specific analysis of the function played by the nation in Canadian literary criticism, is the degree to which Grant's vision — often seen by critics as idiosyncratic, mistaken on important historical points, and overwhelmed by a Christian eschatology that he continually suppresses — is in large part shared by Frye. Frye also suggests that the era for Canadian distinctiveness has passed, even though his work has also been used as the basis for projects to locate Canada's particularity.

In his famous conclusion to the *Literary History of Canada*, Frye raises a number of points about Canadian literature that have since defined the parameters of Canadian literary criticism. In particular, he suggests that Canadian literature must be read with an eye toward the extraliterary features of the text; since "no

Canadian author pulls us away from the Canadian context toward the centre of literary experience itself, then at every point we remain aware of his social and historical setting" (C 821–22). It is the failure of Canada to have produced a major world writer that prompts Frye's suggestion that Canadian writing is over-determined by the context in which it is produced. This in turn leads to two different factors that Frye must attempt to account for in the conclusion. First, he offers a description of the Canadian context that explains why it has been inhos-pitable for literature. Second, he tries to suggest why the literature that nonethe-less manages to be produced is saturated by context. It is, of course, possible to see these factors as interrelated: the inability of Canadian literature to transcend its context, that is, to become universal, moving "toward the centre of literary experience itself," makes it limited and particular, bound by context. As Frye suggests, the lack of a literary tradition in Canada means that Canadian writers borrow literary forms from other traditions; what makes these works "Canadian" can thus *only* be context (C 835). Context-bound literature is what results when formal development is arrested; thus the need for a "thematic" as opposed to a formal mode of interpreting Canadian texts.

For Frye, the facts of Canadian history have made Canada an infertile place for literature. He suggests that what has limited the development of Canadian literature is that it has been crafted within a "garrison mentality" (C 830). The history of Canada is a history of small, isolated communities — isolated from each other as much as from the United States and England — standing against an enormous, threatening, alien physical world that is always ready to annihilate them. In order to survive, such garrisons are "compelled to feel a respect for the law and order that holds them together" (C 830), since in such a landscape, the individual is lost on his own. The specific effects of this mentality on Canadian literature are not explicitly spelled out, though Frye suggests that the need to defend the garrison leads to writing that is more rhetorical than poetical and the need to deal with the environment leads to description rather than metaphor. Though much has been made of this characterization of the origins of the Cana-dian mentality, especially in works such as Margaret Atwood's *Survival* (1972), for Frye it appears that the real problem lies less in the literary outlook or charac-teristics that a "garrison mentality" produces than in the fact that "the Canadian literary mind, beginning as it did so late in the cultural history of the West, was established on a basis, not of myth, but of history" (C 835). It is possible to focus on the division between "myth" and "history" indicated here with reference to Frye's larger body of critical writing. What I want to emphasize instead is the "lateness" of Canada that has produced this division. It is this "belated" Canada that is all too often overlooked in Frye's text. It is overlooked, I think, because it negates the nationalist literary projects that other elements of Frye's conclusion point to: the reading, allegorically or otherwise, of the traces of the garrison mentality in Canadian literary texts, a common currency that establishes the distinctiveness of Canadian literature and thus of the Canadian nation itself; or the tracing of literary attempts to overcome this mentality, the mapping of the movement from "the stage of exploration" to that of "settlement" (C 827), the gradual maturation of Canadian literature to the point where it is no longer delimited by its origins, by its context.

The most famous sentence of the conclusion concerns the vexed question of Canadian identity. Frye writes that the Canadian sensibility is "less perplexed by the question of 'Who am I?' than by some such riddle as 'Where is here?'" (C 826). This characterization of the Canadian imagination has had a tendency to reinforce the priority of content in Canadian literature, particularly a content understood in a brute sense as the appearance of the physical world itself. As suggested by the context in which this statement is made, however, Frye's statement has always been read much too literally. The question, "Where is here?" arises in response to Canada's historical belatedness as a nation. A question that appears to refer to the dominance of space in the Canadian imagination has its origins in time. In the beginning of the paragraph that ends with the question "Where is here?" Frye writes: "English Canada was first a part of the wilderness, then a part of North America and the British Empire, then a part of the world. But it has gone through these revolutions too quickly for a tradition of writing to be founded on any one of them. Canadian writers are, even now, still trying to assimilate a Canadian environment at a time when new techniques of communication, many of which, like television, constitute a verbal market, are annihilating the boundaries of that environment" (C 826). What emerges as a threat to Canadian identity and to the possibility of a unique Canadian literature is a global modernity that is putting an end to whatever connection may have ever existed between Canadian writing and its environment. Canada's colonial situation, which has made it throughout its history a country "treated by others less like a society than as a place to look for things" (C 827), has not made it a place amenable to the production of literature, which is "born in leisure and an awareness of standards" (C 827). But just as important is the historical timing of the project of the Canadian nation, which as Frye suggests elsewhere, begins at the same moment as the modern itself.[53]

Frye returns to this theme at the end of the conclusion when he characterizes the differences between Canada and the United States by reference to two American paintings: Erastus Salisbury Field's *Historical Monument of the American Republic* (1876) and Edward Hicks's *The Peaceable Kingdom* (1830).[54] Frye sees these paintings as representing two different visions of civilization. Field's painting offers "an encyclopaedic portrayal of events in American history, against a background of soaring towers, with clouds around their spires, and connected by railway bridges. It is a prophetic vision of the skyscraper cities of the future, of the tremendous will to power of our time and the civilization it has built" (C 846–47). Hicks's painting, which predates Field's by almost half a century, offers a different vision of the New World whose "mood is closer to the haunting vision of a serenity that is both human and natural which we have been struggling to identify in the Canadian tradition" (C 848). The Canadian tradition is connected to a depiction of a premodern world, a world in which machinery and technology have not yet definitively asserted their place in historical development: "Here, in the background, is a treaty between the Indians and the Quaker settlement under Penn. In the foreground is a group of animals, lions, tigers, bears, oxen, illustrating the prophecy of Isaiah about the recovery of innocence in nature. Like the animals of the Douanier Rousseau, they stare past us with a serenity that transcends consciousness. It is a pictorial emblem of what [Fredrick Philip] Grove's narrator was trying to find under the surface of America: the reconciliation of man with man and of man with nature: the mood of Thoreau's Walden retreat, of Emily Dickinson's garden, of Huckleberry Finn's raft" (C 848).

These are not visions of the New World that can coexist side by side. For what makes Field's prophecy of America's technological will-to-power possible is the end of Hicks's vision of America-Canada. That this end is already near in 1830 is announced by the narratives Frye invokes to describe this vision of a genuine reconciliation of man with man and man with nature — the physical and mental "flights" from the dominant mode of American life in Thoreau, Dickinson, and Twain. The "quest for the peaceable kingdom" in Canadian letters has met a similar end in the worldwide expansion of the technological will-to-power of the American republic, which has rendered anachronistic the idea of the "nation" understood as an organic community of people linked by a common history that is somehow "expressed" through culture. In the conclusion to the first major literary history of Canada, Frye is thus forced to write a requiem to all future national literary projects: "The writers of the past decade, at least, have begun to write in a world which is post-Canadian, as it is post-American, post-British, and post everything except the world itself. There are no provinces in the empire of aeroplane and television, and no physical separation from the centres of culture, such as they are. Sensibility is no longer dependent on a specific environment or even on sense experience itself" (C 848).

Frye's articulation of the place occupied by Canadian literature and culture within modernity in this conclusion is hardly an idiosyncratic position within what might be seen as his broader cultural nationalism. It is, rather, a recurrent theme of his work. In the preface to *The Bush Garden*, a book which collects Frye's writings on Canadian literature, he turns directly and immediately to the question of Canadian identity. This discussion is somewhat more nuanced than that in the conclusion to the *Literary History of Canada*. First of all, Frye explicitly makes a connection between identity and space. He writes that "the creative instinct has a great deal to do with the assertion of territorial rights. The question of identity is primarily a cultural and imaginative question, and there is always something vegetable about the imagination, something sharply limited in range."[55] One of the consequences of this limitation on the imagination is that identity cannot be seen as a *national* question, but at most as a *regional* one. In his best imitation of nineteenth-century European geographers, Frye notes that the numerous cultural and empirical geographies of Canada produce equally numerous points of imaginative identification: the farmland of Southern Ontario, for example, produces a different imagination from the one that the wilderness and mountains of the interior of British Columbia produce. The issue of identity, which is thus regional, has to be separated from the issue of unity, "which is national in reference, international in perspective, and rooted in a political feeling."[56] For Frye, it is in terms of this distinction between identity and unity, between region and nation, that the effects of modernity on the Canadian identity have to be assessed. While identity is primarily regional in nature, Frye admits that there exist national forms of identification as well; at the same time, he claims that national identity is necessarily "negative." It is negative not because it eliminates internal, regional differences, but because, unlike the space of regions, the space of the nation is inevitably modern in a way that corrodes identity. Frye writes that "in our world the sense of a specific environment as something that provides a circumference for an imagination has to contend with a global civilization of jet planes, international hotels, and disappearing landmarks — that is, an obliterated environment. That obliterated environment produces an imaginative dystrophy that one sees all over the world, most dramatically perhaps in architecture and town planning (as it is ironically called), but in the other arts as well. Canada, with its empty spaces, its largely unknown lakes and rivers and islands, its division of language, its dependence on immense railways to hold it physically together, has had this peculiar problem of an obliterated environment throughout most of its history."[57] It is in the perpetual tension between unity and identity—the tension that constitutes federalism in Canada—that Frye finds the essence of the word "Canadian." Correspondingly, it is only when this tension is dissolved that the problems of Canadian national life emerge: "assimilating identity to unity produces the empty gestures of cultural nationalism; assimilating unity to identity produces the kind of provincial isolation which is now called separatism."[58]

Canada's difficult position with respect to modernity also forms the basis of Frye's lectures in *The Modern Century* (1967).[59] Prophetically, what Frye describes in this seldom cited text is the "condition" that would later come to be known as postmodernity: a world dominated by the circulation of simulacra, the waning of the "real" and of depth, the ceaseless play of surfaces, the primacy of desire and seduction as modes of the contemporary subject.[60] This nascent reading of the postmodern is, however, admittedly limited. The vocabulary in which Frye discusses these features of the present remains linked to the modern, existentialist discourse of alienation and the critique of "progress for the sake of progress," placing *The Modern Century* in the company of other works of the 1950s and 1960s such as William Whyte's *The Organization Man* and Vance Packard's *The Hidden Persuaders*, Herbert Marcuse's *One-Dimensional Man*, and Norman O. Brown's *Love's Body*.[61] While the text as a whole offers a general indictment of a degraded present, Frye's specific aim is to assess the possibilities of Canadian culture in the context of larger, global changes in which the ideology of progress has triumphed, producing widespread feelings of individual alienation as a result. Frye presented these lectures in February 1967, at the beginning of Canada's centennial year. In this context, part of his aim seems to be to counteract from the very outset the euphoric discourses surrounding Canadian culture in 1967 that would culminate in the celebration of the World Exposition in Montreal.[62] In opposition to discourses that see a narrative of Canadian cultural maturity in the passage from colony to nation, Frye suggests here that it is "quite clear that we are moving towards a postnational world, and that Canada has moved further in that direction than most of the smaller nations . . . today Canada is too much a part of the world to be thought of as a nation in it."[63] It is the consequences of this claim for Canadian culture that Frye explores at length in the three essays that make up *The Modern Century*.

In the second lecture, "Improved Binoculars," Frye takes up the issue of culture and cultural autonomy most directly. The views that Frye expresses here are more considered and complicated than those offered, for example, in the "Preface" to *The Bush Garden*, even though they may come chronologically earlier. The body of the lecture is a wide-ranging analysis of the "modern" and its meaning in both popular and high art. Frye suggests that "modern" names an "international style" in the arts that is now ubiquitous and inescapable. For Canadian culture, "complete immersion in the international style is a primary cultural requirement . . . anything distinctive that develops within the Canadian environment can only grow out of participation in this style."[64] This would appear to be anathema to any possibility of Canadian cultural autonomy. But if Canada was born at the moment of the modern itself (which Frye marks as 1867), what needs to be asked is what cultural autonomy would Canada have in any case. Frye suggests that the difficulty with this problematic, one in which the notion of cultural specificity (as in the concept of so many "national cultures") must seem of necessity to be aligned against the international character of the modern, is that the idea of culture that it implies remains connected to that of the Romantic idea of folk. Frye writes that "culture, it is often said, in contrast to economic and political developments, is local, regional, and decentralized, as dependent on an immediate environment as a fine wine or a delicate and traditional handicraft like peasant costumes. The first step in the creation of an indigenous culture, therefore, is a firm boundary line, and the next step is the cultural equivalent of high tariffs against foreign influence."[65] While in some limited cases, it might be possible to create such a firm boundary line, it does not seem to make sense to see Canadian culture in this way, especially as Canadian literature and culture have been formed by modern, international styles. Canadian cultural nationalists who continue to see Canada through the lens of Romantic notions about the relationship of culture to definite, determinate spaces, risk misunderstanding the nature of contemporary Canadian cultural forms.

In light of the various formulations that Frye advances about the possibilities of Canadian culture and literature at the end of the century, it is hard to see him as the forefather of a cultural-nationalist literary criticism. As with Grant, Frye appears to occupy the opposing position, arguing repeatedly that there is no specifically *Canadian* literature if this is understood as naming more than the body of texts that can be itemized in national (the space of the nation here being delimited by the state) literary histories. Indeed, what Frye seems to be pointing to is the long-standing presence in Canadian literature of what Timothy Brennan has recently characterized as a "cosmopolitanism" in the texts of postcolonial writers.[66] So another figurehead of thematic criticism has been brought low: first Grant, then Frye. This is not to suggest that thematic criticism should therefore be pronounced dead on arrival — a cultural nationalist practice in a country whose logics of origin cannot possibly sustain such a practice except through bad faith and self-deception. Rather, what needs to be assessed is how the nation functions in thematic criticism and in Canadian literary criticism more generally. How is it possible that a nationalist criticism could have been born out of such anti-nationalist discourses as those of Grant and Frye? I will approach this question through an analysis of Lecker's attempt in *Making It Real* to do away with a nation that stubbornly refuses to be eliminated from the examination of Canadian texts. There are, therefore, two questions that need to be addressed. First, why is it that the nation seems to be an essential aspect of Canadian literature and criticism, especially in the decades immediately following World War II? Second, what are we to make of the persistence of the nation in the discourse of literary criticism in the context of the (apparent) impossibility of the Canadian nation?

The National Text: Canadian Criticism and the People

Withholding the status of "authentic" colonialism from countries such as Canada . . . makes it harder for all Canadians to identify and combat the particular kinds of postcolonial experiences they are currently undergoing as they watch their economy shrink, jobs disappear, and cultural sovereignty erode.

— DIANA BRYDON[67]

There is a contradiction or a gap that has to be explained. On the one hand, Canadian literary criticism, especially of the period from the 1950s to the mid 1970s, but extending up to the present, has been underwritten by a literary nationalism that seeks to make intelligible the special and specific attention to Canadian texts as *Canadian* texts. On the other hand, the work of the intellectual forefathers of contemporary Canadian criticism express forcefully the view that it is no longer sensible to speak of a specifically Canadian sensibility or culture. How and why is it then that the nation became *the* central object of Canadian criticism after World War II? Why has a determination of the "Canadian" qualities of Canadian literature remained an essential element of literary criticism in Canada? Why do the fragile and porous boundaries of late twentieth-century geography retain a primacy in the writing of literary history and criticism in

Canada, even when Canadian literary texts are themselves more cosmopolitan than nationalistic in their outlook?

It seems that as long as the fiction of the nation remains essential to the discussion of Canadian fiction, it is impossible to move away from one version or another of a theory of cultural particularity expressed in the form of the nation, and thus in the literary works that originate in the nation. The question of origin predominates, and consequently literary history remains, in Foucault's sense of these terms, historical rather than genealogical, a teleological story whose origin lies in the native soil. Questions about the "Canadianness" of the text inevitably lead back to narratives about the organic relationship of the community to the earth. This has had very unusual results in Canada. For example, Canadian novelists have often written the history of the country through the body of Native Canadians, incorporating the extended historical relationship of indigenous peoples with the land into their own (generally much shorter) history in Canada, in a process that Margery Fee has described as a "literary land claim."[68] This occurs in official government accounts of Canadian history as well, in which the ethnic diversity of the present Canadian nation is shown to be first exhibited in the numerous Native groups existing in a space that is retrospectively identified as already being Canada.[69]

The persistence of the nation as a theme of Canadian criticism might thus be seen as having had a deleterious effect on the development of Canadian criticism, an effect of arresting it in its tracks and leaving it out of step with the criticism of other, more mature literatures and criticisms. It is for this reason that the need for Canadian criticism to "grow up" has long been an aspect of many of the arguments for abandoning the nation in the consideration of Canadian texts, as reflected by the work of Frank Davey, Barbara Godard, Barry Cameron, Michael Dixon, and others, who have wanted to improve Canadian criticism by introducing the comparatively abstract, universalizing language of contemporary literary theory. From the vantage point of these critics, the period of nationalist criticism seems to have been a mistake that can be rectified by the introduction of new concepts or theories. Yet it is not clear whether it is really so easy to get rid of the nation in Canadian criticism or, for that matter, if it is even desirable to do so. The view taken by many critics that the period of national criticism has been superseded and should give way to other critical tropes and figures reflects a misunderstanding of the structural function of the "national-literary referent" in the practice of literary criticism itself in Canada. Once again, as in the literary fields of the other areas that I have examined in this study, the conjunction of

within the established school and the traditions it has created in order to validate itself and perpetuate its judgements" (MR 42).[73] The result is the production of a canon that has "missed" the nation, that fails, in other words, to reflect anything but the narrow interests of a group of specialists. For Lecker, the problem with this is that the function of the literary canon *should* be to reflect the nation; ironically, the "national-referential aesthetic" fails to do just this.

There are problems with the way in which Lecker understands the process of canon formation. The key insight concerning the canon shared by many of the American critics he cites — John Guillory, Annette Kolodny, Jane Tompkins, and Barbara Hernnstein-Smith — revolves around a realization of the essential arbitrariness of the canon. What these critics hope to do, if it is in fact possible to assign a common purpose to such an ideologically diverse group of thinkers, is to challenge the "natural" character of the canon in order to revise or amend it, or to drain it entirely of its ideological and rhetorical power — its claims to define the essence of a nation or a people. The arbitrariness that Lecker laments with respect to the formation of the Canadian canon is in fact true of all canon formation: *none* of them embody national values in the way he supposes. As with the nation itself, the questions concerning the canon relate to how it transforms artifice into nature. There is another problem with Lecker's understanding of the Canadian canon. Tracy Ware has argued that Lecker's portrayal of a canon dominated by nationalist texts in fact misrepresents the real character of the Canadian canon. He suggests, contra Lecker, that "The Canadian canon has always been fluid: the available anthologies are so inclusive that no course can exhaust their possibilities, and different instructors and institutions use and even construct very different anthologies. Thus Canada has all of the uncertainty but none of the dogmatic resistance necessary for a "delegitimation crisis." Canonical interrogations "have not deconstructed the monolith in any way similar to the way it has been deconstructed in other countries — read 'in the United States' — because there is no monolith here."[74] Ware's criticisms notwithstanding, the conclusions that Lecker draws on the basis of his interrogation of the Canadian canon are innocuous enough. He ends "The Canonization of Canadian Literature," by suggesting that more critical attention should be paid to how the canon was formed. The alarm that he expresses about the construction of a canon dominated by nationalist texts is in the end somewhat tempered. He does not call for a definitive end to nationalism in the canon, but encourages a careful consideration of the values that Canadians want to inform the canon. These may *still* be nationalist values. Lecker simply points out that they don't necessarily have to be:

the necessity that has accompanied the nationalist canon is only a matter of the vagaries of literary critical history.

There is thus already some confusion about the status and meaning of nationalism and the nation in Lecker's book. At first, it appears that nationalism, expressed in terms of the canon, is to be resisted at all costs; by the end of the first essay, it has returned. The relevance of the nation remains framed by the question of the canon, but it has shifted slightly, so that there emerges a distinction between a *genuine* and a *false* literary nationalism. The "genuine" national literature emerges from the people, the false one that currently defines the Canadian canon is violently imposed on the nation by academic critics. The second and third chapters of *Making It Real*, "A Country without a Canon?" and "Privacy, Publicity, and the Discourse of Canadian Criticism," deal explicitly with this division and its consequences for the reading, writing, and interpretation of Canadian literature.

In what might at first seem to be an abrupt and startling about face, in "A Country without a Canon?" Lecker makes the claim that there is *no* canon in Canada. In many ways, this essay constitutes a response to Ware's claims on behalf of the Canadian canon and its essential "fluidity" and malleability. What Ware sees as a positive feature of the Canadian canon, Lecker sees as evidence of the deep problems with Canadian literary criticism. Instead of asserting that there is a canon and that it is scarred by nationalism, Lecker now asks the questions that he sees as emerging out of Ware (and Davey's) criticisms: "What does it mean to be a country without a canon? How does the absence of a canon affect our sense of agency and difference? How does such an absence colour our notions of community, time, and place? Is there any way in which such an absence marks a loss, or gain?" (MR 53)

These questions are meant to prompt an investigation into the significance of the canon for the nation, and more generally of the significance of literature for the nation. In order to support the hypothesis that there is no canon in Canada, Lecker utilizes a distinction between "canonical" and "curricular" value. Following Virgil Nemoianu, Lecker defines curricular literary works as " 'those that are chosen to be taught in class, to be included in anthologies . . . for utilitarian reasons, to satisfy some needs—political, ethical, practical . . . curricula are, in a sense, negotiated accounts between the definitional and hegemonic features of a given historical time and place and the broader and inchoate canonical domain proper.' "[75] By contrast, in defining the meaning of "canonical" value, Lecker invokes Charles Alteri, whose "positivist model proposes that canons provide us with concepts of authority that allow us to resist local and current abuses of power . . . canons promote the recognition of moral categories and therefore have an ethical dimension . . . canon, culture, community; they are all entwined" (MR 54–55). Lecker concludes that "in Canada we have a shifting but identifiable curriculum that is often misread as a canon" (MR 55). Canons are the outcome of numerous forces that democratically mediate between highbrow and lowbrow and are in a sense made up of "popular" works that are "heterogeneous and nonelitist" (54). By this measure, *all* of what supposedly pass for "classic," canonical texts in Canada (for instance, all of the texts of the Canadian literary tradition rapidly invented by the New Canadian Library series in the 1950s and 1960s) cannot claim to be canonical: they have "no claim to public interest," nor do they "mediate between popular and academic demand" (MR 55). As an example of the lack of a Canadian canon, Lecker cites the difference between public and academic views on the status of Sinclair Ross's *As for Me and My House*. He suggests that "while the novel may appear on course curricula throughout the country, and while much has been said about its ostensible excellence, it is not a canonical work. The average, well-read person within the public has never heard of it. In fact, many well-read people within the academy have never heard of it" (MR 55).

For Lecker, the consequences of the absence of a canon in Canada are dire. For it seems that in the canon what is represented is nothing less than (in typical Romantic fashion) the soul of the nation. The literary canon thus assumes in Lecker's essay an enormous and important role with respect to the nation. Indeed, it seems that it *is* the nation, which is why Lecker feels able to claim that "in the absence of a canon, a number of social constructs attached to canonical ideals will also vanish: consensus, community, social responsibility, and ultimately ethical challenge . . . while the country without a canon may be free, plural, ahistorical, and self-conscious of the material conditions that account for its contingent status, it may also be a country without moral conviction, without the means of recognizing difference, without standards against which ethical choices can be judged" (MR 57). A country without a canon is therefore a country that cannot claim to be a nation. As Lecker argues — and the language of Benedict Anderson's "imaginary community" is repeatedly invoked throughout this essay in describing the nation and literature — the canon is "one of the imaginary constructs through which nations articulate their dreams and values" (MR 63). If Canada doesn't have a canon, and Lecker seems to feel that it doesn't, then it desperately needs to "imagine" one; otherwise, the country called Canada risks descending into the ethical and moral wasteland that countries who are not also nations (supposedly) find themselves in. Lecker admits that it may be a lot to ask "that a country as young and regionally diverse as Canada might be expected to produce even one truly canonical text" (MR 56). What he seems to be absolutely certain of, however, is the direct connection between the literary value embodied in the canon and the values of the community embodied in the nation.

One further transformation of Lecker's original points regarding the nationalist basis of the Canadian canon needs to be looked at. For it is only in the third essay of *Making It Real*, "Privacy, Publicity, and the Discourse of Canadian Criticism," that the connections between the nation and literature that underlie Lecker's attack on nationalist criticism become clear. At the heart of the distinction between the canon and the curriculum lies the distinction between the public and the academy. What passes for a canon in Canada — the set of "classics" established by the academic-government-publishing triad — is for Lecker insufficient in yet another way than simply by the fact that it is too weak (more curricular than canonical) to produce or reflect any of the shared values that a nation should possess. The fact that Canada has no canon is also or even primarily due to the professionalization of literary criticism in Canada over the past forty years, which has meant that it no longer speaks of or embodies the values of the public — the only values that could make up a genuine canon.

The substantive part of this long essay traces the way in which "the discourse of Canadian criticism was gradually removed from the public sphere" (MR 70). The turning point of what Lecker describes as the "industrialization" and academic privatization of literary criticism occurs in the period between 1958 and 1965 — the beginning of the period marked by the appearance of the New Canadian Library that allowed Canadian literature to be turned into an academic field studied at universities, the end by the publication of the *Literary History of Canada*, which signified the consecration of this field and it confinement to specialists. To show the effects of the change, Lecker examines the first conference on Canadian literature, held at Queen's University in 1955. This was not a strictly academic conference, but included writers, publishers, editors, librarians, and booksellers, and was "designed to ensure public access" (MR 74). Lecker sees the importance placed on the inclusion of a diverse group of literary professionals and the public-at-large in the debates and discussions at the conference as an example of the fact that the early rhetoric of Canadian criticism "was about much more than making the Canadian writer or Canadian literature accessible to the public. It was also about the political value associated with such publicity" (MR 73). At the Queen's conference at least, it was felt that "the dissemination of a national literature was essential to the recognition of community on a national scale. In other words, the publicity of the nation's literature both formed and publicized the nation" (MR 76).

Beginning in the mid 1950s, this literary nationalism, which Lecker sees as one that perhaps too unproblematically "valorized the transparent equation between critical discourse and nationalist political action" (MR 73), began to be transformed into the basis for the professionalization of the study (and reading) of Canadian literature as part of what he describes derisively as a "state-supported public relations campaign" (MR 82–83). The nationalist, thematic criticism that Lecker saw dominating Canadian criticism up to the present in "The Canonization of Canadian Literature" becomes here simply a phase of professionalism that has culminated in the ascension of theory in Canadian literary criticism, with a result of a further isolation of Canadian literature from the public. On the one hand, "the movement toward privatization allowed the discourse to lose its monologic, nationalist, and hegemonic focus. But the movement away from nationalism was also divisive, both for the social order and for the individual involved in that order" (MR 71). It is for this reason that Lecker claims most Canadian literary critics are uncomfortable with the social positions that they now occupy, since "they are haunted by the idea that criticism is responsible to the public — to the nation" (MR 71).

It would be interesting and useful to critically assess the whole of Lecker's discussion of the professionalization of Canadian literary criticism, but to do so would distract from the point of looking at Lecker's examination of the place of the nation in Canadian literary criticism since the 1950s. While the nation and nationalist criticism in the first essay of *Making It Real* constituted a problem that had to be dealt with, what we are left with here is a sense that the real problem with Canadian literary criticism is that it is *not nationalist enough*. Critics have an important role to play with respect to the nation; it is a role that the professionalization of the academy has not allowed them to play. In the narrative that Lecker presents concerning the professionalization of literary criticism in Canada, it is significant that the thematic critics are now positioned as the last critics to struggle with "the tension between public and private discourse" (MR 86). Atwood's *Survival*, for example, is described as "the expression of a poet who feels victimized by privacy . . . Atwood, an ex-academic, sees the academic walls closing in on Canadian literature. She wants to break the trend toward privacy. She wants a public" (MR 86). By contrast, Canadian criticism is now characterized as private and self-involved: it should be speaking to the public as a whole — to and of the nation, in other words — but instead it confines itself to small intellectual cote-ries. Lecker encourages critics to become public once again. What this seems to mean is that they must perform the essential function that *only* critics can perform with respect to the Canadian nation: produce the public *for* literature, and by so doing, produce the nation that is the culmination of the values embodied and expressed in Canadian literature. And what could this be except the very "Cana-dianness" of Canadian literature, expressed now not through the academic lens of the thematic critics but through a sense of the values of the public? It is not easy to see the difference.

Nation(al) Politics

In the sometimes contradictory positions on the nation that Lecker articulates in *Making It Real*, something important emerges in the anxious reappearance of the nation in the form of a call for a more public criticism. In one of the many summaries of his position that he produces in the introduction, Lecker writes: "If one objects to any formulation of the nation as an entity that can be described — that is *worth* describing — then one has to fall back on a pluralist vision of the country that sees it as a conglomeration of competing forces and centres of power. This is the view endorsed by much contemporary Canadian theory. But if one promotes this view, there is no reason to describe the conglomeration as *Canadian*, and no need to speak to the Canadian public (or students) about it. Only if there is something identifiably Canadian is it worth asking what that identification is all about. Contemporary Canadian literary criticism refuses to speak from where it lives. Yet it still lives — here. This is not just any place. It is a specific place" (MR 9). In what sense can it be said that Canadian literary criti-cism lives "here," in Canada, as opposed to existing at the intersection of nu-merous lines of influence that neither necessarily originate in Canada nor are even identifiably "national" in their determination? While this view of the lines of force that produce the contemporary nation is in some sense "right," Lecker's comments also point to an inescapable fact: it *is* only some conception of the nation that makes Canadian literature a meaningful category, and not just in terms of the divisions that have been established between various national litera-tures; the nation is essential to whatever politics might be imagined for Canadian criticism in the connection of literature to the public. I can't help but wonder if it is not precisely what most contemporary critics have seen as the *immaturity* of Canadian criticism that has already made it potentially more political than is usually thought to be the case. In many ways, the need to think about the function of criticism and literature in the context of the nation has meant that criticism in Canada has long had to worry about the construction of the institution of literature and has had to approach literature as more than an autonomous, self-enclosed practice whose relationship and importance to cultural life are self-evident and unquestionable. This is true of the thematic critics' attempt to make sense of the essence of the Canadian identity as expressed through literature, as much as it is of Lecker's attempt to challenge the supposed hegemony of the particular "national-referential aesthetic" that thematic criticism embodied.

Of course, the centrality of the nation in Canadian criticism has also proved to be parochial and has tended to reinforce a notion of the national literatures as "natural kinds" in a way that has placed limits on effective criticism. While an overly simplistic connection between literature and nation of the kind expressed especially by nineteenth-century critics[76] can be limiting, it should be recognized that it can also be productive; since the category of national literatures has not proved to be very easy to abolish, it is the potentially productive aspects of such a category that may prove important to examine and use. Critics who have chosen to reevaluate thematic criticism, such as T. D. MacLulich, have begun, perhaps without even realizing it, to do just this. MacLulich claims that "Canadian literature is inevitably a subject in which political and literary considerations overlap";[77] removed from their social context, "hybrid literary-political categories such as Canadian literature become meaningless,"[78] that is to say that the contexts that enable the production and circulation of texts necessarily arise in any meaningful study of Canadian literature. While I do not wish to claim an alliance with MacLulich's own particular brand of literary nationalism and while I have my own theoretical reservations about the possibility of locating and identifying the influence of "context" on the text (a procedure that can quickly deteriorate into the most reductive forms of biographical or sociological criticism), what MacLulich identifies in the hybrid category of "Canadian literature" is a dialectic in which each term works continuously to undo the presumptions of the other. That this literature is "Canadian" raises the question of how literature might, or indeed must, be understood as related to broader nonliterary social and political forces, since it is only there that the meaning of "Canadian" can be established, however provisionally. Asking this question also means that one must become aware of the fact that literature is itself constituted within the circuits of ideological operations of which the belief in the ahistorical autonomy of the literary is itself one of the chief and most powerful examples. At the same time, the inevitable lack of identity between works of literature and the national identities that they are supposed to express or participate in reveals the "Canadian" itself to be an ideological construct of some considerable power, even at a time when the influence of the nation is supposed to be on the wane. The fluidity and malleability of "Canada" has, for example, continually produced a sense of the nation that is able repeatedly to mask, under the sign of the "good, caring nation," all sorts of historical and social travesties, such as the unprecedented concentration of wealth and power in a very few hands, the degree to which Canadian society is beset by racism, and the repressive aspects of the state apparatus revealed in the response to the antiglobalization demonstrations in Windsor and Québec City.

The inevitability of having to return continually to the nation in the case of a peripheral country such as Canada rests on the fact that it is only some concept of the nation that enables a sense of national-cultural difference that can potentially be read as a political difference. The sense that it is archaic, pointless, or ideologically suspect to define and defend national characteristics may be theoretically sound. The alternative, however, which is one form or another of internationalism or cosmopolitanism (which now goes by the name of globalization), has a tendency to shelve political struggle (such as the struggle for national sovereignty) and, perhaps unintentionally, to legitimate mass media and cultural imperialism by tacit acceptance. This is a point that has been repeatedly made in other national contexts throughout this century by thinkers as various as Sun Yat-Sen, Fanon, and, more recently, by the Brazilian cultural critic Roberto Schwarz. One solution might be to think of the nation as a potential space for political activity, while at the same time unthinking the unitary vision of the *polis* that it has often implied. This solution has become well recognized, I think, by a number of critics of Canadian literature, who have formulated a similar dialectic with respect to the nation. Lecker himself writes that "the problem today is how to write literary criticism that is postnational and national" (MR 6). With respect to postcolonial criticism, Diana Brydon argues that "the goal throughout is a commitment to establishing and sustaining difference: the differences that make Canada Canada, and the differences that continue to challenge the national formation of an immigrant, capitalist culture."[79] In the work of Neil ten Korteenar, this dialectic takes a new form in which the terms of this postcolonial confrontation with the nation is itself seen as "nationalist in inspiration."[80] This is a claim that can only renew the critical encounter of criticism with the nation. It is perhaps here, in a continual, unending dialectic of literature and the nation, that there remains a politics in the literary critical study of Canadian texts: a politics of the nation and of a place for difference that might distinguish Canada from all other places on the globe.

The sense that the nation might be a positive feature within Canadian literary criticism has, however, to be tempered by the problems that arise in Lecker's "Privacy, Publicity and the Discourse of Canadian Criticism." One of the flaws in Lecker's account of the industrialization of Canadian criticism is that it overestimates the importance of literature in defining the soul of the contemporary Canadian nation; it also offers too limited an analysis of the forces that created a "private" literary criticism in Canada. Lecker's analysis is one-sided. He sees the problems of Canadian criticism originating entirely within the realm of the literary-critical field itself, which means that solutions to the problem — making criticism *and* literature more public — are also expected to be found within the field. For Lecker, it simply comes down to a matter of choice: critics need to become nationalists anew in order to maintain the possibility of a Canadian nation.

Lecker believes that literature can resist the spread of Americanized popular culture into every crevice of Canadian culture. It seems that it is literature alone that is imagined as able to prevent the Canadian community from being stripped of its particularistic charms — whatever these might be. What Lecker seems to be unwilling to admit is that the industrialization of Canadian literature is less a disease than a symptom of a larger "illness" that has already thoroughly lodged itself in the body of the Canadian nation. This is, of course, the "contamination" of the Canadian nation by modernity that Grant and Frye viewed as a fait d'accompli by the time that nationalist criticism began its life in Canada. In part because the professional interests of the literary-critical field in Canada (the study of a specifically Canadian national literature) intersected with a broader set of political and social concerns — the threat of Americanization, the institution of state-sponsored programs of cultural nationalism — thematic criticism seemed content to misread or ignore warnings about the "belatedness" of Canadian nationalism. The professionalization of Canadian criticism since the 1950s should be seen as an index of how a certain notion of the Canadian public, and of the relevance of literature to the definition of the essence of this public, has shifted and changed in such a way that no shift in the practices of Canadian criticism can hope to redress this separation of the public and literature. Another way of putting this is to remember what it was for Grant and Frye that would be a sufficient difference to make a difference in the definition of the Canadian nation. For Grant, this was a substantively different way of life, bolstered by a set of original and intellectually distinct social and political institutions; for Frye the appearance of a unique literary *form*. There seems to be nothing in the character of Canadian literary criticism, either in its understanding of literature, the relationship of literature to the nation, or the character of the nation itself, that seems to suggest it has found what Grant and Frye were looking for. And so its hope for the nation relies on a division that we can now see as fundamental in the literature of the postcolonial situations that I have looked at here: in the absence of a unique national language, literature becomes the spiritual refuge of a nation under constant threat from modernity. Or more precisely, since in Canada literature refused to undertake this particularizing function, the nation's soul had to be safeguarded *and* produced by literary criticism itself.

National Culture and Globalization

In this book I have focused on the different ways in which the notion of the nation has been taken up as an issue for literary production in three postcolonial situations. I argued that the literature and criticism of the period most commonly associated with an explicit nationalism in the projects of political and literary decolonization are both more complex and forward-looking than they are usually thought to be. Literary histories that see the engagement of postcolonial texts with the nation as the expression of a problematic or crude (if perhaps inevitable) politics have not paid sufficient attention to the ways in which the nation names the particular political circumstances of the (post)colonies after World War II: not the problem of how to create a nation-*state*, but the more abstract one of how to create genuine collectivities in the midst of modernity and the developing conditions of what we now refer to as globalization. The literary and intellectual discourses of this period have further to figure out how to address this problem within the framework of an array of paradoxical and often contradictory discourses: those of antiimperialism and imperialism, nativism and modernity, and the possibilities and problems of the nation and national culture, all of which can neither be avoided nor fully embraced. I focused on one axis along which these problems have been taken up: the way in which literature and literary discourses tried to make sense of this discursive and political zone of instability. The writers that I have focused on in this study understand both the problems and possibilities of thinking the nation in the context of these multiple discourses; they also understand, in a way we seem at times to have forgotten, that the writing of literature complicates these issues as much as it clarifies them.

It might seem as if this book introduces another zone of instability — one introduced by the project of the book itself. Even given my articulation of the links between the regions and moments that I've placed side by side at the outset, the ways in which literature articulates the nation (and vice-versa) and the ideologies of literature and nation intersect and connect in these different postcolonial moments may still appear too different to sustain the comparison I have endeavored to make. It's not only the presence of Canada that disturbs the homologies that a comparative project of this kind looks for in disparate national, cultural, and historical circumstances: even Nigeria and the West Indies, connected in so many ways, do not exhibit strict similarities in the ways that literature and the nation intersect in the decades following World War II. Nevertheless, it is Canada that seems most out of place in this triad. Indeed, my own analysis suggests this, since in the chapter on Canada I focus on criticism rather than literature as the site at which discourses of the nation were most prominently articulated. If Canada is postcolonial, it is necessarily so in a very different way from either Nigeria or the Caribbean, a fact that a study like this one has to account for and be clear about; the label "postcolonial" does not do this work all on its own.

I hope that I have been clear in locating and identifying these differences, just as I hope that the reasons for considering these three regions together are apparent. Diana Brydon has argued that "withholding the status of 'authentic' colonialism from countries such as Canada . . . makes it harder for all Canadians to identify and combat the particular kinds of postcolonial experience they are currently undergoing as they watch their economy shrink, jobs disappear, and cultural sovereignty erode."[1] Part of my aim in looking at these particular zones of instability is to offer a slightly different map of the postcolonial that frames the historical, political, and cultural experiences of diverse spaces on the globe against a larger, globally connected set of forces that, in one way or another, produce these experiences *and* their difference from one another. In some respects, it seems absurd to claim the status of postcolonial for a country like Canada. Yet at the same time, as Brydon points out, not doing so can produce a misleading sense of the relationship of different spaces and forces to one another. Canada may belong to the G8 and get high marks on the United Nations Human Development Index. In terms of both its economic and cultural history and its colonial experience, it nevertheless shares a good deal more with the (British) Caribbean than with some of its partners in the G8 such as Germany and France, who have grumbled recently about Canada's membership in this exclusive club as its economy slips out of the ranks of the top ten (as measured in terms of GDP). If we were to rely exclusively on OECD statistics as a guide to the connections that we could legitimately make between different regions of the globe, there is a great deal that we would miss. It is only a crude materialism that would believe the economic to be determinant in this way.

I have explored the way in which, in these three very different places, the general logic linking the nation and literature is remarkably similar, due in part to similarities in the way in which these spaces have been interpellated into the global political-economic system over the past two centuries. In each case, the problem of creating a nation and national cultural in and through literature manifests itself with particular force in the limits and possibilities of intellectual activity. An examination of each situation exhibits no precise homologies between them, but reveals provocative connective strands, both theoretical and empirical. I hope the lack of an overall defining logic (which would produce precise connections rather than broad interconnections) is seen as a virtue of this study rather than a vice. In trying to establish general laws or some larger governing logic out of the consideration of individual cases, the temptation is to locate the cause of everything that happens in each case within a larger metanarrative. The gesture that I want to make here is different from this. My analysis of the recent prehistory of our present moment is meant to help us understand better our own attempts to make sense of the problematic first named in these zones of instability: that of the fate of national cultures (revered and reviled at the same time and for good reason) and of the idea of the nation more generally in the era of globalization, and also the problems and possibilities that literature and criticism face in gauging and making sense of this fate.

It is clear that in many ways we now occupy a very different space (or different spaces) from the ones that I explore here. Provocatively, Fredric Jameson has suggested that recent historical events affirm "the failure and death, not of communism, but rather precisely of federalism as such (the USSR, Yugoslavia, even Canada)."[2] With few exceptions (Australia, Canada, India, and South Africa, for instance), federalisms of the kind that I have been looking at are no longer topics of discussion for politicians or political scientists. In the 1950s and 1960s, the federal model was championed as the political form best able to contain regional and ethnic tensions and conflicts. Yet the recent decomposition of nations into their component parts has been characterized almost exclusively as the reassertion of ethnic and racial identities against the traumas experienced within the confines of the nation-state and *not* as the end of one particular form of nationalism whose decline needs to be better understood: the federation. The global reappearance of the vocabulary of blood and belonging has been seen in part as a series of local reactions to globalization: the reassertion of difference, particularity and identity against the universality of global modernity. But the decomposition of the nation or federation can be read in another way as well. The absence of "intermediary" forms between the local and global has led to the wholesale disappearance of the public sphere: the larger forms of organization available to localities today are no longer primarily political in character, but take the form of agreements (GATT, WTO, NAFTA, etc.) between sovereignties that understand themselves as economic units. Nations relate to one another today as businesses rather than polities, which is another reason why claims about the death of the nation should be understood as ideological rather than empirical statements about the state of the world.

But there is another, even more fundamental way in which things are different now. For those whose profession it is to examine cultural products or even whole cultures (from literary critics to anthropologists), the challenge posed by globalization is that new approaches must be taken and new discourses devised to explain the present. Everything is suddenly up for grabs, open to doubt, in need of revision. It *is* no longer possible to imagine the world as a collection of autonomous, monadic spaces, whether these are imagined as nations, regions within nations, or cultures demarcated by region or nation. Yet it is just this sense of space and, in particular, the intimate relationship of culture and cultural objects to definite, determinate spaces that continues to be presumed in the disciplinary tasks of most of the humanities and social sciences: literary studies are still divided into national specialties; area studies continue to dominate the social sciences; and even cultural studies as a field begins not with a rejection of the nation as an appropriate "field" of study (think of the national cultural histories written by E. P. Thompson, Raymond Williams, and Richard Hoggart)[3] but with a complication of the national field through the introduction of the serious study of popular and mass culture. If culture has for a long time been understood as "the particularizing, localizing force that distinguished societies and people from one another,"[4] globalization has thus forced us to think of a different space for culture — to think of culture as "deterritorialized,"[5] or as something that is not merely "local" "national" or "regional," but which is also already global.[6]

This is one of the reasons why comparative projects like this one are essential. But having said this, it is also important to realize that to think about culture in a world that has been "globalized" is a difficult, complex task, that is full of ideological traps and pitfalls. While it is easy to produce abstract models for culture that emphasize the new translocality or deterritorialization of culture, it is much harder to actually make sense of the complicated ways in which culture is produced at the intersection of a variety of "global" and "local" forces, as well as the way in which culture is constantly being both deterritorialized and reterritorialized. One of the dangers of focusing on globalization as it is either represented in or produced by various cultural objects such as literature, film, music, television programs, and so on, is that it is all too easy to substitute models of global cultural space for the reality of global culture. The existence of all sorts of hybrid cultural forms that we in the West, and particularly in the Western academy, now have access to, from postcolonial literature to fusion music and cuisine to global cinema, along with a transformed global economic system that has become "global" in a different way from what it has been even in the recent past, seems to validate the thesis of a massive transformation of cultural space, its liquidation into flows that intersect unpredictably to produce new cultural forms and identities. If this sense of cultural deterritorialization is intended at least in part to replace a simpler version of cultural imperialism in which resistance to hegemonic cultural forms was futile, it is important not to err too far on the other side as well, seeing resistance in so many locations that it is hard to understand why the world isn't already fundamentally different from what it in fact is.

And this is why it still remains important to think about the nation in literary studies. For even while it might now seem as if postcolonial literature circulates within a very different set of sociohistorical coordinates from those that Fredric Jameson outlines in "Third-World Literature," the nation continues to remain an ineliminable structural presence within the contemporary "cultural pattern." Far from rendering national allegory useless, globalization makes it an increasingly important interpretive mode or problematic; this is no doubt why, seemingly counterintuitively, the nation has become more and more prominent in Jameson's own attempts to make sense of the phenomena associated with globalization.

As everyone knows, the nation has been one of the main sites of struggle in globalization — whether globalization is understood as the name for a set of real, empirical processes that characterize variously the cultural, social, and economic dimensions of contemporary capitalism or as the name for a number of competing narratives about the evolving shape of the contemporary political landscape and of the character of any future polity.[7] It has been frequently suggested that globalization has rendered the nation-state irrelevant, because (for instance) the nation no longer seems to retain any juridical power or control over capital or labor, both of which cross borders and evade state surveillance with increasing ease (though far more so in the case of capital and its associated modes of credit, finance, etc., than in the case of the physical bodies of individual laborers). Then there is the (more or less) antithetical position, which holds that the decline of the nation and nation-state has been much exaggerated. Not only are most companies "tethered to their home economies and are likely to remain so," but also the actions of sovereign nation-states alone have produced new forms of sovereignty through international regulatory mechanisms like the GATT and NAFTA and nation-states have ensured compliance with the global operations of the market at a national level.[8] More recently, commentators have wanted to suggest that neither of these two poles adequately makes sense of the complex, heterogeneous position of the nation-state within globalization. This is, in part, as Jean and John Comaroff point out, because "there is no such thing, save at very high levels of abstraction, as '*the* nation-state'": in many polities, either the "nation" or the "state" doesn't exist as such, while in other places there exists a deep fissure between state and government that makes it impossible to speak of anything that approaches typical ideas about what a functioning nation-state looks like.[9] Put differently, "the processes by which millennial capitalism is taking shape do not reduce to a simple narrative according to which the nation-state either lives or dies, ebbs or flourishes. Its impact is much more complicated, more polyphonous and dispersed, and most immediately felt in the everyday contexts of work and labor, of domesticity and consumption, of street life and media-gazing."[10]

Whether it has died or still lives, the nation-state has long represented the specifically modernist political project of creating citizen-subjects defined through their attachment to national identities. Connected to this project (which on its own is easy to be suspicious of) is a whole history of left political engagement that has made effective use (or so the story goes) of this historical compromise between capital and labor to bring about the social gains associated with left activism over the past one hundred and fifty years or so. Whether or not the powers of the nation-state have declined over the past several decades, the nation as such is frequently evoked or imagined as the only possible site of progressive politics (due largely, it seems, to its scale) and thus as something that should be fought for in order to maintain or preserve the political project of the left.[11] This desire for the possibilities (incorrectly) associated with the nation-state cannot help but be confused with more empirical analyses of its function within globalization, which is perhaps why the defense of the nation continues to be associated with a left that in the past sought to distance itself from nationalism.[12] Against this position, Michael Hardt and Antonio Negri have strongly asserted that "it is a grave mistake to harbor any nostalgia for the powers of the nation-state or to resurrect any politics that celebrates the nation."[13] For them, the relative decline of the sovereignty of the nation-state is the result of a historical, structural process — the globalization of production and circulation, backed up by those supraterritorial agreements that have incurred the wrath of antiglobalization protestors — and is not "simply the result of an ideological position that might be reversed by an act of political will." They also point out that "even if the nation were still to be an effective weapon, the nation carries with it a whole series of repressive structures and ideologies" of which a properly left politics should be appropriately wary.[14] Too simple demands concerning the political or conceptual necessity of the nation or of the nation-state need to be treated with proper caution, or need to be seen as a potentially debilitating form of nostalgia for political possibilities that no longer exist.

It is possible to mistake Jameson's recent interest in the nation as little more than nostalgia for a modernist form of politics (a politics that believes in the citizen rather than the consumer) in very much the same way that some critics have taken his interest in the third (or indeed, the second) world as a search for an Other to a capitalism that "has no social goals."[15] A cursory reading of either of Jameson's most explicit attempts to theorize globalization does little to dispel this impression. In "Notes on Globalization as a Philosophical Issue," he laments the "tendential extinction of new national cultural and artistic production" that is the consequence of the domination of the global cultural industries by the United States and endorses state support of culture in places like France and Canada.[16] He also makes the claim that in the first world the powers of the state "are what must be protected against the right-wing attempts to dissolve it back into private businesses and operations of all kinds," a point he reaffirms in "Globalization and Political Strategy," where he states outright that "the nation-state today remains the only concrete terrain and framework for political struggle," even though the struggle against globalization "cannot be successfully prosecuted to a conclusion in completely national or nationalist terms."[17]

While this might seem to be an affirmation of the kind of view of the nation that Hardt and Negri warn against, in the context of Jameson's supple examination of the contradictions and antinomies of globalization a different reason for foregrounding the nation emerges that is of a piece with its presence in his discussion of third-world literature. In both of his recent articles on globalization, Jameson tries to gauge the significance of the global export of American mass culture (through its intersection with the economic, social, and technological) in order to understand what it might mean to try to oppose or to resist its spread around the world. This is, of course, an expression of the cultural imperialist thesis in a nutshell: an understanding of globalization that, while still predominant in the cultural imagination of academics and the general public alike, has been criticized as misunderstanding the contemporary operations of culture and power.[18] But while on the surface Jameson seems merely to express a Western academic's worries about the disappearance of traditional ways of life, the reappearance of the nation as a conceptual concern complicates our desire to see globalization as something to be either lamented or celebrated. For instance, what Jameson finds disturbing about the global triumph of American cinema is that it marks "the death of the political, and an allegory of the end of the possibility of imagining radically different social alternatives to this one we now live under. For political film in the 1960s and 1970s still affirmed that possibility (as did modernism in general, in a more complex way), by affirming that the discovery or invention of a radically new form was at one with the discovery or invention of radically new social relations and ways of living in the world. It is those possibilities — filmic, formal, political, and social — that have disappeared as some more definitive hegemony of the United States has seemed to emerge."[19] This demand for the persistence of other modes of national culture has little to do with the nation as such. It isn't the case, for example, that Jameson lauds French film because it is formally or thematically richer than American film, either due to its relationship to some purer national essence (say, summer misadventures in the provinces as an adolescent, an apparently inescapable theme for French filmmakers) or because it is produced outside of the strict demands of the market (as a result of state subsidies). Rather, in our present political and cultural circumstances, the nation names for Jameson the possibility of new social relations and forms of collectivity not just "other" to neoliberal globalization, but the possibility of imagining these kinds of relations at all. Such forms of collectivity are not to be found in some actual national space: "today no enclaves — aesthetic or other — are left in which the commodity form does not reign supreme."[20] Rather, the nation is now part of the new problem of contemporary cultural revolution, a part of the problematic of globalization than one cannot avoid even if one shares Hardt and Negri's suspicions about the politics of actually existing nation-states; it once again names a reified "cultural pattern," though with different valences and different connections to other concepts and problems than before.

The nation stands for three things in Jameson's recent reflections on globalization. It identifies, first, the possibility of other modes of social life that are organized in strikingly different ways from the American-led "culture-ideology of consumption." Other "national situations" offer models of different forms of collective and social life — not, it is important to add, in the form of "traditional" or "prelapsarian" modes of social being, but in the form of "rather recent and successful accommodations of the old institutions to modern technology."[21] Second, the nation is the name for a frankly utopic space that designates "whatever programmes and representations express, in however distorted or unconscious a fashion, the demands of a collective life to come, and identify social collectivity as the crucial centre of any truly progressive and innovative political response to globalization."[22] These words at the end of "Globalization and Political Strategy" are actually meant to define the word "utopian" rather than the nation. The link between the two terms is made possible in a note that appears a few pages earlier, where Jameson claims that "the words 'nationalism' and 'nationalist' have always been ambiguous, misleading, perhaps even dangerous. The positive or 'good' nationalism I have in mind involves what Henri Lefebvre liked to call 'the great collective project,' and takes the form of the attempt to construct a nation."[23]

Finally, Jameson discusses the nation not in order to settle the case either for or against globalization — rejecting, for instance, the false universality of the "American way of life" in favor of one of so many other (rapidly evaporating) national models, which themselves have never yet yielded positive social alternatives — "but rather to intensify their incompatibility and opposition such that we can live this particular contradiction as our own historic form of Hegel's unhappy consciousness."[24] If "Globalization and Political Strategy" ends with a discussion of utopia, "Notes on Globalization" ends with a discussion of the necessity of the dialectic, and of the Hegelian dialectic in particular. The aim of the dialectic is to understand phenomena in order, finally, to locate the contradictions behind them: in Hegel's *Logic*, the discovery of the Identity of identity and nonidentity that reveals Opposition as Contradiction. But this is not the final moment. "Contradiction then passes over into its Ground, into what I would call the situation itself, the aerial view or the map of the totality in which things happen and History takes place."[25] Such a map of the moment when the nation is thought to have been superseded once and for all can only be produced if the nation, the Ground of an earlier moment, is put into play in the dialectic rather than suspended from the outset.

And here we find that we have looped back around to Jameson's discussion of the ineliminable horizon of those objective "cultural patterns" that third-world writers have to confront just as much as first-world critics. Which is a long way of saying that far from obliterating the Marxian problematic, especially with respect to the contemporary use and abuse of culture, globalization makes it more important than ever.

Notes

Introduction

Epigraphs: José Martí, *On Art and Literature: Critical Writings*, ed. Philip S. Foner (New York: Monthly Review Press, 1982), 306. Paul Ricoeur, "Civilization and National Cultures," in *History and Truth*, trans. Charles A. Kelbley (Evanston, IL: Northwestern University Press, 1965), 276–77.

1. See especially Bill Ashcroft, Gareth Griffiths, and Helen Tiffin, *The Empire Writes Back: Theory and Practice in Post-colonial Literatures* (New York: Routledge, 1989), who suggest that significant continuities exist not only between the literatures of "settler" colonies such as Canada, New Zealand, and Australia, the British colonies in Asia, Africa, and the Caribbean, and more difficult cases such as Ireland and South Africa, but also between all of these and nineteenth-century American literature (pp. 16, 19–20). The *Encyclopedia of Postcolonial Literatures in English*, ed. Eugene Benson and L. W. Conolly (New York: Routledge, 1994), also implies such continuities in its ascription of the term "postcolonial" to *all* English literature written outside of the United States and Great Britain — with the exception of literature written by minority or immigrant writers *within* these two countries, which is also considered to be postcolonial.

It needs to be mentioned, of course, that there is also a great deal of resistance to such attempts to produce one, unvariegated body of postcolonial texts. See, for example, Arun Mukherjee, "Whose Postcolonialism and Whose Post-modernism?" *World Literature Written in English* 30, no. 2 (1990): 1–9; and Patrick Williams and Laura Chrisman, eds., *Colonial Discourse and Postcolonial Theory* (New York: Columbia University Press, 1994), who in their introduction express doubts about the utility of describing the settler colonies as "postcolonial."

2. "The concerns of the new national literatures are related to the problems of modern western culture . . . although writers from each nation will respond according to their own perspectives, modern means of communication, travel and the effect of industrialization, urbanization and western education on most societies result in similar problems"; Bruce King, *New National Literatures: Cultural Nationalism in a Changing World* (New York: St. Martin's Press, 1980), xi.

3. This issue is addressed, for example, by a number of the essays included in Majorie Garber, Paul B. Franklin and Rebecca L. Walkowitz, eds., *Field Work: Sites in Literary and Cultural Studies* (New York: Routledge, 1996), especially the contributions by Mary Malcolm Gaylord, Judith Ryan, and Stephen Owen; and in *South Atlantic Quarterly* 100, no. 3 (2001), special issue on "Anglophone Literature and Global Culture," ed. Susie O'Brien and Imre Szeman.

4. Paik Nak-chung, "Nations and Literatures in the Age of Globalization," in *The Cultures of Globalization*, ed. Fredric Jameson and Masao Miyoshi (Durham, NC: Duke University Press, 1998), 221, 220.

5. See, for example, Homi Bhabha, *The Location of Culture* (New York: Routledge, 1994); Jon Bird, ed., *Local Culture, Global Change* (New York: Routledge, 1993); James Duncan and David Ley, eds., *Place/Culture/Representation* (New York: Routledge, 1993); David Harvey, *The Condition of Postmodernity* (Cambridge, MA: Basil Blackwell, 1989); Fredric Jameson, *Postmodernism, or, The Cultural Logic of Late Capitalism* (Durham, NC: Duke University Press, 1991); Michael Keith and Steve Pile, eds., *Place and the Politics of Identity* (New York: Routledge, 1993); and Edward Soja, *Postmodern Geographies* (London: Verso, 1989) and *Thirdspace: Journeys to Los Angeles and Other Real-and-Imagined Places* (Cambridge, MA: Basil Blackwell, 1996).

6. Among other works by these authors, see Marshall Berman, *All That Is Solid Melts into Air: The Experience of Modernity* (New York: Simon & Schuster, 1982); Cornelius Castoriadis, *The Imaginary Institution of Society*, trans. Kathleen Blamey (Cambridge: Polity Press, 1987); Michel de Certeau, *The Practice of Everyday Life*, trans. Steven Rendall (Berkeley: University of California Press, 1984); and Jürgen Habermas, *The Philosophical Discourse of Modernity*, trans. Frederick G. Lawrence (Cambridge, MA: MIT Press, 1987).

7. Marc Augé, *Non-Places: An Introduction to an Anthropology of Supermodernity*, trans. John Howe (New York: Verso, 1995).

8. Benedict Anderson, *Imagined Communities* (New York: Verso, 1991), 26. Whether this analogical relationship between the novel and the nation is one that exists in Canada, the Caribbean, and Nigeria in much the same way as in those areas Anderson examines (Europe, Asia, and South America) is one of the issues addressed in Chapter One.

9. As just one of numerous examples, see Paul Carter's discussion of the problems of nomenclature faced by early Australian writers in their attempt to describe the Australian landscape, in *The Road to Botany Bay: An Essay in Spatial History* (Boston: Faber, 1987).

10. Derek Gregory, *Geographical Imaginations* (Cambridge, MA: Basil Blackwell, 1994), 381.

11. Edward W. Said, "Yeats and Decolonization," in Terry Eagleton, Fredric Jameson, and Edward W. Said, *Nationalism, Colonialism, and Literature* (Minneapolis: University of Minnesota Press, 1990), 69–95.

12. Ibid., 76, 77.

13. Frantz Fanon, *The Wretched of the Earth*, trans. Constance Farrington (New York: Grove Press, 1968), 222–23.

14. Said, "Yeats and Decolonization," 77.

15. Ibid., 76.

16. Fanon, *The Wretched of the Earth*, 148–205.

17. Neil Smith, *Uneven Development: Nature, Capital, and the Production of Space* (Oxford: Basil Blackwell, 1984), 146.

18. See Eric Hobsbawm's suggestion that in the late twentieth century, the nation "is no longer a major vector of historical development"; Hobsbawm, *Nations and Nationalism since 1870* (Cambridge: Cambridge University Press, 1990), 163. Michael Hardt and Antonio Negri have also strongly asserted that "it is a grave mistake to harbor any nostalgia for the powers of the nation-state or to resurrect any politics that celebrates the nation"; Hardt and Negri, *Empire* (Cambridge: Harvard University Press, 2000), 336. In an age dominated by multinational corporations and telecommunications, it is nevertheless im-

portant to retain a sense of skepticism about claims that the nation has reached its end. As Timothy Brennan asks, "can't it be said that the recoiling from nationalism is also partly due to the challenge of the rising national movements of the developing world?" See "The National Longing for Form," in *Nation and Narration*, ed. Homi K. Bhabha (New York: Routledge, 1990), 57.

19. Said, "Yeats and Decolonization," 78.

20. Ibid., 79.

21. Fredric Jameson, "Modernism and Imperialism," in *Nationalism, Colonialism, and Literature* (Minneapolis: University of Minnesota Press, 1990), 64.

22. Ibid., 51.

23. Ibid., 60.

24. Ibid.

25. Ibid., 59.

26. For an exploration of the formal links between British and African modernism, see Nicholas M. Brown, *Narratives of Utopia Inchoate: African and British Modernism* (Ph.D. diss., Duke University, October 1999).

27. Benedict Anderson, *Imagined Communities* (New York: Verso, 1991); Ernest Gellner, *Nations and Nationalisms* (Oxford: Oxford University Press, 1983); Eric Hobsbawm, *Nations and Nationalism since 1870* (Cambridge: Cambridge University Press, 1990); and Anthony D. Smith, *The Ethnic Origin of Nations* (New York: Basil Blackwell, 1986).

28. This is the opposite of Hobsbawm's use of the term "negative," when he writes that "the characteristic nationalist movements of the late twentieth century are essentially negative, or rather divisive. Hence the insistence on 'ethnicity' and linguistic differences, each or both sometimes combined with religion"; Eric Hobsbawm, *Nations and Nationalism since 1870* (Cambridge: Cambridge University Press, 1990), 164.

29. Peter Worsley, *The Three Worlds: Culture and World Development* (Chicago: University of Chicago Press, 1984), 22.

30. See Robert Lecker, "The New Canadian Library: A Classic Deal," in *Making It Real* (Concord, ON: House of Anansi Press, 1995), 154–73.

31. Early essays by Achebe, Soyinka, and Lamming, Wilson Harris's extensive body of critical writing, and the work of numerous Canadian writers such as Margaret Atwood, Robert Kroetsch, and Dennis Lee, have all been instrumental in establishing the field of postcolonial theory. More accurately, these earlier writings have been in recent years retrospectively assembled and presented as the "historical past" out of which contemporary postcolonial theory developed. As with all histories, there is an ideological element here that cannot be avoided, an assertion — in the terms of Michel Foucault's distinction between "History" and "genealogy" — of the logics of "origin" instead of the more critical attempt to keep "passing events in their proper dispersion." I am not denying, for example, that Achebe's work on Conrad may have had a decisive impact on Edward Said's work. Yet so has the work of Michel Foucault — but it is Achebe and not Foucault that one will find included in postcolonial theory readers.

For the discussion of the distinction that I invoke here, see Michel Foucault, "Nietzsche, Genealogy, History," in *Language, Counter-Memory, Practice*, ed. Donald F. Bouchard, trans. Donald F. Bouchard and Sherry Simon (Ithaca, NY: Cornell University Press, 1977), 139–64.

32. Kalpana Seshadri-Crooks has spoken recently of a "malaise" that has beset postcolonial criticism as it has become a fixture in the Western academy. See Seshadri-Crooks,

"At the Margins of Postcolonial Studies: Part 1," in *The Pre-Occupation of Postcolonial Studies*, ed. Fawzia Afzal-Khan and Kalpana Seshadri-Crooks (Durham, NC: Duke University Press, 2000), 3–23. The institutionalization of postcolonial criticism can be seen in the almost simultaneous publication of a number of volumes dedicated to making sense of the overall "logic" of the field. See Bill Ashcroft, Gareth Griffiths, and Helen Tiffin, *Key Concepts in Postcolonial Studies* (New York: Routledge, 1998); Ania Loomba, *Colonialism/ Postcolonialism* (New York: Routledge, 1998); Leela Gandhi, *Postcolonial Theory* (New York: Columbia University Press, 1998); and Bart Moore-Gilbert, *Postcolonial Theory: Contexts, Practices, Politics* (New York: Verso, 1997).

33. The term "culturalism" as coined by Arif Dirlik. See Arif Dirlik, "The Postcolonial Aura: Third World Criticism in the Age of Global Capitalism" and Aijaz Ahmad, "The Politics of Literary Postcoloniality," in *Contemporary Postcolonial Theory: A Reader*, ed. Padmini Mongia (New York: Arnold, 1996), 276–93 and 294–321, respectively.

34. For a different genealogy of the postcolonial, see Timothy Brennan, "Meanwhile, in the Hallways," in *Class Issues: Pedagogy, Cultural Studies, and the Public Sphere*, ed. Amitava Kumar (New York: New York University Press, 1997), 221–36.

35. Pierre Bourdieu, *Distinction: A Social Critique of the Judgment of Taste*, trans. Richard Nice (Cambridge, MA: Harvard University Press, 1984).

36. See Peter Bürger, *Theory of the Avant-Garde*, trans. Michael Shaw (Minneapolis: University of Minnesota Press, 1984).

37. Timothy Brennan, *Salman Rushdie and the Third World* (Houndmills, England: Macmillan, 1989), 56.

CHAPTER ONE: The Nation as Problem and Possibility

Epigraphs: Theodor Adorno, "On the Question: 'What is German?'" *Critical Models: Interventions and Catchwords*, trans. Henry W. Pickford (New York: Columbia University Press, 1998), 205. Pierre Elliot Trudeau, *Federalism and the French Canadians* (New York: St. Martins's Press, 1968), 151.

1. There are theories of the nation that trace its roots to a far earlier period in human history, for example, to the Greek city-states. In *The Idea of Nationalism*, for example, Kohn begins his investigation of the origins of the nation in "ancient Judea and Hellas" (27). Even so, Kohn clearly believes that "nationalism as we understand it is not older than the second half of the eighteenth century" (3). This is a definitional point that is shared by most recent theorists of the nation. For Kohn, Herder's addition to the language of nationalism was to substitute "for the legal and rational concept of 'citizenship' the infinitely vaguer concept of 'folk' . . . it lent itself more easily to the embroideries of imagination and the excitations of emotion" (331). See Kohn, *The Idea of Nationalism: A Study in Its Origins and Background* (New York: Macmillan, 1946). In this respect, Herder's contribution was essential, opening the door for appeals to ethnicity and primordialist claims that the language of citizenship alone does not seem to permit.

2. Johann Gottfried Herder, *Outlines of the History of Man*, trans. T. Churchill (London: Johnson, 1800), 166.

3. On the oft-misperceived social and political commitments of Romanticism, see Raymond Williams, "The Romantic Artist," in *Culture and Society, 1780–1950* (New York: Columbia University Press, 1983). The most compelling recent analysis and assessment of the development of culture and the nation-state from the late eighteenth to the late

nineteenth century is found in David Lloyd and Paul Thomas, *Culture and the State* (New York: Routledge, 1998).

4. On the latter, see, for instance, Eugene Weber, *Peasants into Frenchmen: The Modernization of Rural France, 1870–1914* (Stanford, CA: Stanford University Press, 1976), as well as the work of Michel Foucault on the development of the human sciences, as exemplified by *Discipline and Punish: The Birth of the Prison*, trans. Alan Sheridan (New York: Pantheon, 1977).

5. See Hippolyte Adolphe Taine, *History of English Literature*, trans. H. Van Laun (New York: F. Ungar, 1965).

6. Henry Morley cited in Christopher Clausen, " 'National Literatures' in English: Toward a New Paradigm," *New Literary History* 25, no. 1 (Winter 1994): 64.

7. Pattee, in Clausen, " 'National Literatures' in English," 65.

8. For example, see Lauren Berlant, *The Anatomy of National Fantasy: Hawthorne, Utopia, and Everyday Life* (Chicago: University of Chicago Press, 1991); Homi Bhabha, ed., *Nation and Narration* (New York: Routledge, 1990); Anne McClintock, Aamir Mufti, and Ella Shohat, eds., *Dangerous Liaisons: Gender, Nations, and Postcolonial Perspectives* (Minneapolis: University of Minnesota Press, 1997); and Doris Sommer, *Foundational Fictions: The National Romances of Latin America* (Berkeley: University of California Press, 1991).

9. The most frequently cited recent texts concerning the nation remain those of Benedict Anderson, Ernst Gellner, Eric Hobsbawm, and Anthony D. Smith. These works have largely supplanted those written by Hans Kohn and Elie Kedourie a generation earlier. The traumas induced by globalization and by recent nationalist tensions in Africa and the former Soviet bloc have also increased interest in the nation on the part of both academic and popular writers.

10. Anthony D. Smith, *National Identity* (Reno: University of Nevada Press, 1991), 17.

11. As Jean and John L. Comaroff have pointed out, in many polities around the world there is sometimes no state to go along with the nation — or vice-versa. See Jean and John L. Comaroff, "Millennial Capitalism: First Thoughts on a Second Coming," *Public Culture* 12, no. 2 (2000): 291–343.

12. Elleke Boehmer, *Colonial and Postcolonial Literature: Migrant Metaphors* (New York: Oxford University Press, 1995), 180–223.

13. Ibid., 182.

14. This is especially true in the attempt to characterize Latin and South American literature as "post-colonial," since their (formal) colonial status ended much earlier than their counterparts in the British Commonwealth. Ashcroft, Griffiths, and Tiffin have even suggested that "in many ways the American experience and its attempts to produce a new kind of literature can be seen to be the model for all later post-colonial writing"; *The Empire Writes Back: Theory and Practice in Post-colonial Literature* (New York: Routledge, 1989), 16.

15. Properly speaking, there are two common periodizing models that have been conflated. Earlier models, such as those proposed by Fanon and José Carlos Mariátegui *end* with the establishment of a "genuine" national literature after phases of colonial literature and cosmopolitan mimicry. Said and Paul-Marie de la Gorce offer a second model in which this genuine nationalism itself appears as an earlier, mystificatory stage that is ultimately transcended by what Said refers to as "liberation," "a transformation of social consciousness beyond national consciousness"; "Yeats and Decolonization," in Terry Eagleton, Fredric Jameson, and Edward W. Said, *Nationalism, Colonialism, and Liter-*

ature (Minneapolis: University of Minnesota Press, 1990), 83. Said discusses this scheme in further detail in "Resistance and Opposition," *Culture and Imperialism* (New York: Vintage, 1993), 191–281. Barbara Harlow discusses Mariátegui and de la Gorce in *Resistance Literature* (New York: Methuen, 1986), 6–10; Fanon's discussion of the development of literature in the colonies is found in the chapter "On National Culture," in *The Wretched of the Earth*, trans. Constance Farrington (New York: Grove Press, 1968), 206–48.

The sense in which a "postnational" consciousness supersedes a nationalist one is a feature of much recent postcolonial theory. In effect, what has happened is that these two periodizing schemas have been collapsed, so that the freedom that Fanon sought in the nation becomes yet another, perhaps more developed phase of colonial mimicry, with the implication that real liberation can only be found in the *absence* of the nation.

16. This relies on a common assumption in postcolonial theory—however aware it might otherwise be of the continuation of imperialism through various forms of neoimperialism—that the transitional moment from colony to postcolony constitutes some sort of genuine historical break. Fredric Jameson has suggested that "the conception of the Third World 60s as a moment when all over the world chains and shackles of a classical imperialist kind were thrown off in a stirring wave of 'wars of nationalist liberation' is an altogether mythical simplification"; Fredric Jameson, "Periodizing the 60s," in *The Ideologies of Theory* (Minneapolis: University of Minnesota Press, 1988), 2:185. Jameson argues that it is more useful instead to see the 60s as a period characterized by a dialectical combination of decolonization and neocolonialism during which capitalism is in full expansion rather than in retreat. Seen this way, a confusing rhetoric regarding the rise and fall of political hope in the Third World can be dissolved, revealing instead the troubling continuity of problems that have plagued "postcolonial" countries from the colonial period to the present.

17. Boehmer, *Colonial and Postcolonial Literature*, 185.

18. Paul Gilroy, "For the Transcultural Record," in *Trade Routes: History, Geography*, 2d Johannesburg Biennale 1997 (South Africa: Greater Johannesburg Metropolitan Council, 1997), 25.

19. Timothy Brennan, *Salman Rushdie and the Third World* (Houndmills, England: Macmillan, 1989), 18. This claim needs to be off-set with evidence of a simultaneous return to (or, properly, a continuation of) national cultural politics in many parts of the world. Still, it seems to me that these politics are now conducted under a cloud of epistemological "bad faith" as a kind of "strategic" nationalism with the same problems and possibilities as "strategic" feminism.

20. See, for instance, Barbara Harlow's *Resistance Literature*. In almost all of the numerous overviews of postcolonial literature that have recently been written, they continue to be covered in terms of national units. This is reflected as well in Paik Nak-chung's essay, which I discussed in the introduction, and in Geeta Kapur's "Globalisation and Culture." Kapur writes: "Where I speak from there is still ground for debate about the nation-state. With all the calumny it has earned, it may be the only political structure that can protect the people of the Third World from the totalitarian system that oligopolies establish—ironically, through the massive state power of advance nations" (22). Geeta Kapur, "Globalisation and Culture," *Third Text* 39 (Summer 1997): 21–38.

21. See Benjamin R. Barber, *Jihad vs. McWorld: How Globalism and Tribalism Are Reshaping the World* (New York: Ballantine, 1996); Fredric Jameson, "Notes on Globalization

as a Philosophical Issue," in *The Cultures of Globalization*, ed. Fredric Jameson and Masao Miyoshi (Durham, NC: Duke University Press, 1998), 54–77; and Jameson, "Globalization and Political Strategy," *New Left Review* 4 (2000): 49–68.

22. Clausen, " 'National Literatures' in English," 68.

23. Ibid., 69–70.

24. The exception, of course, being the United States. The United States has not been invited to participate in multilateral talks concerning the establishment of a WTO-style organization to protect national cultures from a global monoculture. According to Canadian Heritage Minister Sheila Copps, this is not because of the pre-eminent role of America in the process of global "Americanization," but because the United States is the only nation in the world without a minister or a governmental portfolio dedicated to national cultural development and protection. Suzanne King, "U.S. Not Invited to Copps' Culture Talks," *CBC Infoculture*. June 11, 1998; ⟨http://www.infoculture.cbc.ca/cultpol.html#U STALKS⟩.

25. Richard Collins, "National Culture: A Contradiction in Terms?" *Canadian Journal of Communication* 16 (1991): 225–26.

26. Ibid., 234. Collins suggests that the current surge of separatist sentiment in Québec, as well as among Native groups, represents a failure in *"political* rather than cultural affairs" (234).

27. Appadurai, *Modernity at Large*, 158. This I take to be the aim as well of the collection edited by Bruce Robbins and Pheng Cheah, *Cosmopolitics: Thinking and Feeling Beyond the Nation* (Minneapolis: University of Minnesota Press, 1998).

28. V. I. Lenin, *Imperialism: The Highest Stage of Capitalism* (New York: International Publishers, 1939). On the internationalization of capitalism, see, of course, the "world systems" theory of Immanuel Wallerstein, *The Modern World-System* (New York: Academic Press, 1974); Giovanni Arrighi, *The Long Twentieth Century: Money, Power, and the Origins of Our Times* (New York: Verso, 1994); and Neil Smith, *Uneven Development: Nature, Capital, and the Production of Space* (Cambridge: Blackwell, 1984).

29. Masao Miyoshi, "A Borderless World? From Colonialism to Transnationalism and the Decline of the Nation-State?" in *Global/Local: Cultural Production and the Transnational Imaginary*, ed. Rob Wilson and Wimal Dissanayake (Durham, NC: Duke University Press, 1996), 78–106.

30. On the fictional or discursive character of globalization, see J. K. Graham-Gibson, "Querying Globalization," *Rethinking Marxism* 9 no. 1 (1996–97): 1–27; Arif Dirlik, "Globalization as the End and the Beginning of History," *Rethinking Marxism* 12 no. 4 (Fall 2000); Thomas Peyser, "How Global Is It: Walter Abish and the Fiction of Globalization," *Contemporary Literature* 40 no. 2 (1999): 240–62; and Anna Tsing, "Inside the Economy of Appearances," *Public Culture* 12 no. 1 (Spring 2000): 115–44.

31. Gilroy, "For the Transcultural Record," 26.

32. Anderson, *Imagined Communities*, 3.

33. Régis Debray, "Marxism and the National Question," *New Left Review* 105 (Sept.–Oct. 1977): 26.

34. Henry Giroux, *Fugitive Cultures: Race, Violence, and Youth* (New York: Routledge, 1996), 186. The Brazilian literary critic Roberto Schwarz makes essentially the same point with respect to the discourse of nationalism in Brazil. For Schwarz, nationalism must be seen as "archaic and provincial" (4). Nevertheless, the alternative to nationalism, "an

emphasis on the international dimension" is nothing more than "a legitimation of the existing mass media" (5). Schwarz concludes: "we can see that the imposition of foreign ideology and the cultural expropriation of the people are realities which do not cease to exist just because there is a mystification in the nationalists' theories about them . . . the mass media modernists, though right in their criticisms, imagine a universalist world which does not exist" (5). See Roberto Schwarz, *Misplaced Ideas: Essays on Brazilian Culture*, trans. John Gledson (New York: Verso, 1992).

35. See Stephen Owen, "National Literatures in a Global World? — Sometimes — Maybe," *Field Work: Sites in Literary and Cultural Studies* (New York: Routledge, 1996), 120–24.

36. See, for example, Timothy Brennan, "Cosmopolitans and Celebrities," *Race and Class* 31, no. 1 (1989): 1–19; and Elleke Boehmer, *Colonial and Postcolonial Literature*, 232–43.

37. For example, Chidi Amuta, *The Theory of African Literature: Implications for Practical Criticism* (Atlantic Highlands, NJ: Zed Books, 1989); Georg M. Gugelberger, *Marxism and African Literature* (Trenton, NJ: Africa World Press, 1986), and Abiola Irele, *The African Experience in Literature and Ideology* (London: Heinemann, 1981).

38. Frantz Fanon, "On National Culture," in *The Wretched of the Earth*, trans. Constance Farrington (New York: Grove Press, 1968), 206–48. All further references are indicated in the text by ONC.

39. Frantz Fanon, *Black Skin, White Masks*, trans. Charles Lam Markmann (New York: Grove Weidenfeld, 1963).

40. Anthony D. Smith, "Towards a Global Culture?" *Theory, Culture, and Society* 7 (1990): 171.

41. See Chinua Achebe, *Morning Yet on Creation Day* (Garden City, NY: Anchor Press/ Doubleday, 1975), and Wole Soyinka, *Art, Dialogue and Outrage: Essays on Literature and Culture* (New York: Pantheon, 1993).

42. Léopold Sedar Senghor, "Negritude: A Humanism of the Twentieth Century," in *The Africa Reader: Independent Africa*, ed. Wilfred Cartey and Martin Kilson (London: Vintage, 1970), 179–92.

43. "Theses of the Second Congress of the Communist International on the National and Colonial Questions," in *Nationalism in Asia and Africa*, ed. Elie Kedourie (New York: Meridian, 1970), 544.

44. Sun Yat-Sen, "The Principle of Nationalism," in *Nationalism in Asia and Africa*, 308.

45. Amilcar Cabral, "National Liberation and Culture," Occasional Paper No. 57, Maxwell Graduate School of Citizenship and Public Affairs, Program of East African Studies (Syracuse: Syracuse University, 1970), 9.

46. Ibid., 9.

47. Mao Zedong, *Talks at the Yan'an Conference on Literature and Art*, trans. Bonnie S. McDougall (Ann Arbor, MI: Centre for Chinese Studies, University of Michigan, 1980).

48. It is interesting to note Cabral's similar evocation of biology. For Cabral, culture is the product of history "just as the flower is the product of a plant"; "National Liberation and Culture," 5.

49. See especially "The Pitfalls of National Consciousness," in *The Wretched of the Earth*, 148–205.

50. Benedict Anderson, *Imagined Communities*, rev. ed. (New York: Verso, 1991). Further references will be indicated in the body of the text by IC.

51. Arjun Appadurai, *Modernity at Large: Cultural Dimensions of Globalization* (Minneapolis: University of Minnesota Press, 1996); Stathis Gourgouris, *Dream Nation: Enlightenment, Colonization, and the Institution of Modern Greece* (Stanford, CA: Stanford University Press, 1996); Gregory Jusdanis, *Belated Modernity and Aesthetic Culture: Inventing National Literature* (Minneapolis: University of Minnesota Press, 1991); and Robert Lecker, *Making It Real: The Canonization of English-Canadian Literature* (Concord, ON: Anansi, 1995).

52. One of the most striking recent examples of this is to be found in Stefano Harney, *Nationalism and Identity: Culture and the Imagination in a Caribbean Diaspora* (London: Zed Books, 1996).

53. See Bruce Robbins, "Part 1: Actually Existing Cosmopolitanism," in *Cosmopolitics: Thinking and Feeling Beyond the Nation*, ed. Pheng Cheah and Bruce Robbins (Minneapolis: University of Minnesota Press, 1998), 6–7; Armand Mattelart, *Networking the World, 1794–2000*, trans. Liz Carey-Libbrect and James A. Cohen (Minneapolis: University of Minnesota Press, 2000).

54. Brennan, *Salman Rushdie*, 8.

55. Régis Debray, "Marxism and the National Question," 25–41; and Tom Nairn, *The Break-Up of Britain: Crisis and Neo-Nationalism* (London: New Left Books, 1977), 329.

56. Gopal Balakrishnan, "The National Imagination," and Partha Chatterjee, "Whose Imagined Community?" both in *Mapping the Nation*, ed. Gopal Balakrishnan (New York: Verso, 1996), 198–213 and 214–25, respectively; and Partha Chatterjee, *Nationalist Thought and the Colonial World: A Derivative Discourse* (New York: Zed Books, 1986).

57. Chatterjee, "Whose Imagined Community?" 216.

58. Ibid., 216.

59. Ibid.

60. Ibid., 217.

61. Ibid.

62. On this issue, see Ashcroft, Griffiths, and Tiffin, *The Empire Writes Back*, 38–77; and "Language," Part IX of *The Post-Colonial Studies Reader*, ed. Bill Ashcroft, Gareth Griffiths, and Helen Tiffin (New York: Routledge, 1995).

63. See Chinua Achebe, "The African Writer and the English Language," *Morning Yet on Creation Day*, 91–104; and Wole Soyinka's essays in *Art, Dialogue and Outrage*. The best-known dissenting opinion on the use of English in African writing is offered by Ngugi wa Thiong'o, *Decolonising the Mind: The Politics of Language in African Literature* (Portsmouth, NH: Heinemann, 1986).

64. Pierre Bourdieu makes this claim in his *On Television*, trans. Priscilla Parkhurst Ferguson (New York: New Press, 1998).

65. See John Hutchison's suggestion that cultural nationalism is always the activity of a small "coterie of intellectuals"; *Modern Nationalism* (Hammersmith, England: Harper Collins, 1994), 39.

66. Benedict Anderson, "Imagining East Timor"; available at http://english-www.hss.cmu.edu/theory/anderson.html; originally printed in *Arena Magazine* 4 (April–May 1993): 23–27.

67. Fredric Jameson, "Third-World Literature in the Era of Multinational Capitalism," *Social Text* 15 (1986): 65–88. All further references are indicated in the text by TWL.

68. Aijaz Ahmad, *In Theory: Class, Nations, Literatures* (New York: Verso, 1992), 95–122.

69. Though there has been a good deal of criticism of Jameson's reading of third-world literature, he has also drawn support for his attempt to offer an abstract, general model of literary production in the colonial and postcolonial world. Jean Franco has suggested that Jameson's generalizations are useful because they "provoke us to think of exceptions"; Jean Franco, "The Nation as Imagined Community," in *Dangerous Liasons: Gender, Nations, and Postcolonial Perspectives*, ed. Anne McClintock, Aamir Mufti, and Ella Shohat (Minneapolis: University of Minnesota Press, 1997), 131. With respect to contemporary cultural production in India, Geeta Kapur writes that "Jameson's formulation about the national allegory being the pre-eminent paradigm for Third World literature continues to be valid . . . the allegorical breaks up the paradigmatic notion of the cause . . . it questions the immanent condition of culture taken as some irrepressible truth offering"; Geeta Kapur, "Globalisation and Culture," *Third Text* 39 (1997): 24–25. Michael Sprinker has misgivings about some of Jameson's claims, but finds that he nevertheless puts forward a "provocative hypothesis" that needs to be carefully considered: "Is it not possible, as Jameson here maintains, that certain forms of collective life have until now persisted more powerfully outside the metropolitan countries? And if this be so, of what value are these, perhaps residual but still vital forms of social practice?" Michael Sprinker, "The National Question: Said, Ahmad, Jameson," *Public Culture* 6 (1993): 7–8.

70. It is important to recognize just how foreshortened the history of postcolonial studies is within American academic discourse. For instance, two of the formative essays in the field, Spivak's "Can the Subaltern Speak? Speculations on Widow Sacrifice," *Wedge* 7/8: 120–30, and Bhabha's "Signs Taken for Wonders" *Critical Inquiry* 12, no. 1: 144–65 were published in 1985. Jameson's essay is roughly contemporaneous with these essays and should be taken as an attempt to situate Marxist criticism within the general problematic being developed within postcolonial studies at the time.

71. All uses of the terms "first world" and "third world" should be understood, following Santiago Colás's suggestion, as being used *sous rature* so as to mark "both the inadequacy and the indispensability of the terms and the system of geo-political designations to which they belong"; Santiago Colás, "The Third World in Jameson's *Postmodernism, or The Cultural Logic of Late Capitalism*," *Social Text* 31–32 (1992): 259.

72. Kalpana Seshadri-Crooks, "At the Margins of Postcolonial Studies, Part 1," in *The Pre-Occupation of Postcolonial Studies*, ed. Fawzia Afzal-Khan and Kalpana Seshadri-Crooks (Durham, NC: Duke University Press, 2000), 19.

73. This is one of Ahmad's major criticisms of Jameson. By utilizing the "three worlds theory" as his primary interpretive matrix, Ahmad suggests that Jameson is unable to see that capitalism, socialism, and colonialism are *all* present within the third world. Colás also points out that there are "not only many 'Third Worlds' and many 'First Worlds'; but there are also 'Third Worlds' within the 'First World' and vice-versa"; Colás, "The Third World in Jameson's *Postmodernism*," 259. It is worth mentioning here Colás's examination of the paradoxical function of the third world in Jameson's *Postmodernism*, which is more or less repeated in his essay on third-world literature: "It is *both* the space whose final elimination by the inexorable logic of late capitalist development consolidates the social moment — late capitalism — whose cultural dominant is postmodernism, *and* the space that

remains somehow untainted by and oppositional to those repressive social processes which have homogenized the real and imaginative terrain of the 'First World' subject"; ibid., 258.

74. Sprinker suggests that:

We may wish to inquire, are First World allegorical forms so utterly unconscious of their potential transcoding into political readings? Leaving aside the whole rich territory of contemporary science fiction, about which Jameson himself has taught us so much, what about so-called film noir? Surely Fritz Lang, Billy Wilder, and the other émigrés who pioneered this form understood perfectly well that they were making sociopolitically coded films. On the contemporary scene, there is the massive presence of Francis Ford Coppola, not to mention David Lynch, filmmakers whose affinities with the supposedly disreputable mode of social allegory Jameson has discussed with great insight.

It is probably possible to cite endless counterexamples in this way; and yet it is important to note that this is also to have somehow missed Jameson's fundamental point entirely. Sprinker, "The National Question," 6.

75. Recently Jameson has noted that "It is very easy to break up such traditional cultural systems, which extend to the way people live in their bodies and use language, as well as the way they treat each other and nature. Once destroyed, those fabrics can never be recreated. Some third-world nations are still in a situation in which that fabric is preserved"; Fredric Jameson, "Notes on Globalization as a Philosophic Issue," in *The Cultures of Globalization*, ed. Fredric Jameson and Masao Miyoshi (Durham, NC: Duke University Press, 1998), 63.

76. Johannes Fabian has described this "time lag" as "allochronism" — a denial to the "other" of any possible contemporaneity with the West. See Johannes Fabian, *Time and the Other: How Anthropology Makes Its Object* (New York: St. Martin's Press, 1983).

77. Dipesh Chakrabarty's work has engaged directly with the need to both "think" and "unthink" modernity in the conceptualization of third-world histories and third-world politics. See Chakrabarty, *Provincializing Europe* (Princeton, NJ: Princeton University Press, 2000), especially chapter 1.

78. See Fredric Jameson, "Modernism and Imperialism," in Terry Eagleton, Fredric Jameson, and Edward W. Said, *Nationalism, Colonialism, and Literature*, (Minneapolis: University of Minnesota Press, 1990), 43–66.

79. Julie McGonegal has shown how Jameson's mode of national-allegorical interpretation reveals narratives that reading strategies that focus on "manichean" allegories cannot. Part of her point is that critics of Jameson have confused Jameson's elaboration of an interpretative hermeneutic ("third world texts are . . . *to be read* as national allegories") with the thing itself (third-world texts *are* national allegories, the nation still has significance in the third world, the third world is homogeneous, etc.), and in so doing have missed Jameson's metacritical emphasis on the way in which third-world texts necessarily appear to us as "already read"; Julie McGonegal, "Post-Colonial Contradictions in Tsitsi Dangaremba's *Nervous Condition:* Toward a Reconsideration of Jameson's National Allegory," unpublished manuscript. It is worth remembering that Jameson's comments concerning third-world literature arise out of meditations on a different matter entirely (i.e., the debates in the American academy in the mid 1980s over the revision of the literary canon).

80. Raymond Willliams provides an account of the historical development of the concept of literature in *Marxism and Literature* (Oxford: Oxford University Press, 1977).

81. This is intimated in the final footnote of "Third-World Literature": "What is here called 'national allegory' is clearly a form of just such a mapping of the totality, so that the present essay—which sketches a theory of the cognitive aesthetics of third-world literature—forms a pendant to the essay on postmodernism which describes the logic of cultural imperialism of the first world and above all of the United States"; Jameson, "Third World Literature," 88 n. 25.

82. Fredric Jameson, *Fables of Aggression* (Berkeley: University of California Press, 1979), 90. All further references are indicated in the text by FA.

83. See Fredric Jameson, "Modernism and Imperialism."

84. Antonio Gramsci, "The Intellectuals," in *Selections from the Prison Notebooks*, ed. and trans. Quintin Hoare and Geoffrey Nowell Smith (New York: International Publishers, 1971), 5–23; and Michel Foucault and Gilles Deleuze, "Intellectuals and Power," in *Language, Counter-Memory, Practice*, ed. Donald F. Bouchard, trans. Donald F. Bouchard and Sherry Simon (Ithaca, NY: Cornell University Press), 205–17. For a comparison of these positions, see R. Radhakrishnan, "Toward an Effective Intellectual? Foucault or Gramsci?" in *Intellectuals: Aesthetics, Politics, and Academics*, ed. Bruce Robbins (Minneapolis: University of Minnesota Press, 1990).

85. Chatterjee, *Nationalist Thought and the Colonial World*.

86. Seshadri-Crooks, "At the Margins of Postcolonial Studies, Part 1."

87. This is essentially the critique that Spivak makes of Jameson's theory of the postmodern in her *A Critique of Postcolonial Reason* (Cambridge: Harvard University Press, 1999), 312–37. See also Dipesh Chakrabarty's challenge to the "politics of historicism" in *Provincializing Europe*.

88. Fredric Jameson, *Postmodernism, or, The Cultural Logic of Late Capitalism*, 5.

89. For example, Philip Darby has pointed to the failure of postcolonial theory to engage with international relations theory; Darby, *The Fiction of Imperialism: Reading between International Relations and Postcolonialism* (London: Cassell, 1998). Chakrabarty's analysis of the politics of historicism, including those historicisms such as Ernst Mandel and Jameson's, which remain indebted to Marx's placement of capitalism at the leading edge of historical time, foregrounds the theoretical problems that arise in attempts to think a global totality. While he is right to criticize the Eurocentrism of historicism, the difficulty of developing a different model of history that does not reduce it to "sheer heterogeneity" can be seen in his unproductive attempt to develop an alternative model of historicity that enables one to "think about the past and the future in a nontotalizing manner" by passing through the ontological dead zone of Heidegger's thought; Chakrabarty, *Provincializing Europe*, 249.

90. Michael Hardt and Antonio Negri, " 'Subterranean Passages of Thought': *Empire*'s Insert," *Cultural Studies* 16, no. 2 (2002): 196.

91. "Every individual interpretation must include an interpretation of its own existence, must show its own credentials and justify itself: every commentary must be at the same time a metacommentary"; Fredric Jameson, "Metacommentary," *PMLA* 86 (1971): 10.

92. "Though there is no shortage of criticism of postcolonial studies—even or especially from within its own ranks—no other critical practice has foregrounded the links between cultural forms and geopolitics to the degree that postcolonial studies has over the past four decades. No other materialist practice has considered the modalities of race, nation, gender, and ethnicity, in relationship to global activity of hegemonic cultural,

political and economic forces, with the degree of complexity and sophistication that have come to be associated with the best work in the field. Before postcolonial studies, Western scholarship was an embarrassment"; Susie O'Brien and Imre Szeman, "Introduction: The Fiction of Globalization/The Globalization of Fiction," *South Atlantic Quarterly* 100, no. 3 (2001): 603–26.

CHAPTER TWO: Caribbean Space

1. Allison Donnell and Sarah Lawson Welsh, eds., introduction to *The Routledge Reader in Caribbean Literature* (New York: Routledge, 1996), 7.
2. For a definitive account of the 1930s, see Reinhold Sander, *The Trinidad Awakening: West Indian Literatures of the Nineteen-Thirties* (Westport, CT: Three Continents Press, 1988).
3. Stefano Harney, *Nationalism and Identity: Culture and the Imagination in a Caribbean Diaspora* (London: Zed Books, 1996).
4. Benedict Anderson, *Imagined Communities* (New York: Verso, 1991), 30.
5. Western political scientists who wrote about the prospect of a West Indian federation saw it as assuming a place alongside Canada and Australia in the British Commonwealth. See, for example, the essays collected in H. D. Huggins, ed., *Federation of the West Indies* (Mona, Jamaica: University of the West Indies, 1957).
6. Simon Gikandi, *Writing in Limbo: Modernism and Caribbean Literature* (Ithaca, NY: Cornell University Press, 1992), 33.
7. Ibid., 26.
8. In Pierre Bourdieu, *Distinction: A Social Critique of the Judgement of Taste*, trans. Richard Nice (Cambridge, MA: Harvard University Press, 1984).
9. Edward Said, "Reflections on Exile," *Granta* 13 (Autumn 1984): 159.
10. Mao Zedong, *Talks at the Yan'an Conference on Literature and Art*, trans. Bonnie S. McDougall (Ann Arbor, MI: Center for Chinese Studies, University of Michigan, 1980), p. 60.
11. With respect to literature, see Edward Said's suggestion that "exile, far from being the fate of nearly forgotten unfortunates who are dispossessed and expatriated, becomes something of a norm, an experience of crossing boundaries and charting new territories in defiance of the classic canonic enclosures"; Edward W. Said, *Culture and Imperialism* (New York: Vintage, 1993), 317.
12. Ibid., 332.
13. Edward Said, "Reflections on Exile," and Gikandi, *Writing in Limbo*.
14. Gikandi, *Writing in Limbo*, 66–106.
15. George Lamming, "The Occasion for Speaking," *The Pleasures of Exile* (London: Michael Joseph, 1960), 23–50. All further references are indicated in the text by OS.
16. See Fanon's discussion of the phenomenological and psychological effects of the colonial experience in *Black Skin, White Masks*, trans. Charles Lam Markmann (New York: Grove Weidenfeld, 1963). See also recent discussions of Fanon, including Alan Read, ed., *The Fact of Blackness: Frantz Fanon and Visual Representation* (Seattle, WA: Bay Press, 1996); Lewis Gordon, T. Denean Sharpley-Whiting, and Renée T. White, eds., *Fanon: A Critical Reader* (New York: Blackwell, 1996); and Ato Sekyi-Otu's superb *Fanon's Dialectic of Experience* (Cambridge, MA: Harvard University Press, 1996).
17. Fanon, *Black Skin*, 72.

18. Ibid., 11–12.

19. Lamming tempers this claim later in the essay: "At this point the whole truth must be told. The political constitutions have been improved on; standards of living may have gone up. These standards will probably get better as more emigrants leave the land, and more foreign capital takes their place" (OS 47). Nevertheless, as he goes on to say, "little has really changed in the West Indies in the last ten years. The colonial structure of our thinking at home has not been touched. Nothing has really happened" (OS 47).

20. Ngugi wa Thiong'o, *Decolonising the Mind: The Politics of Language in African Literature* (Portsmouth, NH: Heinemann, 1986), 168.

21. Gordon Rohlehr, "The Folk in Caribbean Literature," in *Critics on Caribbean Literature*, ed. Edward S. Baugh (New York: St. Martin's Press, 1978), 29.

22. Fredric Jameson, *Marxism and Form* (Princeton, NJ: Princeton University Press, 1971), 195.

23. Gikandi, *Writing in Limbo*, 67.

24. Ngugi wa Thiong'o, *Decolonising the Mind*, 63–86.

25. Rohlehr, "The Folk in Caribbean Literature," 27.

26. George Lamming, *Coming Coming Home: Conversations II* (St. Martin, Caribbean: House of Nehesi Publishers, 1995), 16–17.

27. George Lamming, *The Emigrants* (Ann Arbor, MI: University of Michigan Press, 1994), 65. All further references are indicated in the text by E.

28. See Selwyn Cudjoe, "Towards Independence," *Resistance and Caribbean Literature* (Athens: Ohio University Press, 1980), pp. 179–211; Margaret Paul Joseph, "The Tormented Spirit: George Lamming and the Tragic Sense of Life," *Caliban in Exile: The Outsider in Caribbean Fiction* (New York: Greenwood Press, 1992), 51–82; and Ian Munro, "George Lamming," in *West Indian Literature*, ed. Bruce King (Hamden, CT: Archon Books, 1979), 126–43. This reading positions *The Emigrants* as "a phase of discovery that leads back to the West Indies and the rejuvenation of the spiritually moribund society the emigrants fled" (Munro, "George Lamming," 132) in Lamming's next novel, *Of Age and Innocence*. A more sophisticated and thorough reading of Lamming's oeuvre is offered in Supriya Nair's superb *Caliban's Cure: George Lamming and the Revisioning of History* (Ann Arbor: University of Michigan Press, 1996).

29. George Lamming, *The Pleasures of Exile* (London: Michael Joseph, 1960), 18–22, and *Of Age and Innocence* (London: Michael Joseph, 1958), 94–102.

30. Gikandi, *Writing in Limbo*, 89–98.

31. Cudjoe writes that "Although Aimé Césaire develops the theme of the colonizer and the colonized in *Discourse on Colonialism*, Lamming is the first writer in the British Caribbean to explore seriously the relationship between them at the psychological level" ("Towards Independence," 179).

32. Munro writes that "Of the twenty-one scenes that follow their arrival in England, only two occur outside, in contrast to *In the Castle of My Skin*, where most of the action takes place in backyards, on street corners, or beaches, where the villagers are free to move about" ("George Lamming," 131). Munro notes this as a way of highlighting the increasingly confined world of *The Emigrants*. I see its significance differently: in *The Emigrants*, setting is strangely unimportant. One is reminded of György Lukács's discussion of Flaubert's "incidental" use of the setting of the fair in the decisive love scene of *Madame Bovary*. England is used in the same way in Lamming's novel: incidentally. It is not central to the narrative in the way that Lukács suggests the marksmanship contest is in Walter

Scott's *Old Mortality*. See György Lukács, "Narrate or Describe?" in *Writer and Critic, and Other Essays*, ed. and trans. Arthur D. Kahn (New York: Grosset & Dunlap, 1971), 110–48.

33. Gikandi, *Writing in Limbo*, 72.

34. Mervyn Morris, "The Poet as Novelist: The Novels of George Lamming," *The Islands in Between: Essays on West Indian Literature*, ed. Louis James (Oxford: Oxford University Press, 1968), 73–85.

35. C. L. R. James, "A National Purpose for the Caribbean Peoples," *At the Rendezvous of Victory: Selected Writings* (London: Alison & Busby, 1984), 155.

36. George Lamming, *The Pleasures of Exile*, 37.

37. V. S. Naipaul, "Our Universal Civilization," *New York Review of Books* 38, no. 3 (January 31, 1991): 23.

38. As a recent example of the kind of ad hominem attacks that Naipaul has suffered, see Paul Theroux, "The Enigma of Friendship," *New Yorker* 84, no. 22 (Aug. 3, 1998): 44–55.

39. V. S. Naipaul, *The Middle Passage* (London: Penguin, 1969). All further references are indicated in the text by MP.

40. The lone reference to the West Indies Federation occurs in a popular Lord Blakie song that Naipaul quotes: "Move, lemme get me share. / They beating Grenadians down in the Square. / Lemme pelt a lash, lemme get a share. / They beating Grenadians down in the Square. / Since they hear we have Federation / All of them packing up in this island" (MP 47).

41. Stefano Harney has characterized the whole of Naipaul's work as exhibiting this antinationalist stance: "Naipaul's pessimism is so totalizing that any discussion of his situation in the discourse of race and class in Trinidadian nationalism breaks down. His work has to be discussed not as a reading of the nation, but as an attack on the possibility of reading a post-colonial state as a nation at all"; Stefano Harney, *Nationalism and Identity*, 140. It has also been suggested that Naipaul not only rejects the possibility of postcolonial nationalism, but of nationalism in toto. See Victor Ramraj, "V. S. Naipaul: The Irrelevance of Nationalism," *World Literature Written in English* 23, no. 1 (1984): 187–96.

42. These are now almost too numerous to cite, but see, for example, *Among the Believers: An Islamic Journey* (London: A. Deutsch, 1981), *India: A Million Mutinies Now* (New York: Viking, 1991), *The Loss of El Dorado* (New York: Knopf, 1970), and most recently, *Beyond Belief: Islamic Excursions among the Converted People* (New York: Random House, 1998).

43. Indeed, as Selwyn Cudjoe points out repeatedly, there is little attempt on the part of Naipaul to make sure that he has his facts straight on the matter under consideration in his "nonfiction" work; Selwyn Cudjoe, *V. S. Naipaul: A Materialist Reading* (Amherst, MA: University of Massachusetts Press, 1988). Writing about Naipaul's *Among the Believers*, Salman Rushdie suggests that his claims about the Islamic revival are "powerful indictments, and there is much truth in them. The trouble is that it's a highly selective truth, a novelist's truth masquerading as objective reality"; Salman Rushdie, *Imaginary Homelands: Essays and Criticism, 1981–1991* (New York: Penguin, 1991), 374.

44. V. S. Naipaul, *The Mystic Masseur* (London: A. Deutsch, 1957), 143.

45. Gordon Roehler, "The Ironic Approach: The Novels of V. S. Naipaul," in *The Islands in Between: Essays on West Indian Literature*, ed. Louis James (Oxford: Oxford University Press, 1968), 132.

46. James Anthony Froude, cited in MP 7. As important as Froude's *The English in the*

West Indies (1888) is a book written one year later, J. J. Thomas's *Froudacity*. Thomas's book provides an "energetic defense [that] makes one of the most positive early statements by a West Indian of the validity of his differentness. It is very significant that in this defense there is no sense of apology or inferiority"; see Anthony Boxill, "The Beginnings to 1929," in *West Indian Literature*, ed. Bruce King (Hamden, CT: Archon Books, 1979), 31. The same cannot be said of Naipaul's book.

47. Partha Chatterjee, "Whose Imagined Community?" in *Mapping the Nation*, ed. Gopal Balakrishnan (New York: Verso, 1996), 214–25.

48. "As we penetrated deeper into Brazil I felt as a fact, what the maps had already told me, that the savannah was really Brazilian and the British Guianese portion of it trifling" (MP 113).

49. Naipaul, *The Middle Passage*, 44.

50. C. L. R. James, *Beyond a Boundary* (Durham, NC: Duke University Press, 1993), 233 and 49, respectively. All further references are indicated in the text by BB.

51. Arjun Appadurai, *Modernity at Large*, 113.

52. For that matter, it is hard to find anyone with comparable intellectual credentials in the entire world, much less the Caribbean: writer of an astonishing array of books and articles, from books on the development of the dialectic (*Notes on the Dialectic* [1948] and *State Capitalism and World Revolution* [1950]) to a famous history of the Haitian revolution (*The Black Jacobins* [1938]) to a study of the work of Herman Melville (*Mariners, Renegades, and Castaways* [1952]); world-famous socialist and political activist, who was delegate to the Fourth International, chairman of the International African Friends of Abyssinia during the Italian invasion, initiator of the English translation of Marx's *Economic and Philosophic Manuscripts of 1844* and translator himself of Boris Souvarine's *Stalin*, the first exposé of the abuses of the Soviet leader's regime; actor, with Paul Robeson, in *Touissant L'Ouverture* (1936), a play, which he also wrote; sports writer and literary critic; etc.

53. C. L. R. James, "Lecture on Federation," in *At the Rendezvous of Victory*, 90.

54. Ibid., 90.

55. A selection of James's speeches and letters are reproduced in the section entitled "On Federation," in *At the Rendezvous of History*, 85–128.

56. The letter from Nkrumah was solicited by James, who gave him instructions on the issues and themes to be addressed. The relationship between James and Nkrumah was established through James's work in the late 1930s with the International African Service Bureau, under whose auspices Nkrumah returned to the Gold Coast from London in 1947 to prepare for the Ghanian revolution. James visited Ghana several times during the early years of the Nkrumah regime, and later wrote *Nkrumah and the Ghana Revolution* (Westport, CT: L. Hill, 1977), an account of the events leading up to the establishment of the first African country to gain independence.

57. C. L. R. James and Kwame Nkrumah, *Kwame Nkrumah and the West Indies* (San Juan, Trinidad: Vedic Enterprises, 1962).

58. Ibid.

59. C. L. R. James, "The Mighty Sparrow," in *The Future in the Present: Selected Writings* (Westport, CT: L. Hill, 1977), 191–201, and "A National Purpose for Caribbean Peoples," in *At the Rendezvous of Victory*, 143–158.

60. C. L. R. James, "The Artist in the Caribbean," in *The Future in the Present*, 185.

61. Ibid., 185.

62. Ibid., 187.

63. "365" refers to Sobers's extraordinary score in a Test Match — a world record until it was recently surpassed by another West Indian batsman. "Maple," "Shannon," and "Queen's Park" refer to Trinidadian cricket clubs. James himself was a member of the Maple Cricket Club. James writes that "the cricket field was a stage on which selected individuals played representative roles which were charged with social significance" (BB 72). Each club had its own particular racial and class affiliations and largely defined the professional circles within which its members were able to move. Maple was the club of the brown-skinned middle class, and though dark-skinned, James was admitted on the basis of his professional affiliations. It was a decision he regretted: "Faced with the fundamental divisions in the island, I had gone to the right and, by cutting myself off from the popular side, delayed my political development for years" (BB 53).

64. Neil Lazarus, "Cricket and National Culture in the Writings of C. L. R. James," in *C. L. R. James's Caribbean*, ed. Paget Henry and Paul Buhle (Durham, NC: Duke University Press, 1992), 94.

65. Hazel Carby writes that *Beyond a Boundary* is "one of the most outstanding works of cultural studies ever produced"; Hazel Carby, "Proletarian or Revolutionary Literature: C. L. R. James and the Politics of Trinidadian Renaissance," *South Atlantic Quarterly* 87 (Winter 1988): 51.

66. Lazarus, "Cricket and National Culture," 108.

CHAPTER THREE: The Novel after the Nation

Epigraphs: G. W. F. Hegel, *The Philosophy of History*, trans. J. Sibree (New York: Prometheus Books, 1991), 99. Frantz Fanon, *The Wretched of the Earth*, trans. Constance Farrington (New York: Grove Press, 1968), 212.

1. Basil Davidson, *The Black Man's Burden: Africa and the Curse of the Nation-State* (New York: Times Books, 1992).

2. Ibid., 290. Achille Mbembe has thoroughly analyzed the symbolic operations that have helped to perpetuate and maintain the nation-state's "shackle on progress." See Achille Mbembe, "The Banality of Power: Aesthetics of Vulgarity in the Postcolony," *Public Culture* 4, no. 2 (Spring 1992): 1–30.

3. Craig Calhoun, *Nationalism* (Buckingham, England: Open University Press, 1997), 6. The nation is a project in the form of "social movements and state policies by which people attempt to advance the interests of the collectivities they understand as nations, usually pursuing in some combination (or in a historical progression) increased participation in an existing state, national autonomy, independence and self-determination, or the amalgamation of territories" (6). It is an evaluation in the sense of "political and cultural ideologies that claim superiority for a particular nation" (6).

4. The usual number that is cited is over 250 ethnic groups, of which nine account for 80 percent of the population: Hausa-Fulani, Yoruba, Ibo, Kanur, Tiv, Edo, Nupe, Ibibio, and Ijaw.

5. Africa is not necessarily unique in this respect. Once again, as Calhoun reminds us, "Though nationalist self-descriptions generally emphasize mass participation and cross-class unity, for example, nationalism is often an elite project structured in ways which maintain or institute patterns of domination. This is nowhere more true than in those post-colonial states where it is most vociferously denied"; Calhoun, *Nationalism*, 111.

6. Davidson, *The Black Man's Burden*, 295.

7. Chinweizu cited in Wole Soyinka, "Neo-Tarzanism: The Poetics of Pseudo-Tradition," *Art, Dialogue, and Outrage: Essays on Literature and Culture* (New York: Pantheon, 1993), 315–16.

8. Fanon, *The Wretched of the Earth*, 216.

9. Soyinka's antipathy toward political "ideologies" in general and Marxism in particular is expressed most explicitly in "Who's Afraid of Elesin Oba?" *Art, Dialogue and Outrage*, 110–31; nothing since has suggested that he has changed his political outlook.

10. What is missing in this account is the complicated story of the factionalization of the major political parties into numerous smaller parties whose fierce rivalries intensified what was an already difficult political situation.

11. Chinua Achebe, *Anthills of the Savannah* (London: Picador, 1987), 124. All further references are indicated in the text by AS.

12. Bertolt Brecht, *Diaries, 1920–1922*, ed. Herta Ramthun, trans. John Willett (New York: St. Martin's Press, 1979).

13. Chinua Achebe, *Hopes and Impediments: Selected Essays* (New York: Doubleday, 1988), 96.

14. Ibid., 99.

15. Though, as Achebe points out, it isn't clear what constitutes a non-African language: "As you know, there has been an impassioned controversy about an African literature in non-African languages. But what is a *non-African* language? English and French certainly. But what about Arabic? What about Swahili even? Is it then a question of how long the language has been present on African soil? If so, how many years should constitute *effective occupation?* For me it is a pragmatic matter. A language spoken by Africans on African soil, a language in which Africans write, justifies itself"; Chinua Achebe, *Morning Yet on Creation Day* (New York: Anchor Press/Doubleday, 1975), 83.

16. Chinua Achebe, *Morning*, 100.

17. Chinua Achebe, *A Man of the People* (New York: John Day, 1966), 122.

18. Neil ten Kortenaar suggests that "*Anthills of the Savannah* is a fictional working out of Achebe's concerns in *The Trouble with Nigeria*"; see Neil ten Kortenaar, " 'Only Connect': *Anthills of the Savannah* and Achebe's Trouble with Nigeria," *Research in African Literatures* 24, no. 3 (Fall 1993): 60. My feeling, however, is that *Trouble* represents a summation of Achebe's views on Nigeria from the disappointments of Biafra to the disappointments of the Second Republic, a summation which allows him to move on to a different set of concerns in *Anthills*.

19. See Michel Foucault, *The History of Sexuality*, I: *An Introduction*, trans. Richard Hurley (New York: Vintage, 1978), 81–91, and "Two Lectures," *Power/Knowledge: Selected Interviews and Other Writings, 1972–1977*, ed. Colin Gordon (New York: Pantheon, 1980), 78–108.

20. Chinua Achebe, *The Trouble with Nigeria* (London: Heinemann, 1983), 1.

21. Ibid., 2.

22. Achebe, *Morning*, 137.

23. Ibid., 147.

24. Achebe, *Hopes and Impediments*, 146.

25. Achebe, *Morning*, 72.

26. Achebe, *Hopes and Impediments*, 100–112.

27. Chinua Achebe, *A Man of the People* (New York: John Day, 1966), 128.

28. Michel Foucault and Gilles Deleuze, "Intellectuals and Power," in *Language*,

Counter-Memory, Practice, ed. Donald F. Bouchard, trans. Donald F. Bouchard and Sherry Simon (Ithaca, NY: Cornell University Press), 207.

29. From 1954 to 1966, Achebe was first Talks producer and later director of external broadcasting for the Nigerian Broadcasting Corporation. During the Biafran War, Achebe spoke extensively on behalf of the Biafran cause in Africa, Europe, and North America.

Although the character of Chris Oriko is meant obviously, at least in name, as a tribute to the Ibo poet Christopher Okigbo, who died while fighting with the Biafran army, there is a sense in which this character also "stands in" for Achebe — the "official" Achebe in his role as a senior executive in the NBC in the pre-Biafran government.

30. An attitude that mirrors Odili's in *A Man of the People*, when he describes Edna as possessing "just the right amount of education" (143). He continues: "I had nothing against professional women — in fact I liked them in their way — but if emancipation meant people like that other lady lawyer who came to sleep with illiterate Chief Nanga for twenty-five pounds a time (as he confided to me next morning), then they could keep it" (143).

31. Neil ten Kortenaar, " 'Only Connect'," 62.

32. Wole Soyinka, *The Open Sore of a Continent* (Oxford: Oxford University Press, 1996), 153.

33. Wole Soyinka, *Aké* and *Season of Anomy* (New York: Vintage, 1994), 261; *Season of Anomy* runs from 231–554 in this joint volume.

34. What little attention has been paid to it consists mainly of rather straightforward overviews of the plot and the tracing of its (obvious) connection to the civil war. See, for example, Eldred Durosimi Jones, *The Writing of Wole Soyinka* (London: Heinemann, 1973), 201–12, and Abdulrazak Gurnah, "The Fiction of Wole Soyinka," in *Wole Soyinka: An Appraisal*, ed. Adewale Maja-Pearce (London: Heinemann, 1994), 61–80. Abiola Irele does not even mention *Season of Anomy* in his discussion of Soyinka's literary reactions to Biafra, choosing to focus instead on *Madmen and Specialists, The Man Died*, and scattered examples of poetry; see Irele, "The Season of the Mind: Wole Soyinka and the Nigerian Crisis," *The African Experience in Literature and Ideology* (Bloomington: Indiana University Press, 1990), 198–212. The most substantive critical discussion of the novel remains the chapter devoted to it in Obi Maduakor's *Wole Soyinka: An Introduction to His Writing* (New York: Garland, 1986), 113–52.

35. Derek Wright, *Wole Soyinka Revisited* (New York: Twayne, 1993), 118.

36. Wole Soyinka, *The Interpreters* (London: Andre Deutsch, 1965).

37. For a discussion of this distinction, see K. E. Agovi, "The African Writer and the Phenomenon of the Nation State in Africa," *Ufahamu* 18, no. 1 (1990): 41–62.

38. Wole Soyinka, "The Writer in a Modern African State," *Art, Dialogue and Outrage*, 18.

39. Ibid., 20.

40. It might be argued that the play *Madmen and Specialists* (London: Methuen, 1971), which examines the disintegration of humanity in a totalitarian society and is also a response to consequences of the Nigerian Civil War, is just as explicit as *Season of Anomy*. Yet by comparison, *Madmen* is exceedingly abstract at every level: setting, characterization, narrative, and the like. Approvingly, Irele notes that in *Madmen* there is "no longer a direct preoccupation with social problems and human types, but rather a passionate and consuming obsession with the problem of evil" (*The African Experience*, 202). For a writer whose

politics is always in danger of running afoul of the Nigerian authorities, such abstractness can be useful. At the same time, the result in this play at least seems to be the production of a fable or a morality play that aims for such a degree of universality that it is effectively stripped of its ability to act as a political allegory of the events that had just transpired in Biafra. All further references to *Season of Anomy* are indicated in the text by SA.

41. Wole Soyinka, *The Man Died: Prison Notes of Wole Soyinka* (New York: Harper & Row, 1972), 8. This is also the manner in which Soyinka wrote *The Man Died* and the poems that appeared in *Shuttle in the Crypt*.

42. Soyinka was detained for his public opposition to the civil war and because of his visit to the Biafran leader, Colonel Ojukwu in Enugu. (This is the same Ojukwu that Soyinka attacks in *The Open Sore of a Continent* as demonstrating "a remarkable involvement with the project of browsing where the pasture appears greenest" [45]). Prior to his arrest, Soyinka was already seen as a suspicious figure by Nigerian authorities. Though he was acquitted in 1965 for his supposed role in originating a pirate radio broadcast denouncing Chief Akintola's election victory, successive Nigerian governments have from this incident on viewed Soyinka as a persistent political threat.

43. Maduakor, *Wole Soyinka*, 121.

44. Wole Soyinka, *The Open Sore of a Continent*, 35. All further references are indicated in the text by OSC.

CHAPTER FOUR: The Persistence of the Nation

Epigraphs: From Section 1 of "Civil Elegies," in Dennis Lee, *Civil Elegies and Other Poems* (Toronto: Anansi, 1972). William Lyon MacKenzie King, address at the Canadian National Exhibition, July 1927, cited in Bill McNeil and Morris Wolfe, *Signing On: The Birth of Radio in Canada* (Toronto: Doubleday Canada, 1982), 190.

1. Northrop Frye, *The Bush Garden: Essays on the Canadian Imagination* (Toronto: Anansi, 1971), iii.

2. Maurice Charland, "Technological Nationalism," *Canadian Journal of Political and Social Theory* 10, no. 1–2 (1986): 197.

3. For a discussion of the long history of technologically mediated nationalisms, see Armand Mattelart, *Networking the World, 1794–2000*, trans. Liz Carey-Libbrect and James A. Cohen (Minneapolis: University of Minnesota Press, 2000). In Canada, the need for a cultural nationalism in addition to technological nationalism should not be surprising. As Charland points out, it is precisely because Canadian identity has been premised on technological nationalism that it has been an identity in perpetual crisis. Charland notes that "technological nationalism promises a liberal state in which technology would be a natural medium for the development of the *polis*. This vision of the nation is bankrupt, however, because it provides no substance or commonality for the *polis* except communication itself. As a consequence, technological nationalism's (anglophone) Canada has no defense against the power and seduction of the American cultural industry or, indeed, of the technological experience. Canada, then, is the 'absent nation'"; "Technological Nationalism," 198.

4. Tabled as *Royal Commission Studies: A Selection of Essays Prepared for the Royal Commission on National Development in the Arts, Letters and Sciences* (Ottawa, 1951).

5. Paul Litt, *The Muses, the Masses and the Massey Commission* (Toronto: University of Toronto Press, 1992), 4–5.

6. Raymond Williams, *Marxism and Literature* (Oxford: Oxford University Press, 1977), 17.

7. Litt describes this tension between culture as "the arts" and culture as "whole ways of life" as a tension between a populist nationalism and a cultural elitism that persisted throughout the commission's hearings:

> The popular appeal and Canadian emphasis which nationalism demanded some-times threatened the critical standards and cosmopolitan outlook of the cultural elite. The claims of nationalism wrestled with those of elitism within the minds of individuals and between different factions of the culture lobby. Organizations that had cultural interests but were not closely linked to the elite tended to be more nationalistic than elitist in their views. Some regarded the elitist emphasis on the broad context of Western culture as a form of colonialism . . . the elite leadership of the culture lobby, however, feared that emphasizing nationalism over cultural ex-cellence would breed and inferior and parochial culture in Canada. (Litt, *Muses*, 109–10)

8. B. W. Powe, *A Climate Charged* (Oakville, ON: Mosaic Press, 1984), 65.

9. Ibid., 62.

10. Robert Lecker, *Making It Real: The Canonization of English-Canadian Literature* (Concord, ON: Anansi, 1995). All further references are indicated in the text by MR. On the involvement of the federal government in the establishment of Canadian literature, see also W. J. Keith, "The Function of Canadian Criticism at the Present Time," *Essays on Canadian Writing* 30 (Winter 1984/85): 1–16; and T. D. MacLulich, "What Was Cana-dian Literature? Taking Stock of the Canlit Industry," *Essays on Canadian Writing* 30 (Winter 1984/85): 17–34.

11. The critical texts most commonly included as examples of thematic criticism in-clude Margaret Atwood, *Survival: A Thematic Guide to Canadian Literature* (Toronto: Anansi, 1972); D. G. Jones, *Butterfly on Rock: A Study of Themes and Images in Canadian Literature* (Toronto: University of Toronto Press, 1970); and John Moss, *Patterns of Isola-tion in English Canadian Fiction* (Toronto: McClelland, 1974) and *Sex and Violence in the Canadian Novel: The Ancestral Present* (Toronto: McClelland, 1977). Warren Tallman's influential essays in the 1960s are precursors to these book-length studies. See "Wolf in the Snow. Part One: Four Windows onto Landscapes," *Canadian Literature* 5 (1960): 7–20, and "Wolf in the Snow. Part Two: The Home Repossessed," *Canadian Literature* 6 (1960): 41–48.

12. Northrop Frye, conclusion to *Literary History of Canada: Canadian Literature in English*, gen. ed., Carl F. Klinck (Toronto: University of Toronto Press, 1965), 835. All further references are indicated in the text by C.

13. Fredric Jameson, "Third-World Literature in the Age of Multinational Capital-ism," *Social Text* 15 (1986): 65–88.

14. Donna Pennee, "Canadian Letters, Dead Referents: Reconsidering the Critical Construction of *The Double Hook*," *Essays on Canadian Writing* 51–52 (1993/94): 233–57.

15. Stephen Scobie, "Davey, Frank," in *The Oxford Companion to Canadian Literature*, ed. William Toye (Toronto: Oxford University Press, 1983), 173.

16. Frank Davey, *Surviving the Paraphrase* (Winnipeg: Turnstone, 1983), 1.

17. John Moss, ed., *Future Indicative: Literary Theory and Canadian Literature* (Ottawa: University of Ottawa Press, 1987); Barbara Godard, ed., *Gynocritics: Feminist Approaches to*

Canadian and Quebec Women's Writing (Toronto: ECW Press, 1987); Sylvia Söderlind, *Margin/Alias: Language and Colonization in Canadian and Québécois Fiction* (Toronto: University of Toronto Press, 1991); and Barry Cameron and Michael Dixon, "Minus Canadian: Penultimate Essays in Literature," *Studies in Canadian Literature* 2, no. 2 (1977): 137–45.

18. Diana Brydon, "Introduction: Reading Postcoloniality, Reading Canada," *Essays on Canadian Writing* 56 (1995): 1–19.

19. As but a few examples of a growing body of work, see Cyril Dabydeen, ed., *A Shapely Fire: Changing the Literary Landscape* (Oakville, ON: Mosaic Press, 1987); Linda Hutcheon, ed., *Other Solitudes: Multicultural Fiction and Interviews* (New York: Oxford University Press, 1991); Arun Mukherjee, *Towards an Aesthetic of Opposition: Essays on Literature, Criticism and Cultural Imperialism* (Toronto: Williams-Wallace, 1988); and W. H. New, ed., *Native Writers and Canadian Writing* (Vancouver: University of British Columbia Press, 1990).

20. See my "The Persistence of the Nation: Interdisciplinarity and Canadian Literary Criticism," *Essays on Canadian Writing* 65 (1998): 16–37.

21. Frank Davey, *Post-National Arguments: The Politics of the Anglophone-Canadian Novel since 1967* (Toronto: University of Toronto Press, 1993), 266.

22. Ibid., 15.

23. Ibid., 16–17.

24. Ibid., 18.

25. Davey, *Surviving*, 4.

26. T. D. MacLulich, "Thematic Criticism, Literary Nationalism, and the Critic's New Clothes," *Essays on Canadian Writing* 35 (Winter 1987): 17.

27. Ibid., 33.

28. Ibid., 17–18.

29. MacLulich, "What Was Canadian Literature?" 27.

30. Northrop Frye once commented, "I imagine in another ten years there will be very little different in tone between Canadian and American literature." What is most interesting about this assertion, especially in the context of the discussion that will follow in this chapter, is that Frye believes this will happen because the entire world will become more *Canadian* rather than becoming Americanized. He writes: "The Canadian recurring themes of self-conflict, of the violating of nature, of individuals uncertain of their social context, of dark, repressed, oracular doubles concealed within each of us, are now more communicable outside Canada in the new mood of the world"; Northrop Frye, "National Consciousness in Canadian Culture," in *Reflections on the Canadian Literary Imagination* (Rome: Bulzoni Editore, 1991), 177.

31. Davey, *Post-National Arguments*, 266.

32. Boehmer, *Colonial and Postcolonial Literature* (New York: Oxford University Press, 1995), 184.

33. As exemplified by T. D. MacLulich's *Between Europe and America: The Canadian Tradition in Fiction* (Toronto: ECW Press, 1988). This is a very common way of envisioning the landscape of Canadian literature. For example, the Prairie Work Group's *New Land, New Language* (Toronto: Writers' Development Trust, 1977), which was written as a curriculum guide for the teaching of Canadian literature in high schools, begins with the following assertion: "Canadian writers have been faced with two overwhelming alterna-

tives: the cultural tradition of England (and later the United States) and the vast, empty land they inhabit" (1).

34. Which places Margaret Laurence's oft-cited connection between Canadian and third-world writing—the common quest, in her words, to "find our own voices and write out of what is truly ours in the face of overwhelming cultural imperialism"—in a different light. See "Ivory Tower or Grassroot? The Novelist as Socio-Political Being," in W. H. New, ed., *A Political Art* (Vancouver: University of British Columbia Press, 1978), 17.

35. Leslie Monkman, "Canada," in *The Commonwealth Novel since 1960*, ed. Bruce King (London: MacMillan, 1991), 34–35.

36. Hugh MacLennan, *Two Solitudes* (Toronto: Macmillan, 1957), 412.

37. The general attack announced in *Refus Global* on an increasingly utilitarian modern culture that had no place for art and culture was transformed in the more political climate of the 1960s "Quiet Revolution" into a manifesto concerning the differences between French and English culture in Canada. See Paul Émile Borduas, *Refus Global: Projections Libérantes* (Montréal: Parti Pris, 1977). As the work of Max Dorsinville has shown, it is much easier to make the case for significant points of connection between Québécois fiction and the fiction of other former colonies. See *Caliban without Prospero: Essays on Quebec and Black Literature* (Erin, ON: Press Porcepic, 1974), and *Le Pays Natal: Essais sur les littératures du Tiersmonde et du Québec* (Dakar: Les Nouvelles Editions Africaines, 1983).

38. For a thorough investigation of the nation and nationalism in Canadian literature, see Jonathan Kretzer's *Worrying the Nation* (Toronto: University of Toronto Press, 1998).

39. Frank Davey, "It's a Wonderful Life: Robert Lecker's Canadian Canon," *Canadian Literary Power* (Edmonton: NeWest, 1994), 45–78; and Tracy Ware's superb, "A Little Self-Consciousness Is a Dangerous Thing: A Response to Robert Lecker," *English Studies in Canada* 17, no. 4 (December 1991): 481–93.

40. Marshall McLuhan, "Epilogue: Canada as Counter-Environment," in *The Global Village: Transformations in World Life and Media in the Twenty-First Century* (New York: Oxford University Press, 1989), 147–66.

41. Paul Valéry, "America: A Projection of the European Spirit," *History and Politics* (New York: Bollingen, 1962), 329–30.

42. These programs—which reached an apex in the Trudeau years with the founding of the Canadian Development Corporation (1971), the Foreign Investment Review Agency (1974), Petro-Canada (1974), and the National Energy Program (1980) and were all subsequently undone by the signing of the Free Trade Agreement in 1990—were intended to combat Canada's "branch-plant" economy and its role as a primary provider of raw materials to the American economy. These programs mark the high point of the temporary "triumph of the political imagination over cold economic reality" in Canada, the "attempt to create an economic foundation for a political structure that otherwise would be dangerously weak"; Robert Chodos, Rae Murphy, and Eric Hamovitch, *The Unmaking of Canada: The Hidden Theme in Canadian History since 1945* (Toronto: Lorimer, 1991), 86.

43. Dennis Lee, "Cadence, Country, Silence: Writing in Colonial Space," *boundary 2* 3 (1974): 159.

44. Powe, *A Climate Charged*, 74. Although Eli Mandel is critical of Grant, he also concedes that "the subtlety and power of Grant's argument has been fully evident in the degree to which it spoke to Canadian nationalists and, through the sixties, gave vivid force

to their views"; Eli Mandel, "George Grant: Language, Nation, the Silence of God," *The Family Romance* (Winnipeg: Turnstone, 1986), 97.

45. George Grant, *Lament for a Nation: The Defeat of Canadian Nationalism* (Toronto: McClelland and Stewart, 1970). All further references are indicated in the text by LN.

46. Although Grant is the product of a very different philosophical tradition, it is difficult to avoid comparing his lament over Canada's possibilities with the later Heidegger's repeated lament over the decline of the Western spirit in essays such as "The Question Concerning Technology" and "The Nature of Language." If Heidegger locates possibilities for "thinking" in a world rapidly being overtaken by "the technical maximization of velocities" ("The Nature of Language," 62) (as exemplified by the ominous image of the Sputnik) in a renewed experience with language, Grant localized these possibilities in Canadian space. For this to be possible, the entire nation has to be thought of as a sort of Heideggerian fieldpath or "neighbourhood," which seems to introduce a philosophical difficulty from the outset in a country that has already launched its own version of the Sputnik into outer space. In a sense, then, Grant finds himself in a much more compromised position with respect to modernity than Heidegger. While the latter famously ended his lifelong reflections with a lament about the absence of gods on the earth, Grant begins with this knowledge: there is no Canadian equivalent of Stefan George or Georg Trakl to offer him even a glimmer of hope. See Martin Heidegger, "The Question Concerning Technology," *The Question Concerning Technology and Other Essays*, trans. William Lovitt (New York: Harper, 1977), 3–35, and "The Nature of Language," *On the Way to Language*, trans. Peter D. Hertz (New York: Harper & Row, 1971), 57–110.

47. For an intriguing analysis of this crisis, see Chodos, Murphy, and Hanovitch, *The Unmaking of Canada*. The authors are correct in their view of Grant's treatment of the Diefenbaker government in *Lament for a Nation*. Grant's book, they suggest, "serves as something of an antidote to the approved Liberal histories of the Diefenbaker-Pearson years. But when Grant portrays Diefenbaker as something approaching Canada's last best hope, the eulogy becomes a little tattered. John Diefenbaker had no clear national vision, or at least none that bore any resemblance to the twentieth century" (*Unmaking*, 25).

48. See Linda Hutcheon, *The Canadian Postmodern* (New York: Oxford University Press, 1988), and "Circling the Downspout of Empire: Post-colonialism and Postmodernism," *Ariel* 20, no. 4 (October 1989): 149–75. Jacques Derrida has argued, however, that *"what is proper to a culture is to not be identical to itself"* (9), which would mean that Canada is hardly exemplary in this respect; Jacques Derrida, *The Other Heading*, trans. Pascale-Anne Brault and Michael B. Naas (Bloomington, IN: Indiana University Press, 1992).

49. George Grant, "Canadian Fate and Imperialism," *Technology and Empire* (Concord, ON: Anansi, 1969), 74. All further references are indicated in the text by CFI.

50. See, for instance, Mandel's criticisms of Grant's "imperial connections," in "George Grant," 91–93.

51. *OECD Observer*, no. 215, January 1999. Canada spends 20% of its GDP on social programs; Denmark and Sweden both spend over 35%.

52. Northrop Frye, "National Consciousness in Canadian Culture," 172.

53. In *The Modern Century*, Frye identifies the "second phase" of the modern with 1867, the year of the publication of the first volume of *Das Kapital*, the death of Baudelaire, and the passage of the British North America Act, which established Canada as an independent nation.

54. It is important to point out that there is no one version of *The Peaceable Kingdom*

that was produced with certainty in 1830. Hicks painted sixty versions of the *The Peaceable Kingdom* between 1820 and 1849. By contrast, twenty-one years after first painting *Historical Monument of the American Republic,* Salisbury returned to the same canvas in 1888 to add even *more* towers and details to the painting.

55. Frye, *The Bush Garden,* i.

56. Ibid., ii.

57. Ibid., iii.

58. Ibid., iii.

59. Northrop Frye, *The Modern Century* (Toronto: Oxford University Press, 1967).

60. For example: "In a world where dynasties rise and fall at much the same rate as women's hemlines, the dynasty and the hemline look much alike in importance, and get the same amount of featuring in the news" (*Modern Century,* 20–21); "The variety of things that occur in the world, combined with the relentless continuity of their appearance day after day, impress us with the sense of a process going by a little too fast for our minds to focus on anything in it" (22); "Advertising implies an economy which has some independence from the political structure, and as long as this independence exists, advertising can be taken as a kind of ironic game . . . it creates an illusion of detachment and mental superiority even when one is obeying it exhortations" (26).

61. William Whyte, *The Organization Man* (New York: Simon & Schuster, 1956); Vance Packard, *The Hidden Persuaders* (New York: D. McKay Co., 1957); Herbert Marcuse, *One-Dimensional Man* (Boston: Beacon, 1964); and Norman O. Brown, *Love's Body* (New York: Random House, 1966).

62. Expo'67 provides evidence of all sorts of national anxieties that had yet to be adequately resolved. First, it is a coming-out party for a mature nation, but one that has to affirm its maturity by celebrating its centennial under the gaze of an international audience. Second, it anxiously reaffirms the ties that bind English and French Canada, taking place in a Québec whose political and social fabric was just about to come undone. Third, the specificity of the Canadian space in which the Expo took place was established through the construction of numerous modernist (international) monuments, for example, Moshe Safdie's Habitation, the Buckminster Fuller dome that was Expo's symbol, and so on. As reflected in Prime Minister Lester B. Pearson's remarks, for Canada, Expo'67 was a symbol of both the universal and the particular: "The lasting impact of Expo '67 will be in the dramatic object lesson we see before our eyes today — that the genius of man knows no national boundaries, but is universal . . . anyone who says [Canadians] aren't a spectacular people should see this. We are witness today to the fulfillment of one of the most daring acts of faith in Canadian enterprise and ability ever undertaken"; *Time,* May 5, 1967, p. 48.

63. Frye, *The Modern Century,* 17–18.

64. Ibid., 57.

65. Ibid., 53.

66. Timothy Brennan, "Cosmopolitans and Celebrities," *Race and Class* 31, no. 1 (1989): 1–19.

67. Brydon, "Introduction," 11.

68. Margery Fee, "Romantic Nationalism and the Image of Native People in Contemporary English-Canadian Literature," in *The Native in Literature,* ed. Thomas King, Cheryl Calver, and Helen Hoy (Oakville, ON: ECW Press, 1986), 26.

69. Canada, Parliament, Standing Committee on Multiculturalism, *Multiculturalism: Building the Canadian Mosaic* (Ottawa: Minister of Supply and Services, 1987), 13.

70. Robert Lecker, ed., *Canadian Canons: Essays in Literary Value* (Toronto: University of Toronto Press, 1991).

71. Frank Davey, "It's a Wonderful Life: Robert Lecker's Canadian Canon," *Canadian Literary Power* (Edmonton: NeWest, 1994), 45–78.

72. W. J. Keith, "Canadian Tradition and the (New) Canadian Library," *American Review of Canadian Studies* 21 (1991): 71.

73. The citation from Keith is taken from "The Quest for the (Instant) Canadian Classic," in *The Bumper Book*, ed. John Metcalf (Toronto: ECW Press, 1986), 163.

74. Tracy Ware, "A Little Self-Consciousness Is a Dangerous Thing," 487. To this may be added Frank Davey's comments on Lecker's essay: "Canadian criticism is nowhere near as monolithic as Lecker depicts it"; "Critical Response I: Canadian Canons," *Critical Inquiry* 16 (1990): 680; and "Lecker gave unsupportable weight to the decade of influence of the thematic critics, and ignored the cumulative discrediting of these critics from 1973 onward, a discrediting that had led Heather Murray — with some ironic hyperbole, I admit — to remark in 1986 that 'thematic criticism is of course now universally despised' "; "It's a Wonderful Life," 53.

75. Virgil Nemoinanu cited in Lecker, *Making It Real,* 53–54.

76. In Canada, see, for example, the comments of Edward Hartley Dewart: "A national literature is an essential element in the formation of national character"; Edward Hartley Dewart, *Selections from Canadian Poets with Occasional Critical and Biographical Notes and an Introductory Essay on Canadian Poetry* (Toronto: University of Toronto Press, 1973), ix; originally printed in 1864.

77. MacLulich, "Thematic Criticism," 17.

78. Ibid., 33.

79. Brydon, "Introduction," 16.

80. Neil ten Kortenaar, "The Trick of Divining a Postcolonial Canadian Identity: Margaret Laurence between Race and Class," *Canadian Literature* 149 (1996): 12.

Conclusion

1. Diana Brydon, "Introduction: Reading Postcoloniality, Reading Canada," *Essays on Canadian Writing* 56 (1995): 11.

2. Fredric Jameson, "Notes on Globalization as a Philosophic Issue," in *The Cultures of Globalization,* ed. Fredric Jameson and Masao Miyoshi (Durham, NC: Duke University Press, 1998), 74.

3. I invoke here some of the precursors to the Birmingham cultural studies movement: E. P. Thompson, *The Making of the British Working Class* (New York: Vintage, 1966); Raymond Williams, *Culture and Society: 1780–1950* (New York: Columbia University Press, 1983); and Richard Hoggart, *The Uses of Literacy* (New York: Oxford University Press, 1958).

4. Anthony D. King, *Culture, Globalization, and the World-System: Contemporary Conditions for the Representation of Identity* (Binghamton: SUNY Binghamton, 1991), 8.

5. This is not to invoke the precise use of this term in Deleuze's work, but to signal in a general manner all of the variety of ways this term has been used, e.g., in political science, as a way of signaling challenges to accepted definitions of citizenship and political sovereignty.

6. Anthony D. King, *Culture, Globalization, and the World-System,* 8.

7. For a perceptive taxonomy of the latter, see Michael Hardt, "Globalization and Democracy," McMaster University Institute for Globalization and the Human Condition Working Paper series, May 13, 2001 (http://www.humanities.mcmaster.ca/"global/work papers/wp.htm).

8. Paul Hirst and Grahame Thompson, *Globalization in Question: The International Economy and the Possibilities of Governance* (Cambridge, UK: Polity Press, 1996), 2.

9. Jean Comaroff and John L. Comaroff, "Millennial Capitalism: First Thoughts on a Second Coming," *Public Culture* 12, no. 2 (2000): 325.

10. Ibid. The complexities that exist here can be seen in the way in which globalization itself sometimes provides the basis for the reconstitution or concentration of national energies. Frederick Buell has suggested recently that in the United States globalization seems to be a form of "cultural nationalism for post-national circumstances"; Buell, "Nationalist Postnationalism: Globalist Discourse in Contemporary American Culture," *American Quarterly* 50, no. 3 (1998): 550. R. Radhakrishnan makes a similar point when he suggests that "postnational developments are never at the expense of nationalist securities; if anything, they *foundationalize* nation-based verities and privileges to the point of invisibility"; Radhakrishnan, "Postmodernism and the Rest of the World," in *The Pre-Occupation of Postcolonial Studies*, ed. Fawzia Afzal-Khan and Kalpana Seshadri-Crooks (Durham, NC: Duke University Press, 2000), 42.

11. See Timothy Brennan's "Cosmo-Theory," *South Atlantic Quarterly* 100, no. 3 (2001): 659–91.

12. See Rosa Luxemburg, *The National Question*, ed. Horace Davis (New York: Monthly Review Press, 1976). In Canada, for example, left nationalism represented by groups such as the Council of Canadians seems to have experienced a revival within the antiglobalization protest movement more generally.

13. Michael Hardt and Antonio Negri, *Empire* (Cambridge, MA: Harvard University Press, 2000), 336.

14. Ibid.

15. Fredric Jameson, "Globalization and Political Strategy," *New Left Review* 4 (2000): 62.

16. Fredric Jameson, "Notes on Globalization," 61.

17. Ibid., 72; Jameson, "Globalization and Political Strategy," 65, 66.

18. See especially John Tomlinson, *Cultural Imperialism* (Baltimore: Johns Hopkins University Press, 1991). For an ethnographic consideration of the limits of the cultural imperialist thesis, see James L. Watson, ed., *Golden Arches East: McDonald's in East Asia* (Stanford, CA: Stanford University Press, 1997).

19. Jameson, "Notes on Globalization," 62.

20. Ibid., 70.

21. Ibid., 63.

22. Jameson, "Globalization and Political Strategy," 68.

23. Ibid., 64, n. 11.

24. Jameson, "Notes on Globalization," 64.

25. Ibid., 76.

Index

velopment of, 184; as defensive posture, 188; focus on the nation in, 158–59, 183–85; government-funded, 155; politics of, 158–59, 194–95; professionalization of, 192–93; and the structural function of the nation, 184–85

Literary History of Canada, The, 17, 155–56, 175–83, 187, 192; nationalist literary projects of, 178; as seminal text for thematic criticism, 175

literary nationalism, 190, 193

literature: and the creation of national space, 66, 87; as enduring colonial pattern, 63; and globalization, 8; as ideological, 195; and the nation, 1, 22–31, 39, 40–48, 50–51, 64, 99, 102, 106–7, 114, 119, 140, 190; as privileged form of writing, 79, 104, 119; as producing cultural self-reflection, 187, 195; relationship to politics, 1, 5, 37, 47, 49, 72–73, 104, 140; as resisting imperialist forces, 197; role in creating a collectivity, 151. *See also* Canadian literature

Litt, Paul, 153

Living Novel, The, 88, 97

Logic, 207

"low" cultural forms, importance of, 112

Lukács, György, 76

MacLennan, Hugh, 162

Maclulich, T. D., 159, 195

Madmen and Specialists, 148

Making It Real, 164, 185–98

Man of the People, A, 123–25, 127–28, 139

margins, focus on, 113

marketing, 142

Martí, José, 1–2

Martinique, 101

Marxism, 129, 170

Marxist criticism, 30, 42

mass culture, 206, 216n. 34

masses, the. *See* people, the

Massey, Vincent, 153

Massey (Commission) Report, 4, 16; influence of, 153–54, 166

material, the, 43, 52

materialist approach: to postcolonial text, 49, 62

McLuhan, Marshall, 165–66

Middle Passage, The, 66, 98–107; and federation, 68

Mighty Sparrow, 110

Miguel Street, 100

military, the, 140

mimesis: as characteristic of Canadian literature, 187

Mobutu regime, 116

modern, the, 181

Modern Century, The, 181

modernism, 11, 58

modernity: ambivalence of, 175; belated, 52; concept of, 6; as cultural system, 2, 101; as desirable, 102–3; effects of, 83, 180; as embodied in the nation, 71; as global space, 8; as imitative and false, 103; as inevitable, 119, 173; multiple, 104; postcolonial, 103, 219n. 77; as a threat to the nation, 163, 165, 167–68, 173–74, 197–98

Modernity at Large, 27–28

Modern Politics, Party Politics in the West Indies, 110

Monkman, Leslie, 162

Morning Yet on Creation Day, 122

Morris, Mervyn, 87

Moss, John: as thematic critic, 155–56, 187

multiculturalism, 16

Munro, Alice, 162

Mystic Masseur, The, 100

NAFTA, 160, 231n. 42

Naipaul, V. S., 15, 66, 97–108, 223n. 41

Nation, The, 109, 111

nation, the: as artificial, 13, 117; as constituted in the literary canon, 189–90; critical approaches to, 22–24, 117; as discursive problematic, 59–62, 98, 117; as economic unit, 202; failure of, 148; formation of, 13, 22–23; as historical idea, 10, 212n. 1; impossibility of, 167; as inevitable, 143, 150; limits of, 35, 49, 101; as linking literature and politics, 165, 196; as literary theme, 26, 56, 59; and new forms of collectivity, 206–7; persistence of, 118, 164–65; as product of imperialism, 26, 34;